BETTER KITCHENS

W9-ARI-388

BETTER KITCHENS

CECILE SHAPIRO

CONTRIBUTING AUTHORS
DAVID ULRICH, CKD
NEAL DeLEO, CKD

A DIVISION OF FEDERAL MARKETING CORPORATION,
24 PARK WAY, UPPER SADDLE RIVER, NEW JERSEY 07458

CREATIVE HOMEOWNER PRESS®

COPYRIGHT © 1980 CREATIVE
HOMEOWNER PRESS®
A DIVISION OF FEDERAL MARKETING CORP.,
UPPER SADDLE RIVER, NJ
This book may not be reproduced, either in part
or in its entirety, in any form, by any means,
without written permission from the publisher,
with the exception of brief excerpts for purposes of radio, television, or published review.
Although all possible measures have been
taken to ensure the accuracy of the material
presented, neither the author nor the publisher
is liable in case of misinterpretation of directions, misapplication or typographical error.
All rights, including the right of translation, are
reserved.

Manufactured in United States of America

Current Printing (last digit)
10 9 8

Editor: Shirley M. Horowitz
Assistant Editors: Marilyn M. Auer
  and Gail Kummings
Art Director: Leone Lewensohn
Designer: Paul Sochacki

Technical Review and Assistance:
  Edwin Giese,
  University of Wisconsin-Milwaukee;
  Kenneth Rademacher,
  Electrical Engineer
  Robert Schmitt,
  University of Wisconsin-Milwaukee

Cover photograph courtesy of Allmilmo Corporation

We wish to extend our thanks to the many designers, companies, and other contributors
who allowed us to use their materials and gave
us advice. Their names, addresses, and individual indentifications of their contributions can
be found on *page 158*.

LC: 80-617151
ISBN: 0-932944-24-8 (paper)
      0-932944-23-X (hardcover)

CREATIVE HOMEOWNER PRESS®
BOOK SERIES

A DIVISION OF FEDERAL
MARKETING CORPORATION
24 PARK WAY,
UPPER SADDLE RIVER, NJ 07458

SELECTED PROJECTS

FOREWORD

Better Kitchens has been created in order to answer a broad range of homeowner needs, with varying viewpoints and expertise from the author, Cecile Shapiro, and contributing authors David Ulrich and Neal DeLeo. We have tried to be precise regarding cost breakdowns, and to give dollar-cutting or time-saving options whenever possible — such as building a pass-through serving latch rather than tearing out a wall. We have compiled a broad-based selection of products and materials available, with source listings and addresses provided in the appendices. In as many cases as possible, we have tried to discover desirable and unusual kitchens, in order to photograph and present them.

Author Cecile Shapiro sets the foundation, presenting the concerns of the knowledgeable consumer and homeowner. As a book reviewer of books for *House and Garden*, she has seen many publications on kitchens and related topics, but few that she felt attacked most of the problems faced by both average kitchen users and serious cooks. Her careful research, and consideration of function in design, resulted in useful analysis of various aspects of the remodeling process: how to plan, how to cope, and how to creatively use products and arrangements in order to solve irritating kitchen problems.

Cecile Shapiro, an enthusiastic cook who has now thoroughly remodeled and renovated two kitchens, offers procedures and arrangements while always keeping in mind the point of view of the cook. Creative and low-cost options are presented as alternatives to extensive re-

modeling, based upon a problem/solution approach.

Contributing author David Ulrich is owner of and designer for Ulrich, Inc., located in Ridgewood, New Jersey. He has directed and produced kitchen remodelings for a wide range of budgets and tastes, winning several design awards in the process. In addition to contributing nearly all of the artwork and many of the step-by-step procedures included in this book, he has been called upon many times to review and instruct on the technical aspects of design and construction.

In addition to informative presentations of the various tasks, Mr. Ulrich has made available many before-and-after floor plans and photographs of his own as well as those of other designers.

Some of the undertakings included in

Better Kitchens are purely decorative and cosmetic — such as adding an arch, putting up wallpaper, or refinishing kitchen cabinets — but most combine functional improvements with the decorative aspects — replacing a hood or fan, tiling a countertop, or building a pass-through for improved foot traffic patterns and increased light.

Contributing author Neal DeLeo also has served as a technical consultant, as well as providing photographs and product information based upon his years of experience as a designer.

By drawing upon the different backgrounds and viewpoints of these three professionals, we at Creative Homeowner Press have tried to offer a wide selection of solutions and choices for any homeowner desiring a better kitchen.

CONTENTS

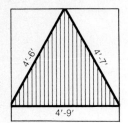

1
KEEPING COSTS DOWN

A homeowner remodeling a kitchen can economize and yet be indulgent. That may sound contradictory, but few home improvements add so much to the value of a house or so enhance its sales potential as will a convenient kitchen. Real estate investors who buy old houses to modernize and resell know this, which is why they take the trouble to install attractive kitchens. Remodeling a kitchen not only can add to the resale value of a house but also can provide interim satisfactions such as convenience and ease of use, reliable appliances, plus the visual and aesthetic rewards of improving one of the most important rooms in the house.

ESTIMATES

How much should it cost to remodel a kitchen? Several rules of thumb are used, but none might apply to you. Ask yourself how much you would pay for a new car — or paid for your last one. A new kitchen, according to many designers and contractors, often will cost about the same amount. Other family budget advisors suggest spending about 10 percent of the value of the house for kitchen improvements.

Because so many possibilities exist, there is probably no accurate way of determining how much a family ought to spend. You might need everything new, from floor covering to windows — not merely appliances, cabinets, plumbing, and electrical work. You may decide to take this opportunity to insulate the exterior kitchen walls to modern standards, since the old cabinets will be torn out.

Normally this involves taking down wallboard or plaster walls as well; the latter is one of the dirtiest jobs known to remodelers. On the other hand, you might plan just to refurbish the kitchen with new or repainted doors for the cabinets and a spray job for the appliances.

For example, you can buy a refrigerator for anywhere from $300 to $1,200. The remodeler who dreams of an expensive stove may be satisfied with an inexpensive countertop. Another person might settle for nothing less than Dupont's Corian as a work surface, yet insist on keeping an old kitchen floor made of wood, refinished and highly polished.

However, you can develop rough estimates by adding up the costs of new features you want. The distribution of costs

The hood over this tiled cooking island incorporates spotlight task lighting. There is sufficient preparation space for the cook to work next to the cooking grill. The heat resistant tiles cannot be damaged by hot pots.

for the kitchen pictured can be taken as an example and breaks down in the table below. The costs depend heavily on how much of the work you do yourself.

FINANCING

Financing is available for kitchen renovation, but renting money can be expensive. If you can stagger costs, or find the cash,

DISTRIBUTION OF COSTS*

Allocation	Percent of Total
Appliances (oven, top burners, refrigerator, dishwasher)	33%
Stock cabinets (unpainted), countertop plastic laminate, sink installed fixtures, dishwasher installation, oven and top burner installation	36%
New plasterboard ceiling over old ceiling	4%
Electrical work (3 high hats over sink and counter) sink and counter, 2 exhaust fans and ducts, ceiling fixture	10%
Flooring (vinyl sheet roll) over masonite underlayment, installed	10%
Wood and materials for built-in cabinet, open shelves, radiator cover, wall paneling in dining area	6%
Paint	1%

* The costs and their allocation will vary, according to how much of the work you handle yourself.

The collection of blue and white china keyed Cecile Shapiro's choice of countertop material with a pattern similar to Delft tiles. A brick-red floor adds a contrasting third color.

A brick wall housed a coal stove, but now sports a mantel for dish display over cooktop.

Painted pine paneling hides uneven plaster on the wall of the family dining area; the soffit in the kitchen is covered with the same paneling for a unified decorative scheme.

or use a portion of your existing savings, your total expenses may be reduced substantially. Many families still find it necessary to borrow, however, feeling that interest charges are worth their additional cost.

Money-Saving Options

You can save by doing as much as possible yourself, both the simple and complex tasks. Removing old fixtures and appliances, for instance, might be an easy job for you. A dealer installing new cabinets or appliances might charge a substantial sum for removing and disposing of them. (Such charges are sometimes hidden in the cost of labor.) You may have little difficulty installing ready-made cabinets and countertops, or you may have the skills to construct your own from basic materials. (Plans are given later in this book.) You might prefer mainly open shelves to show off dishes and other items. They are less expensive than the wall cabinets you see in showrooms. Cosmetic improvements such as paint and wallpaper may suffice; these usually call for little professional aid. A partial remodeling may transform your kitchen to suit you — or you may find a firm specializing in kitchen remodeling that encourages homeowners to do the finish work after they install the basic cabinets and countertops.

Total cost rests with the choices of each homeowner. While one family may insist on a round dozen fixtures designed for specific lighting jobs, another may be satisfied with one or two fluorescent fixtures. The latter costs much less to install and maintain, and can be satisfactory. You also have choices in cabinets, which come in both stock and custom grades. Generally, custom ones cost more but are of better quality. However, a stock cabinet with special trim may cost more than a simple custom cabinet.

The countertops, backsplashes, and hooded work island are all surfaced in brilliant ceramic tile. Such brightly colored tile and wood can be combined with either a clean-lined contemporary design or a more formal, traditional one.

Newly painted cabinets and bright vinyl wallpaper combine for a low-cost but appealing result. Painted moldings accent the cabinets.

A U-shaped kitchen provides valuable additional counterspace while minimizing the number of steps taken in the work triangle. The extra counter area enables the cook to set up specialized food preparation centers, as indicated by the butcher block inset and the unusually large sink.

2
KITCHEN PRIORITIES

PLANNING CHECKLIST

Compile a questionnaire; this can be a family project. Answers to the questions will create a useful checklist of what you need for the kitchen remodeling, as well as provide a guide and timetable for the work. It also can become a tool to help you determine the total cost. Following are types of questions you might list and then answer.

Cooking Needs

Do you like to cook and do other members of the family cook?
Does more than one person work in the kitchen at the same time?
Do you do much baking?

Dining Needs

Do you usually eat in the kitchen?
Do you prefer having meals there to eating in a dining room or separate dining area?
How many people regularly sit down to meals?

Storage Needs

Do you like kitchen gadgets?
Do you own a food processor, blender, mixer, crockpot, electric can opener, knife sharpener, juicer or coffee mill?
What other small electric appliances do you consider necessities? Are you satisfied with the space you have for them now?
Do you expect to buy any other small cooking appliances?
Do you own an assortment of large or odd-shaped pieces, such as a fish poacher or a wok?

Canning or Freezing Needs

Do you freeze or can produce?
Do you need extra space and equipment for annual harvest periods?
Will you store frozen, canned, or dried food in the kitchen or in a separate pantry or cellar?
Does anyone in the family bring home

When you enjoy and practice a type of cooking that calls for unusually shaped cooking utensils, you can plan for it when designing your kitchen. Wok cooking requires very high heat; tile is a good choice for the surrounding material because it is heat resistant and easily cleaned.

fresh fish; if so, where is it prepared for cooking?
Are tasks such as scaling fish or butchering meat ever part of the kitchen work?

Display Needs

Do you collect pottery or prints, copper or tinware, china or silver spoons?
Do you collect anything that might be displayed or used in the kitchen?
Do you collect cookbooks? If so, you will need an expandable storage space.

Entertaining Needs

Do you entertain in the kitchen; do your guests seem to congregate there?
Do you serve drinks there?
Do you have company often or occasionally?
Do you serve buffet or sit-down company dinners?
Does it upset you if people talk to you while you are trying to cook?

Though herbs and spices keep best in a dark cupboard, shelves above kitchen counters offer quick access to those used daily. The clear bottles can serve as decorative accents.

Room for dining space can be found even in a space-restricted one-wall kitchen.

Brick and wood contrast with the laminate covered counters and cooking island.

Though function and convenience were the primary considerations in the design of this kitchen, the glass-fronted, built-in cupboards allow the china and crystal to lend their sparkle to the room. The varnished wood combines well with the patterned walls and brightly colored laminate.

Activities

If you like to listen to the radio while you work in the kitchen, consider where to put it. Give the same consideration to a television set in the kitchen. If the kitchen is where you sit to plan meals, make marketing lists and write letters, also plan in space for that kind of activity. Decide also whether the kitchen would or should be a family room. If your old one has been, you may want to separate the activities of food preparation and family entertainment.

Today's lifestyles indicate you should decide if your new kitchen will have access to outdoor dining. Supervising the play of small children indoors or outdoors from the kitchen becomes another important factor.

Growing plants or herbs and other edibles in the kitchen requires special attention. Natural light and sunshine are necessary, as well as perhaps artificial light for plants.

When remodeling, decide how to heat your kitchen, without heating the whole house. In very cold climates you might desire a wood or coal stove in the kitchen. You might like to have one to supplement other cooking and heating fuels. If so, you must build a safe chimney and install the heat unit properly for efficiency.

Identifying Kitchen Routine

Once you ask yourself the above and other questions, you begin to have a clearer idea of what you want in a kitchen. Think about your answers and those of everyone else who lives with you before designing your kitchen, or engaging a professional kitchen designer, architect or interior designer.

Storage Planning. To help clarify your needs, let us outline the many detailed movements you carry out in the kitchen. Include in the list utensils used to prepare food, where the items come from (cabinets, shelves, and other storage areas) and their progress through the work areas.

Food Preparation. During food preparation, the sink and the stove come into use. Using water in preparing a meal means repeated trips to the sink. You may use water to boil or steam vegetables, to add to the stew, to make tea or coffee. For each of these foods, too, you have to get the appropriate stove-top utensil from a cabinet or a fixture from which it may hang. Dishes used in preparation are soiled and no longer needed — the bowl in which we beat the eggs, the board on which we sliced the onions — are set in or near the sink. The bowl that held the eggs is filled with cold water; the board is rinsed, if time permits. Going back and forth to the stove from time to time, stirring one dish, lowering the heat under another, you will watch the clock on the wall to check the timing or set an automatic timer, sometimes both. If using a written recipe, room for that must be found on the counter, possibly a cook-book holder is the answer.

While the food cooks, you can set the table. Dishes, glasses, flatware, place mats, napkins come from kitchen cupboards to the table. For a company dinner, out comes the best linen, silver, and china which may not be stored in the kitchen. Flowers and candles may be added. If the meal is to be served outside the kitchen, each of these table-setting steps will be that much more time-consuming and involve that much more walking.

During Meals. With the meal ready and diners seated, the food must be transported from the stove or work counter to the table. If the eating place is nearby, the work counter might be used as a serving counter. If the dining space is in another room, or in another section of the same room but nearby, a serving pass-through with a counter at both sides makes it easy to transfer food to the table. Those with separate dining rooms can use trays or

wheeled carts, as they also might do if serving on a porch or patio or in a garden.

After the Meal. When the meal ends, repeat your steps in reverse. You won't use the stove, of course, although pots and pans still on the stove have to be taken to the sink, filled with water and set aside, usually to the left of the sink. The table is cleared, and everything removed to the serving counter or cart or tray. Dishes are scraped and stacked. The garbage goes into the disposer, if there is one, or into a garbage can under the sink. Gardeners often divide their garbage for use in compost, putting most scraps into a container kept in the kitchen for that purpose. Dish-

This wet bar is equipped with a built-in re-frigerator for handy beverage storage and readily available ice, a small sink for easy cleanup, and a blender motor built into the countertop.

es are next placed in the dishwasher if they are not rinsed under running water. Leftovers go into storage dishes and into the refrigerator. Utensils that are too large, too dirty, or too fragile for the dishwasher are washed by hand and left to dry on the drainboard. Now the stove needs to be wiped, the counters rinsed, the sink scoured, and when the dishwasher finishes its cycle, everything has to be put away.

Visualizing Needs. Try to watch yourself mentally doing the job from beginning to end on the floor plan. It might help to draw a diagram. Pencil in the floor plan, draw lines showing movements from one place to another: preparing, cooking, serving, and tidying up. This exercise could help you locate equipment for better efficiency in a remodeled kitchen.

In compiling food sequences, don't overlook how you enter the kitchen with groceries from the store. If access is inconvenient, you might want a new entry into the remodeled kitchen.

As a further aid to help you with decisions, compile a list of your present kitchen utensils. To this assortment add items you hope to acquire. Add to these two sets of dishes, one of which is probably complete with assorted serving pieces, an oversize salad bowl or two, one or two sets of flatware, placemats and table cloths, pitchers large and small, dozens of glasses, and all the other pieces of kitchenware accumulated over the

Adjacent to the kitchen on the facing page, this breakfast corner is given continuity by repeating the kitchen color scheme. The built-in bench saves floor space.

The clean lines of this kitchen are emphasized by the expanse of white cabinets and counters. The peninsula sink backs up to the cooking area for fast progression from food preparation to cooking center, while the shelf above speeds service to the dining area on the other side.

years. Get rid of those that are never used. Some see use once or twice a year; store those in the least accessible places. There is no rule as to how much storage space a family of four needs, since every family of four (or two or six or eight) differs. But you can benefit by thinking carefully about where all the possessions will be stowed in the new kitchen.

TIMING

How long does it take a kitchen to go from planning to completion? "That depends" sounds like a weaseling answer, but it does depend on many variables. If once your plans are complete you hand your drawings to an architect or a kitchen designer, along with the necessary money, you will surely spend less time looking around for materials, accessories, and appliances than if you function as your own contractor.

The end base cabinet in this kitchen serves as both a storage unit and a room divider.

Scheduling

The following guidelines cannot be applied indiscriminately; choose the items which apply to your situation.

Appliances. Appliances displayed in the showrooms of department stores, kitchen shops, home centers, discount houses, and appliance distributors usually can be delivered within two weeks. However, to avoid unexpected delays that could destroy your arrangements with your other suppliers, try to order a month ahead. Appliances which must be

special-ordered, but which appear in manufacturers' catalogs, cannot be predicted as easily. You may have to check several times after ordering due to factory delays. Catalog firms such as Sears & Roebuck and Montgomery Ward usually state how long it takes for delivery, but if the information does not appear, phone your nearest catalog store.

When you order from any source, ask about the delivery date and include the information in your schedule. If possible, have the salesperson note on your receipt the date of promised delivery. If ordered through the mail, laws have been passed enforcing delivery within 30 days. If the product does not arrive, the supplier must inform you and offer your money back.

There is always the possibility that you will be without a stove (or, less frequently, a refrigerator) for a day, a week or more. (The last is rare.) Or there may simply be too much mess and confusion to perform all the usual kitchen chores. Plan now for substitute ways of managing. If you own or can borrow a camp stove or a hot plate, decide where you will keep it should it become your temporary kitchen stove. You may want to set up the bathroom for dishwashing. It may be possible to stock the freezer with readymades that require heating or defrosting only. Try to plan cookouts.

Cabinets. Stock cabinets are usually delivered within a few days to a few weeks, while custom cabinets may take from 6 to 14 weeks. Special-order custom cabinets may take even longer. European-made custom cabinets can require up to 10 to 16 weeks for delivery, although some manufacturers, such as Allmilmo, are stocked in the United States.

It is usual to pay at least 20 percent (sometimes one-third) on order and the balance on delivery of stock cabinets. For custom cabinets, be prepared to put down 30 to 50 percent on ordering, and the balance when they have been installed. Special custom orders may require higher first payments.

Utilities and Construction. Electricians, masons, plumbers, and other special craftspeople whose services you may require all need to plan their work in advance. Since it is impossible to know exact dates far in advance, you cannot ask them in March to schedule work for you on a particular day in May. But you can phone to ask how long a specific job might

This kitchen is a raised island in an open plan house. The cooking units are built into one circular component, the food preparation center and refrigerator into the other.

Varnished wood, plank flooring, rough-finished plaster, clay, and glass — all unadorned materials presented in natural finishes — combine to give this room an easy, comfortable feeling.

take and how much it is likely to cost. Then you can say that you expect to need such work done some time near the middle of May, and that you will let them know exactly when as soon as you have more specific information. Confirm this in a note to the supplier, and ask him to respond in writing. If you plan ahead in this way, the workers are much more likely to pencil you into their schedules, and you are much more likely to have the work done promptly.

This kitchen in a finished attic did not require costly cabinets or finishing. It features a stainless steel countertop with a wood inset, and lots of light, as well as cabinet doors painted in various bright, arresting colors.

White cabinets, hood, molding, and cooking appliances give the eye a rest from patterns in the flooring, wallpaper, and ceiling. The white becomes a unifying force that draws the eye around the room. High shelves keep cookbooks away from damaging ingredients but still close at hand.

Try to schedule do-it-yourself jobs realistically. Estimate how many hours it will take to remove the sink or install the tile or build a countertop. Then work out how many hours per day, including weekdays, evenings and weekends, you and other members of the family will be able to give to this task.

Realistic time estimates are another contribution that the professional can offer. He or she can give guidelines for various segments of the job, which will of course have to be adjusted according to your particular time and material availability.

Many steps in the sequence of kitchen remodeling are likely to result in confusion and disorder. Be prepared for them. Here are some of the situations that will affect your life during this time.

Electricity and water (and gas, if you use it) will each have to be shut off at some point during a complete renovation, though probably they'll phase out one at a time, not all at once. Also, each will probably continue to function in other parts of the house.

Whether you are merely repainting cabinets or replacing them, all articles tucked into them will have to be emptied out and set aside. Pick a place where they will not be in your way if the job drags on. Keep enough available for skeleton operations. Eventually, everything that has been removed will have to be washed and stowed away again.

Kitchen table and chairs, plus any wall or shelf decorations, will have to be removed. Furniture, rugs, and decorations in adjoining rooms should be protected with a covering of sheets, plastic, or newspaper to cut down on the dirt and plaster that can sift through the house. Dripped paint can be found in remarkably remote places. It is a good idea to cover doorways with plastic to keep the dust from spreading.

Large amounts of debris and old kitchen fixtures will pile up before disposal. Contractors or plumbers will usually agree (if the matter is discussed in advance) that it is their responsibility to take away anything they have removed. If you are not using them, check in advance with your public or private rubbish company about the removal of large items and building debris. Plan to give anything usable to friends, acquaintances, or a charity-sponsored thrift shop.

3
PLANNING AND EVALUATING LAYOUT

A peninsula offers several practical benefits; feeling of openness; separation of the eating area from the food preparation spaces; additional counter space; and, a more effective and convenient work triangle.

All homeowners face limitations to some degree because of space, time, money, or the size or arrangement of the house on its lot. In designing the kitchen, give yourself the greatest latitude, along with the cheapest and best remodeling tools: pencils and paper. Use your imagination. Pretend that what you sketch in your first drawings are, indeed, a kind of make-believe. Mentally put appliances where you think they might function best. Tear down walls and build new ones. After you have planned without restrictions, begin to consider your actual limitations.

To your pencils and paper, add graph paper, a pair of scissors, ruler and yardstick or measuring tape.

MEASURING AND PLANNING

Once you have taken the measurements of your kitchen as described in the following paragraphs, you will be all set to use the movable paper model units.

Most graph paper comes scaled ¼ inch to the foot. That means that each quarter-inch represents a foot of actual floor space. Every fourth line on the graph paper will be darker and heavier than the others. This indicates that the space between the heavy lines measures four feet on the quarter inch scale. The heavy lines serve as a convenience and a check, allowing you to skip some counting of lines. Use either a ¼-inch or ½-inch-to-the-foot scale. Draw kitchen fixtures to same measure; see page 34 for

samples. These can serve as your scale models for trial layout designs and for layout drawings. Trace the model fixtures through ordinary inexpensive typing paper, or if you prefer, use a sturdy tracing paper. Once you have made a scaled outline on graph paper of the kitchen, these templates can be moved around for trial plans.

Begin by making a rough freehand pencil sketch of the kitchen on any sheet of paper. Draw it to more or less the same shape as the actual kitchen, but do not measure for this sketch, and do not worry too much about accuracy. The purpose of the rough sketch is to give you a place to jot down measurement information and related details. After making your sketched outline on plain paper, draw lines indicating every door and window in the room — again, without measuring. Next draw the shape and place of jogs or recesses, closets, radiators, and any other permanent features in the room. (You may want to remove or add to any of these later, but now you want to make a schematic version of what is actually there.)

Once you have made the sketch, measure the room with the ruler. Start at any corner of the room. Measure from the corner to any logical point — for example, the stove — and then from the stove to the radiator, the radiator to the window, and so on. When you get to windows, as well as doors, measure the frames and moldings around them. Measure any jogs, too. Jot down each measurement you make on your freehand sketch in the appropriate place. Go around the room until you come to the place at which you started. Your rough sketch is complete.

Now measure the length and width of your kitchen. The figures you get will serve as a check on your first drawing. They will also serve as the outline for the room dimensions you will use in making a scale drawing on graph paper. Add up the measurements you have just made for the rough sketch, wall by wall — corner to stove, 7 inches; stove, 36 inches; stove to radiator, 47 inches; radiator to window molding, 29 inches; window molding, 2 inches; window, 24 inches; molding, 2 inches; molding to corner, 12 inches. You have one wall 159 inches long (13 feet 3 inches). This should tally with the overall measurement you made. If the figures do not check, measure again until you find your error.

You are now ready to transfer your freehand sketch to graph paper. First, draw an outline of the outer dimensions. As an example, let us suppose that your kitchen is 13 feet, 3 inches long and 10 feet wide. Count off 13 squares, then make a dot a fraction beyond it to represent one-quarter of a foot. Use a ruler to draw a line to represent the wall. (If you are familiar with using a scale ruler and you have one, use it.) Lay out all four walls of the room.

Once the rectangle has been completed, look at your rough sketch. Working to scale, draw in the irregularities — the closet that projects into the kitchen, the alcove that once held an icebox, the half-wall that separates the old dining

nook. Put in the existing doors and windows, to scale, even if they will be changed in the remodeled kitchen. A clean eraser will be helpful to make adjustments. Now add the measurements of the doors, windows, moldings, projections and so on that were itemized on the rough sketch. Leave out of this scale drawing all appliances. You can, however, show which way doors open with the symbol below.

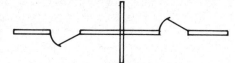

You are now ready to experiment with kitchen layouts. Look at the basic plans suggested in this chapter. Then draw scaled templates for all of the appliances and cabinets you hope to include. Move them around on the graph paper. Try various sizes of equipment. Give yourself every chance to experiment with any idea that occurs to you. None need be considered final until you are absolutely satisfied with the plan. You can always redraw on fresh graph paper when a new idea or better layout occurs to you. Later, after you have worked out a floor plan, you can follow the same procedure to make measured drawings of each wall.

BASIC KITCHEN LAYOUTS
The basic layouts that have been devised in the last decades are tools for designing and planning kitchens. Concepts such as the "U-shaped" kitchen or the "L-shaped" kitchen began with home economists. They analyzed the steps necessary in meal preparation and realized how much zig-zagging was required in what had hitherto looked like adequate kitchens. They then applied a variant of industrial time-motion studies in an attempt to work out "scientifically" the best way to eliminate excess motion and wasted energy. Since then kitchen designers, architects, appliance manufacturers, and homeowners have worked out refinements that are generally applicable. They now agree on four basic kitchen types — the one-wall kitchen, the galley or Pullman kitchen (referring to boat galleys and Pullman trains), the L-shaped kitchen, and the U-shaped kitchen. There are many variations and combinations. Each can be the basis of an excellent kitchen.

The Work Triangle
Kitchen efficiency experts have come up with a set of numbers and a concept called the "work triangle." Since there are three necessities in every kitchen — stove, sink, and refrigerator — these should be grouped in a triangular pattern which requires those working within it to do the least possible walking between one point and another, and have adequate workspace on adjacent counters.

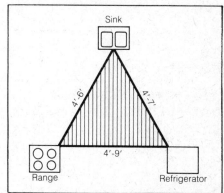

This work triangle shows convenient maximum and minimum dimensions. A larger work triangle will require too much walking; a smaller one will be work-efficient, but will result in a cramped kitchen with insufficient counterspace.

Minimums and Maximums. The distance between the sink and the refrigerator has a recommended range of between four and seven feet. Between the sink and the range, the recommendation is four to six feet. Between the range and the refrigerator, the ideal is four to nine feet. The minimums add up to a total of twelve feet of counter space, the maximum to twenty-two. To some degree these figures are arbitrary. Clearly, a good kitchen would not be ruined if for some reason the work triangle included as little as 11 feet or as much as 23, nor would the design necessarily be perfect even if the golden mean of 17 feet were designed.

One-Wall Kitchen
The kitchen with all its equipment and appliances lined up along one wall is used mainly in two ways: in a large room that serves also as the family or living room or one that is the only room in a studio apartment, serving as living/dining/bedroom. It is used too, when space is limited and there is no room for any other sort of kitchen.

One-wall kitchens have certain inherent problems. If the sink is made the center or hub of the kitchen, as is usually recommended, the distance between the refrigerator at one end and the stove at the other can be much too long if appropriate work spaces are left in between. When a one-wall kitchen is part of a large room, the cook's back is to the guests. However, the kitchen can be hidden easily. A Venetian blind, a folding or sliding door or a curtain, can close it off from view if so desired when the room is used for another purpose. Even without a visual barrier, such a kitchen can be unobtrusive. When a one-wall kitchen is placed in a small, separate enclosure it can be claustrophobic as well as tiring, and should therefore be avoided if at all possible.

Galley or Pullman Kitchens

The galley or Pullman kitchen, also called the corridor kitchen, is a narrow kitchen in which all equipment and appliances are

if at least some portion of the aisle is wider.

A corridor kitchen should not have more than one entry doorway, if at all possible. Two doors are almost certain to ensure its being used as a passageway between rooms — an irritant to any cook.

If you face the design problem of remodeling a small one-wall or two-wall Pullman kitchen, determine whether you can borrow space from an adjoining room. Removing a non-bearing wall is not necessarily expensive. Perhaps you can expand outward, or even use your present kitchen for some other purpose and equip a different room as a kitchen. It might be worthwhile to add a new room to the house.

Should you decide on a corridor kitchen, however, it will be relatively simple to conveniently arrange all your

the room, usually a long and a short, while U-shapes run along three walls. In both a third or fourth "wall" can be created by a peninsula or an island. Neither shape need be pure. An L-shape that continues beyond a peninsula may turn into an F-shaped or even E-shaped kitchen. An L or U-shape may be broken by a door.

With L and U shapes it is usually simple to place the sink at the center of the work triangle, where it functions best. In planning any kind of kitchen, especially the L or U-shapes, try to place the sink under a window.

The Final Sketch

After you have decided upon one kitchen layout that you like and think will work, you are ready to draw your plan for a remodeled kitchen. With pencil, eraser,

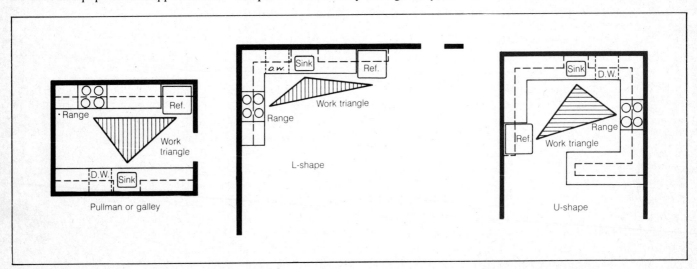

These floor plans exhibit three common kitchen layouts and their corresponding work triangles.

placed on two facing walls. It has basic advantages over the one-wall kitchen — both types are often found in small apartments — but there are problems, nonetheless. These difficulties can be especially severe if more than one person works in the kitchen.

Base cabinet built-ins should have a minimum aisle of four feet between them in order to allow doors of the cabinets, refrigerator, and oven to be opened and for an adult to maneuver around them. Since standard base cabinets are two feet deep, this would require the corridor kitchen to be at least eight feet wide. There are times when space is so extremely tight that a remodeler might narrow the aisle to the bare minimum of three feet, or even shave a little off that, and narrow down to 32 inches. This can work

workspace. You also can avoid one problem in kitchen design — corners — since you will have none. Corners require accessibility, which is why we have a special section on them. Galley kitchens have another problem which must be watched — doors. Make sure the oven and refrigerator are not opposite each other, since they both have large doors that at some time might both need to be opened at the same time. In any kitchen, no cabinet or refrigerator or oven doors should open into the paths of entry and exit doors. In the corridor kitchen this may be difficult to avoid.

L-Shaped and U-Shaped Kitchens

Both L-shaped and U-shaped kitchens lend themselves to triangulation. L-shaped kitchens run along two walls of

The addition of a new section of countertop to the left of the built-in refrigerator created a U-shaped kitchen by connecting the original countertops to the peninsula.

graph paper, and ruler, draw in the lines representing the base cabinets. Include all doors and windows, but leave out the wall cabinets above until you are ready to draw plans for each wall. Erase jogs or walls you plan to remove. Place your appliances, continuing to work to scale. It will not do any good, for instance, to plan for a 20-inch refrigerator if no such unit exists.

MEASUREMENTS THAT HELP
Kitchen Cabinets

Most base cabinets are 30½ inches high as manufactured. Toe space and the base on which they rest brings them up to 34½ inches. Another 1½ inches is allowed for the countertop base and materials, bringing the standard height to 36 inches. However, toe space may be varied from a low (a minimum) of three inches to as much as eight inches, if greater height is wanted. A shallow or deep drawer may be added to the top or the bottom of the standard 30½ inch base cabinet for additional height.

Some studies indicate that the standard height of most base cabinets, 36 inches, is too low for most people, and that 37½ inches would be better. Such chores as pastry rolling apparently demand less height than the standard. Most designers, however, do not like to change or vary countertop heights in any one run of cabinets, or even in any single kitchen. If you should decide to vary countertop height, plan for the greater height to be at the corner. To do otherwise could create an odd-looking wall. Drawers added to base cabinets to increase height may have to be made to order.

Standard base cabinets are 24 inches deep. Standard wall cabinets are 12 to 13 inches deep, although some of the European lines vary from this. The distance between base and wall cabinets is usually 14 to 18 inches. The latter allows more room for appliances that stand at the back of the work counter. The former height makes wall cabinet shelves more accessible to shorter people. The maximum height that a person 5 feet 4 inches can reach with ease is 66 to 68 inches, though according to studies this person can place objects on or remove them from shelves up to 71 inches high. After that, step stools are required.

Wall units may be hung higher or lower for people above or below average height. Eye-level for a person 5 feet 4 inches is 4 feet 11 inches. Wall-hung base units may be hung at any convenient height.

Appliances such as dishwashers, washing machines, dryers and ovens can be installed at a higher level in taller base cabinets.

Custom and stock cabinets progress in three and six-inch increments. For example, one company manufactures sink bases that are 24, 27, 30, 33, and 36 inches wide. Another company produces them 54, 60, 66 and 72 inches wide.

Corner cabinets are made four ways: blind or not usable, dead storage, dead corner turnouts and carousels. The drum carousels are made in 33, 36 and 39 inch sizes, with 36 inches the most popular size.

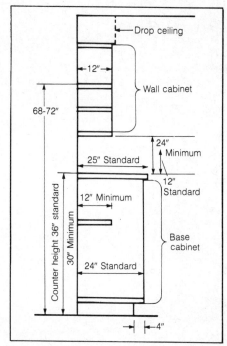

Here are the most common cabinet heights and proportions. These standard dimensions can be adjusted depending upon the height of the person who will be working in the kitchen and upon types of cooking activities.

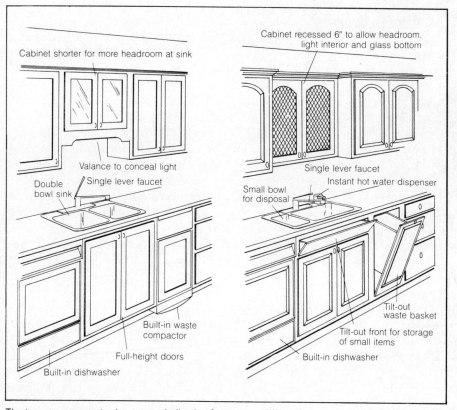

The two arrangements shown are similar, but feature two different types of cabinet treatments over the sink. One layout has a trash compactor where the other has a built-in wastebasket. Full-height doors in the drawing at left give better access than the shorter doors at right, but the tilt-out front with a stainless steel liner will hold small, useful items.

Set apart higher or lower counter, or as an island, so height difference is less apparent.

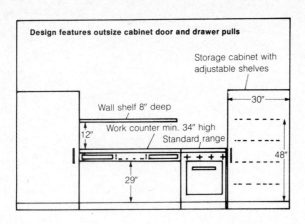

Design features outsize cabinet door and drawer pulls

Storage cabinet with adjustable shelves

Wall shelf 8″ deep

30″

12″

Work counter min. 34″ high

Standard range

48″

29″

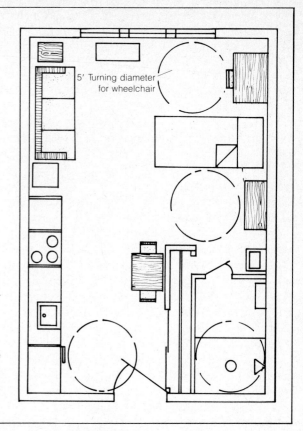

5′ Turning diameter for wheelchair

The elevation above has a storage cabinet with 6 inch deep shelves on its door. The work counter is open at the front and high enough to clear wheelchair arms. The range must always have controls on the front, not on top. The sink includes a 4 inch deep undercoated bowl, a single-lever faucet, a drain at either the side or the rear, with any exposed hot-water piping well insulated for safety.

The floor plan at right shows a kitchen designed for the handicapped (also see elevation above). One of the features is a chopping board that can be held on the lap or rest on the arms of a wheelchair. If two boards are feasible, one should have an 8 inch diameter cut-out that can hold a mixing bowl. The counter is usable by either a wheelchair-bound person sitting or a crutch-bound person standing.

Sinks

Open sink fronts that allow handicapped people or those in wheel chairs to sit down while they work are ready-made in 18, 24 and 30 inch sizes. Many sizes and variations of single, double, and triple corner sinks are manufactured.

Standard sinks are 21 inches deep, including the ledge for the faucet. The 30-inch-wide single-bowl sink is the most popular with consumers. Double-bowl sinks are usually 32 or 42 inches across. The double bowls may both be equal in size or one may be considerably larger than the other. Triple-bowl sinks may be up to 43 inches wide, or larger when made with attached drain boards.

Good sink planning requires 30 inches of countertop space on one side, 24 inches on the other.

Stoves

Cooktops are usually about 22 inches deep. Width ranges from 15 inches for small two-burner tops to the popular 30-inch width, and on by degrees up to 46 inches. Commercial stoves can be considerably wider.

Gas and electric wall ovens are made to fit either 24-, 27-, or 30-inch cabinets, with many variations in height. Standard stock and custom cabinets are made to accept them. It is usually recommended that the base of the oven be set at counter-top height, with the door opening out flat to a level with the countertop. Some people may find it more comfortable to drop the wall oven a few inches lower in order to see inside more easily. If there are two ovens, the top one may have to rise so the bottom oven is not too low.

If a separate oven is used infrequently, it may be placed outside the work triangle when necessary, but there should be at least 12 inches of heatproof countertop to one side, with a minimum total of 24 inches with both sides combined.

The recommended height for vent hoods is 56 inches to the bottom of the hood, except when the person who does most of the cooking is more than six feet tall. In that case, it should be higher. Vent hoods should not protrude outward more than 21 inches.

Cooktops require a minimum of 18 inches on each side. It is preferable if the countertop on one side is heatproof. A built-in range also requires 18 inches on either side, although it is preferable to allow at least 24 inches on the side toward the inside of the work triangle.

Refrigerators and Freezers

Refrigerators are usually 58 to 72 inches tall, as are most upright freezers. The standard widths are 28 to 35¾ inches. Allow 18 to 46 inches of countertop on the side of the refrigerator toward which the door opens. Make sure the door opens toward the inside of the work triangle, not away from it. Built-in refrigerators, such as sub zero, require very specific cabinet planning.

Dishwashers

Dishwashers are designed to fit under the standard 36-inch high, 24-inch deep countertop. They may be installed higher under a countertop that is greater in height. The usual width is 24 inches, although at least 2 companies (Sears and Admiral) manufacture a narrow dishwasher 18 inches wide. Portable dishwashers may have different dimensions, as do the larger, commercial dishwashers. Portable dishwashers may be toploading, but built-in dishwashers are front-loading, with doors that open out into the kitchen and occupy at least 20 inches of floor space.

Washing Machines and Dryers

A washing machine and dryer placed side by side will occupy approximately 60 inches of floor space if they are of standard dimensions. They are usually 27 to

30 inches deep — making them noticeably deeper than standard base cabinets. Models that can fit below countertops are manufactured, however, as are stacking models, which require more height and less floor space.

Small Kitchens

Very small kitchens can't be avoided sometimes in small apartments, vacation houses, in-law quarters. Appliances are manufactured for such places. If you are creating or remodeling a tiny kitchen, you should be aware that special appliances exist, even if you do not see them when you begin shopping. One type of space-saver is the all-in-one unit. Some of them are quite luxurious. They may be as small as two feet overall or as long as six feet. They combine sink, stove, refrigerator, cabinets, and work counter. Not all the components are necessarily of standard size. The stove may have three or only two burners; the sink may be considerably narrower than standard; and the refrigerator may be under the counter. In certain situations, individual miniature units may be preferable.

One manufacturer, for example, makes a dishwasher that fits directly under a shallow-bowled kitchen sink. Another makes a dishwasher topped by four standard-size burners, above which there is an oven at wall-cabinet height. Narrow dishwashers, refrigerators, and ranges are also on the market.

The difficulty in small kitchens is not so much fitting in the basic three necessities — sink, stove, and refrigerator — but in allowing sufficient space between them for anyone to work and enough storage space to make the kitchen realistic. Extra storage might be gained by examining every wall for its potential. Is there a place for pegboard on which to hang pots, pans, cutting board, orange juicer, food mill, can opener? Will utilization of the backsplash create space? A shallow cabinet over the doorway might be an answer. Perhaps another spot could take a six, twelve, or fifteen-inch deep unit. Instead of a soffit over the wall units, consider open or closed storage there.

Shallow and Recessed Storage. Space between studs sometimes can be used on interior walls. (Exterior walls in your remodeled kitchen will presumably

Wood-grain front panels for dishwashers are offered to match nearly any cabinet.

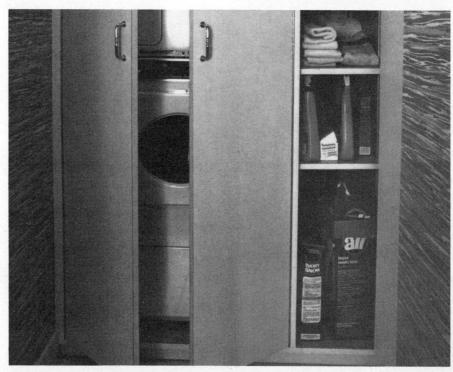

A closet near the kitchen hides a small but convenient laundry center with open shelving for kitchen linens and cleaning products.

A triangular desk and special cabinet were chosen to meet the needs of this problem area.

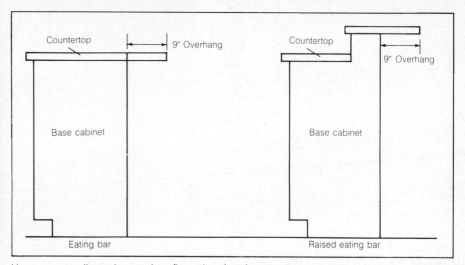

Countertop   9" Overhang   Countertop   9" Overhang

Base cabinet   Base cabinet

Eating bar   Raised eating bar

Here are some dimensions and configurations for a freestanding counter that doubles as an eating bar by addition of an overhang — or raised overhang — on the countertop.

This slide-out table on casters not only provides extra counter space and an eating surface, but it also integrates with the design of the deep drawer for unusually large items.

Extra storage can be gained by adding shelves which have been raised or lowered for the particular items to be kept there. The shelves on top are slightly recessed to allow room for the shelves on the inside of the door.

be filled with insulation.) This extra, shallow space can be squeezed into the kitchen by removing the wallboard between two studs and building shelves to the same depth. The opening may go from floor to ceiling, or be only a foot or two high. A niche or a series of them could be used for display. They could even be specially lighted. An entire wall, once opened up, has depth adequate for most canned and bottled foods.

This sort of recessed storage built above head height can be closed off with doors. No one could inadvertently bump into them when they were open. (Such storage near the ceiling would require the use of a step-stool or ladder.) If the studs are opened for storage lower on the walls, sliding doors can be used. Before you go ahead with this space stretcher, check your plans, and your kitchen, to make sure that no plumbing or electrical lines must travel through the section of wall selected.

The effect of shallow, between-studs storage need not be makeshift. Each section can be framed and finished with appropriate molding, which will make it appear to be the deliberate part of the plan that it is. The interiors can be backed with plastic laminates or with

Shallow shelves in the pantry and on the door make it easy to find things quickly.

specially finished hardboard, which will ease cleaning.

Full-size doors have storage possibilities. Shallow cabinets can be built on the inside or the outside of doors. Shallow racks can hold such hard-to-store things as pot lids or magazines.

Think in inches rather than feet. Removing moldings around windows and doors can provide a few inches more for storage. It may also be visually effective.

Extra Measures. Consider angling cabinets or counterspace into the room. This can add to counterspace as well as cabinet storage. Use whatever pull-out workspaces you can. Cutting boards that pull out, for instance, are excellent work tops. The same is true for hinged counters where they do not interfere with base cabinets.

Look at the Ceiling. If it is too high to hang things from, perhaps you can attach a dowel or hooks from which to hang attractive items. Possibly a ready-made unit with long chains will bring it low enough. Conversely, a low ceiling may be a place to hang smaller items.

Counters. Consider base or wall units of smaller than usual depth. Instead of base cabinets 24 inches deep, plan for cabinets 22 inches or 20 inches deep. They will hold almost as much, yet their size can make the kitchen appear visually enlarged. Similar wall cabinets can be used. Drop-in stove tops in units of two, placed parallel to the wall, can forestall a cramped countertop when it is of less than standard depth. Exercise care when choosing shallow-base cabinets, since most appliances and free-standing ranges are 24 inches or more in depth.

Door Placement

Doors should be thought through individually as you are drawing kitchen plans. Virtually all cabinets and appliances offer either right-hand or left-hand openings, sometimes on special order. This includes refrigerators, freezers, base, and wall cabinets. Make sure they open in ways that ensure their usefulness — refrigerators opening to a counter where foods can be put down, as as example. Guard against doors that hit each other when they are opened or those that obstruct passage past them. The door(s) in and out of the room are equally important. Sometimes all that is required to solve a problem door is to change it from a right-hand hinge to a left-handed one. In other situations, it may be best to remove a kitchen door, leaving an open doorway. Draw in door opening directions on your working plans so that you will be alert to potential difficulties. Sliding doors on cabinets reduce swing-out space needs, but are often not as convenient as doors which allow full access to the interior.

SINKS

If the location of your sink is to be changed more than four feet from its present location, you may run into problems involving the vent stack. Changing vent lines can be costly. So can moving water lines. Generally, a plumber must do the work. It is expensive; however, if the sink's new location is superior, and the budget permits it, the expense can be justified.

Sink Functions

No matter where the sink is placed, it must have adequate space on either side, on the left (if you are right-handed) for stacking soiled dishes, on the right for draining anything washed by hand. The countertop near the sink also will be used during food preparation, for washing fresh vegetables and fruits, arranging flowers in vases and other tasks. If you use a folding dish drainer or provide a place to hang out of the way a traditional plastic drainer, the worktop to the right of the sink will be doubly useful. In England, as a matter of fact, dish drainers are suspended over the sink or counter, or at the bottom of a wall cabinet, arrangements we can copy.

Sink on Wall Away from Window

When a sink is integrated in a run of base cabinets with wall cabinets above, and there is no window behind the sink, headroom must be provided. This can be done several ways. Shallow wall cabinets, 6 inches deep rather than the standard 12½ inches, may be placed above the sink. Or cabinets of the usual depth may be placed higher on the wall. Or wall cabinets can be eliminated completely, with a shallow shelf or two between cabinets on either side of the sink. A shallow cabinet, with sliding glass doors as a change of pace from the other might be used as a contrast to the regular cabinets. A cabinet containing a set of small shallow drawers would work. The wall above the sink also might

This cabinet arrangement alternates open and closed shelving and then squeezes in additional shelving. The dividers at both ends of the open kitchen double as storage and display shelves.

Kohler's Epicurean sink has a raised center disposal basin and an outsized washing basin. The set-in cutting board and the dish-draining unit can free valuable counter space.

One of the two windows in this kitchen was closed in to create a U-shaped cabinet/counter setup. The window was wallboarded and covered with Z-brick that was used for the backsplash. The remaining window provides light for plants, but a shade can control glare.

be used to hang colanders, strainers, salad spinners and other implements used around the sink. A shelf over the kitchen sink could be used to display non-electric coffee and teapots, or mugs hung on cuphooks.

Corner Sinks

Planning advice used to warn against placing a sink or a stove in any corner of the kitchen, but designers now feel that corners can be used successfully. A corner can be widened, or flattened, by placing a base cabinet at an angle to the wall, allowing its back to become the third side of a triangle. When a stove or sink is situated in this way, the extra countertop space behind is also triangular. It would normally be surfaced with whatever countertop material has been used elsewhere.

The space behind a corner sink can be used to hold useful or decorative ware, for a raised platform for plants or other objects. A small cabinet can be fitted into the angles. The space under a corner sink can be deeper than under a sink placed along a wall, depending on whether you choose a cabinet that follows the wall, back to the corner or not.

When placing a sink in a corner, be sure to allow adequate space. The angles can be tricky. Single bowls are often placed diagonally, as double bowls may be. Double corner sinks are available from several manufacturers, some with the bowls at right angles to each other, others curved to the same basic arrangement. Finding base cabinets for corner sinks is no problem.

Corner sinks are still relatively unusual but can be attractive. Don't place a sink in a corner arbitrarily or just to be different. But if it will provide more counterspace, or better placement of appliances or the dining table and chairs, then it could be beneficial.

Above the Corner Sink. A corner sink may also prompt you to weigh the possibility of a new corner window, on one or both walls over the sink. These may be of fixed glass or may open and close for ventilation. Over a corner sink you might be tempted to install or to build a variation of the upper half of the old-fashioned corner cupboard. The extra, deep space behind a corner sink may encourage you to design a raised, artificially lit plant niche behind the faucets, or to build a

dramatic recess for display. Wall cabinets above an angled base may follow the lines by being similarly angled.

Contoured Sinks

Contoured sinks provide focus for a large kitchen. They work especially well with long runs of countertop. The idea is similar to making a fireplace the central focus in a living room. With a contoured sink, it or one of its surrounding elements is pulled out into the room, out of line with the adjacent built-ins. For instance, the sink cabinet can be canted into the room, with one corner projecting about six inches. If the dishwasher is angled in the same way, projecting no farther than six inches, the effect is similar. If the work counter and cabinets on both sides of the sinks are angled equally, a niche for the sink is formed that emphasizes its central function. Conversely, the sink itself may be pulled out three to six inches from the surrounding cabinetry, giving it visual prominence.

In a small or even middle-sized kitchen contouring will rarely be attractive, for its effect can easily seem cramped. Keep in mind that contouring makes cutting and fitting countertop materials more difficult, especially for amateurs. Standard base cabinets may also require certain alterations. Contouring, therefore, should be reserved for kitchens where it enhances function.

Peninsula and Island Sinks

Peninsula and island sinks are another modern option. These can work only if sufficient space exists for passage on both sides of the peninsula or island, as there is in the accompanying photograph. Peninsulas and islands can be very useful by making the work triangle more compact, eliminating unnecessary steps. They are often used to separate the working part of the kitchen from the dining area. Frequently, one side serves as breakfast-and-snack bar. At dinner it becomes the serving counter. Both peninsulas and islands also increase countertop work space and undercounter storage areas.

Island or peninsula sinks involve moving plumbing lines out from the side walls into the center of the room, not always easy or worthwhile. The proper venting mandated by plumbing codes may not be possible, since most codes require pipes to rise vertically from floor to ceiling.

A corner sink takes advantage of the view while reducing the sink space necessary. The tile is impervious to any drainage from the plants, which are positioned to utilize the light and the space otherwise wasted behind the sink.

This dual-level island has a sink, stove and ample space for snacks and meal preparation.

Sometimes the solution is to enclose pipes within cabinets, beams, or other housing. Because of the labor required in moving waste and intake plumbing lines away from the side walls, island and peninsula sinks inevitably result in higher installation costs than other types.

FOOD PREPARATION — COUNTERS

If you asked remodelers what was wrong with their old kitchens, most would say, "There isn't enough counter space." No matter how small, spacious, or equipment-saturated your kitchen, sufficient countertop workspace is essential.

Certain sections of the kitchen countertop are determined by the appliances near them. A section of heat-proof countertop, for instance, is ideal on one or both sides of a stove or top burners. Counter space on one side of the refrigerator, the one on which the door opens, is necessary to conveniently hold foods being removed. Sinks must have free counter space on either side, one for stacking soiled dishes before placing them in the sink or dishwasher, the other for draining and airdrying anything washed by hand. Some of the planned counter space must serve several uses. A sink counter space filled with soiled dishes hinders the cook. If the cook has to move a toaster, blender, and a jar of wooden spoons in order to assemble and mix a salad, efficiency drops.

Mixing and Baking Centers

If you bake breads, pies, or cakes, you need more countertop space. Rolling pastry dough, kneading bread dough, or cooling cakes on racks all need elbow room. When space permits, many planners advise including special mixing and baking centers in kitchens if they will be used. All the equipment, tools, and ingredients commonly used in baking can be kept in such a center. You can store your full-size mixer, there, either on the counter of in a base cabinet. A few manufacturers make mixers designed for permanent installation in special base cabinets which they provide. The mixers can be raised and lowered without being removed from the platforms to which they are attached. Other mixers may be similarly affixed to platforms in base cabinets provided by kitchen cabinet manufacturers, or they may be made by the handy home carpenter.

You will also want to keep small tools within arm's reach of your mixing and baking space — your rolling pin, measuring cups and spoons, mixing bowls, flour sifter, cake, pie, muffin, and bread tins. In the best of all possible kitchens, a mixing center would also have storage room for flour and sugar, not to mention baking

powder and soda, nuts, raisins, vanilla, chocolate, and the host of other supplies used mainly in baking. If your kitchen plan does not permit storing such ingredients at the baking center, provide enough room on the countertop for the many items you need to use in preparing a recipe.

Freeing Countertops from Clutter

Some people design and build enviable counter space only to crowd it to inefficiency with clutter. Toasters, blenders, can-openers, bread boxes, knife-holders, food processors, mixers, freestanding ovens and broilers, rotisseries, electric coffeemakers, cookbook stands, scales, dish racks — some or all of them steal workspace in many kitchens.

To avoid this, plan ahead for places for each piece of equipment you now own or plan to buy. Try to find places in kitchen cabinets for everything except what you use daily. Use your walls to hang or shelve items you want to keep handy. Can openers and knife racks, for example, can be attached to the wall. Perhaps the toaster would be more serviceable on the kitchen table or a nearby shelf. Bread boxes can be built into base cabinets. A shelf above the sink can offer quick access to items or spices you use often. Planning a new kitchen should also spur you mentally to review all your old kitchen items and decide which no longer are useful.

Planning Center

Do you plan meals in the kitchen — or would you if everything were at hand? Do you have one worn old cookbook stuffed

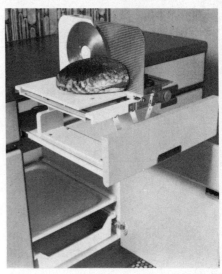

A fold-out cutting unit, coming from a kitchen drawer and projecting beyond the counter, enables convenient slicing and saves needed counter space.

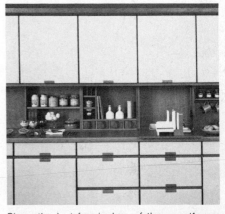

Since the last few inches of the counter are rarely used, they can take shallow modular display shelves. A fold-out cutting board projects beyond the counter for additional depth.

Knives retain a sharp edge when kept in a wood knife holder. This is safer and faster when looking for a particular knife.

Paper towels are located in the bottom half, with waxed paper and plastic wrap stored in the top section of this recessed unit.

into a drawer or a shelf full of cookbooks in another room to which you must dash to consult your recipe? Do you sit at the kitchen table for menu planning or use one of the children's desks upstairs? Where do you make out shopping lists? Do you like to use a bulletin board or a wipe-off slate to jot things down? Where do you put all the recipes clipped from newspapers and magazines?

All these and other tasks can be simplified by including a planning center in the kitchen. It may be as modest as a shelf for cookbooks and recipe files, or it may be a complete work center with a desk, shelves, and telephone.

STORAGE ARRANGEMENTS
Displays — Open Shelves

Open display of kitchenware is a noticeable and welcome trend today. It can help make the room warm, colorful, and personal. Collections and individual pieces picked up here and there make the room more truly yours and visually lively.

Open storage can be a single shelf tucked into a kitchen. Open storage can

You can build an activities center and desk from the same materials used for the kitchen cabinets.

be designed to hold just about everything portable, with no closed cabinets at all except base cabinets. Most remodelers want some combination of closed and open storage.

Open storage has advantages and disadvantages. Choices depend on your style of living and working as much as on the wall space and dimensions of the kitchen. Open shelving of any type is much easier for the do-it-yourselfer to build, because building, hanging and fitting doors often prove difficult. Shelving costs less than cabinets no matter what wood is used, even if the shelving is cut to order at the lumberyard. Open shelves give families with attractive possessions a chance to display them as well as have them convenient for use.

Much of the contemporary kitchen equipment can be stored on open shelves. Perhaps this has contributed to the trend toward open wall storage above closed base cabinets in kitchens. Some kitchenware lends itself to open shelves along the wall. Some of the most mundane items create an attractive display. Save objects that look disorganized, or are not lovely in themselves, for closed cabinets and cupboards.

Disadvantages. A drawback to open storage is that it collects dust and grease. Some may contend that dust and grease cause no problems when items are used frequently, but that holds true only when an item is used almost daily. Although

cups, saucers and plates used every day will be clean enough, the row of plates taken down only for company dinners, or the mold or platter used rarely, will need rinsing. If extra washing and dusting make open shelves unpleasant, but you like the sight of the objects, try to limit open storage to things used daily or to those for which dust is not a particular problem, such as vases (with or without fresh or dried bouquets), baskets, decorative pieces not used in cooking or eating, or perhaps even packaged and bottled foods.

People disturbed by rooms that are not orderly and neat rarely are happy with open-shelf storage.

Pegboard. Pegboard, whether in traditional white or in colored metal and plastic, is well suited to kitchen walls. Prongs on pegboard enable it to hold racks, shelves, easels, jars, bins. An entire wall or just a portion of one can be made of pegbord. One system uses outline drawings of every item to be hung on the board, from frying pan to rolling pin, for orderliness. Julia Childs uses the system in her own kitchen. Above the pegboard she has a shelf holding a few colored glass wine flasks which are very attractive. Under the shelf a light is hidden by a board attached to the shelf.

Racks. Whether pots and pans are hung on pegboards or from overhead or wall racks, they should be within easy reach from the stove and sink. Many spe-

This country style kitchen is unified by the use of materials. The cabinets, beams, post and window screen are of wood. Tile has been used on the floor, countertops, backsplash and toe space. The decorative face of the cooktop could be done with brick, Z-brick or ceramic tile.

cial devices intended for hanging utensils are now being manufactured, most commonly of black metal. Adequate hardware must be used, for a falling pot or pan can be dangerous. These ceiling racks come in several configurations — straight-line, semi-circular, and rectangular. The type you choose depends on where you intend to put it. Devices for hanging cooking ware can also be made at home quite simply with a minimum of skill and equipment by attaching a dowel to supports. Such a unit can run along a wall, a few inches in front of it, or can be hung over a peninsula or island.

Variations. Open shelves are often constructed as complete fixed cases, like traditional bookcases, or with heavy metal strips along the uprights that are designed to allow shelves to be moved up and down. Shelves can be designed to emphasize a strong horizontal line to unify a room, or to intensify the vertical and visually raise ceiling height.

Open kitchen shelves have no standard depth, just what best suits your purpose. Six-inch-deep shelves work very well for most grocery storage. With this depth, no package will disappear behind another, so you won't have to move cans to find other smaller ones. A shelf deeper than the standard 12½-inch-deep wall cabinet can accommodate large items like an old crock, terracotta strawberry jar, or over-size cannister.

The height between open shelves can vary, permanently or temporarily. Graduated shelves on a wall, with the deepest and tallest at the bottom and the most shallow in depth and height at the top can be effective looking as well as practical. A distance of only a few inches between shelves works best for herbs and spices, while tall bottles — which might contain anything from vinegar to vodka — require extra height.

Herbs and Spices. Some designers treat herbs and spices as purely decorative materials and place shelves of them directly above or alongside stoves. Actually seasonings lose their flavor more quickly when exposed to excess heat. Unless they are stored in opaque containers that shut out light, herbs and spices should be kept inside a cool, closed cupboard.

Often-Overlooked Spaces. The undersides of built-in wall cabinets usually are unused, as is the wall space between base cabinets and wall cabinets, the 12-to-18-inch wall space generally termed the backsplash. Both of these can be used for open or closed storage. A shallow, closed cabinet under the base cabinet near the food preparation area can hold seasonings. Cup hooks under a cabinet can hold cups or potholders, measuring spoons, or what-have-you. A magnetic knifeholder on the wall between counter and wall cabinet keeps knives sharp and out of a cluttered drawer (where they'll get knicked) and off of the counter (where they will be in your way). Two or more magnetic racks can be used for small metal tools — vegetable scraper, apple corer, or manual can-opener. A narrow shelf on this "extra" wall could hold a pepper mill or miniatures. Pegboard can work in this space, too, and a continuous run of it as backsplash between the work counter and the wall cabinets can answer many needs.

Wine Storage. Wine bottles are sometimes displayed in contemporary kitchens in open racks and bins that hold a half-dozen bottles or several cases. But wine

Spice holders set into wall tiles above the counter serve as decorative and practical assets.

Pegboard mounted on furring strips holds an assortment of frequently used cooking necessities.

Base cabinet drawers should come in graduated sizes. The open sides of this bottom drawer prevent seldom-used items from becoming "lost" in a back corner.

that is stored for any length of time should be kept at temperatures cooler than that of most homes. Further, a dark storage place is preferable to a light one. The hazard is that wine kept under improper conditions will turn — lose its bouquet or become vinegary. The same is true for wine stored upright. When wine is horizontal the liquid is always in contact with the cork, which keeps it from drying out and losing its seal. If the seal is broken and air reaches the wine, it is ruined. Therefore, although wine racks look good it is not a good idea to place them in the kitchen. Use a base cabinet set against an outside wall, away from the oven, refrigerator or hot water pipes, if you don't have a cool cellar or closet.

Specialty Cabinets

There are as many styles of "hutch" cabinets, buffets, antique "dressers," Hoosiers, and pie safes as there are varieties of period furniture. Almost all of these many types have one characteristic in common: they provide some sort of open display.

Rearrangement of Interior Cabinet Space

Remodelers who plan to refurbish rather than replace older cabinets can get many usable interior fittings in department, hardware, and furniture stores. They are usually plastic, plastic-coated wire, or enameled steel in primary colors or white. One company, which distributes through hardware stores, is Elfa Trading Company (395 Broadway, New York City). It produces free-standing baskets and racks, and white enameled steel runners that can be cut to size and mounted on the wall of a cabinet or under a shelf. Another maker is Rubbermaid, whose products are widely distributed. Their pull-out drawer units on runners can be screwed to the bottom of a base cabinet. These hard plastic ivory-colored drawers are 19½ inches deep, which allows a roomy fit in the standard 24-inch base cabinet. The drawer comes in two widths, 12 inches and 16 inches, and both are 2¾ inches high. Two of these drawers can be stacked with Rubbermaid's stacking kit. Several kits may be stacked one on top of another. (See also Chapter 6.)

Bins. Stackable plastic bins are made by several manufacturers. Some are of solid sheets (as for a plastic dishpan), and some of grids or other kinds of openwork which might be good for storing vegetables that need air — such as onions or potatoes. Generally, their corner posts protrude to permit stacking. The least expensive bins, which would probably not stack satisfactorily, are those made as kitty litter pans, but with the potential to hold kitchen sundries. Inexpensive open-front stacking bins made in six colors by Hammerplast are sold in hardware stores. Beylerian makes stackable bin drawers that are as enclosed as any other sort of drawer. These polypropylene drawers come in sets of three, and can be joined into stacks of six, nine, twelve or even more drawers. Workbench, a retail furniture store with outlets on the East Coast, the Midwest, Canada, the South and California, sells 19-inch deep wire baskets in units with two baskets each, which in turn may be stacked. Each basket is 14½ inches wide and 14½ inches deep. Their distinction is that they pull out like drawers. Matching, nonstacking, open-fronted bins in five graduated sizes are made in polypropylene by Mail Order Plastic.

This island with a butcher block surface can be used as a chopping board/food preparation area or as an additional eating counter, whichever is most in demand at the moment.

Heights of slide-out bins (these are from Wood Mode) can be varied to hold particular types of foods. Another advantage is that storage space toward the back becomes accessible.

New Cabinets — Styling

Most manufacturers of custom or stock cabinets make styles labeled "Colonial," "modern," "provincial," "Spanish," or whatever. All are misnomers. No citizen of pre-Revolutionary America or of Spain would recognize a single detail in the kitchen units that bear their respective names as labels. The entire concept of built-in kitchen cabinets as we know them today is very much a product of the twentieth century. Until the 1920s and 1930s most American kitchens were designed as a series of free-standing parts.

Choose designs you like and ignore the labels, since they do not describe the real thing anyway. Buyers of kitchen cabinets will soon realize that standard wall and base cabinets are modular units offered in an almost infinite choice of materials, finishes, colors, and decorative details.

Bar or Hospitality Center. Modern kitchen cabinets allow you to easily create a hospitality center. Sufficient space must be provided for the extra cabinet or two necessary. Leave enough room around them the host or hostess can prepare drinks without interfering with the activities of another person working in the kitchen at the same time. Ideally, space would also be adequate for one, two, or more guests to assist or gather 'round, since sociability is part of hospitality. A hospitality center set up elsewhere in the house would have the same needs as one in the kitchen.

Wherever a home bar is set up, a base cabinet or its equivalent is fundamental. It may be a custom or stock kitchen cabinet, or may be a bar created from another piece of furniture.

The further away your bar is from the kitchen refrigerator, (and the more space and money you have), the more tempting it becomes to include a small under-counter refrigerator. Mini-refrigerators are a luxury, but they can save steps and ease entertaining by keeping cold mixers and ice readily at hand. Small under-counter machines ice are said to make cubes that are clearer than those produced by regular refrigerators.

An extra sink is also a luxury, but it can be small and need not have a hotwater connection, just a high faucet. For a professional type of bar there are small machines called glasswashers. These are useful for families which give frequent cocktail parties for 25 guests or more. A glass can be pushed down over the outlet and then, in a few seconds, removed sparkling and sanitary. Mini-hot-water heaters are also now on the market. Designed primarily for occasional use, they are activated only when the hot water tap is turned on. It's an apparatus that can save energy when used in the right situation.

A pantry storage closet need not be deep to provide space for box and canned goods. This closet has both deep and shallow shelves to hold small appliances as well as pantry goods.

A serving unit slides out on casters from under the countertop. The front wood-grain panel and toe-space trim match the facing of the cabinets for a built-in look.

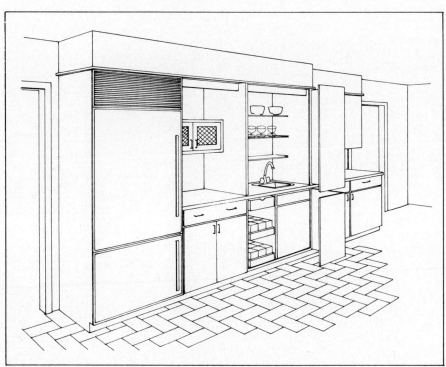

Folding doors hide bar accessories, storage and a preparation center, with recessed lighting built into the soffit above.

A lazy Susan offers almost 360 degrees of usable storage space and will fit into a corner so its height is just below the counter level. The cabinet framing acts as support for the counter. If counter material will be heavy — such as tile or butcher block — cross-braces are added.

"Blind" Base Cabinets

Two base cabinets of equal depth can abut each other in the corner. One of them would then be what is termed a "blind" base cabinet. A blind base cabinet is one whose access is partially blocked by the abutting cabinet. It does allow storage but does not offer easy access. This limits the corner storage possibilities.

Three possible solutions to wasted space in base cabinet corners are manufactured in stock and custom cabinets, two of them for cabinets of standard depth and width. One calls for two identical quarter-round shelves, one mounted on the cabinet door, the other on the stile. This allows either door to swing out. The second practical solution calls for several pie-cut circle shelves that are attached to the cabinet door. A third solution to corner waste in base cabinets is the lazy

This open kitchen has been modified with the addition of a floor-to-ceiling partition and a ceiling-hung cabinet. The counter extending out from the base cabinet/divider serves as an eating bar on one side and a cooking facility on the other. Note the dropped ceiling over the eating area.

Susan, offered by many manufacturers. This usually calls for a larger base cabinet occupying up to 36 inches of wall space on each side of the corner. Its interior is fitted with a device variously called a lazy-Susan, merry-go-round, or carousel. These full-circled shelves can be rotated to bring any portion to the front. Similar carousels are available in wall-hung units, although they are used less frequently. Carousels are satisfying to users because they bring everything to the front at the turn of the wheel, but the design mechanics are such that even they waste some space.

Space Behind or Under Corner Stoves

Try not to place anything behind a corner stove, since reaching across a lighted stove can be hazardous. The triangular space behind a full-size stove placed at an angle to the corner is not accessible and must be wasted. But it is too little an area to worry about. A drop-in corner burner top, on the other hand, allows full access to whatever base cabinet is below.

Corner Conflicts. Always be alert to corner conflicts. For example, avoid placing two appliances, such as a refrigerator and oven, catty-cornered to each other. Their doors, when open, will interfere

This closet wet bar utilizes every inch of space. Shelves for glassware climb the back wall, freeing the cabinet space below the bar for sink plumbing and liquor storage.

with each other, as will two people working in the kitchen. When considering the possibility of a flip-down table or flip-down bar in a corner, plan so it is not in the way of kitchen appliances or cabinets.

Testing the Floor Plan

Whenever you consider a design, especially one that angles out or has other unusual features, you can visualize it better if you try it out with a paper pattern. Cut out newspaper or brown wrapping paper to scale and lay it on the floor according to your plan. A similar sort of dry run can be experimented with by tacking up string in simulated dimensions. Leave these in place for a day to two, as you use the room. You will soon learn whether or not your plan is realistic.

DRAWING CABINET ELEVATIONS

If you are replacing the old kitchen cabinets, or simply adding cabinet space, you will need to draw elevations of the new cabinets. On a sheet of vellum or graph paper measure in two inches (actual size) from the top and left borders and draw very light lines. The horizontal line will represent the ceiling. Using a ½ scale (½ inch = 1 foot), measure from the ceiling line and draw the floor line. The ½ scale will be used on all cabinet elevations.

If you will be ordering prefabricated cabinets — a less expensive alternative to built-on-site cabinets — work from the manufacturer's brochure as to exact sizes.

Some custom-made cabinets can also be ordered this way. Although we will use stock sizes in the examples in this chapter, you should substitute the exact sizes once you are sure of them.

Each wall of cabinets in the kitchen will be drawn as a separate elevation. From the new floor plan find the cabinet end that would be on your left if you were standing in the middle of the remodeled kitchen, as shown in the illustration. This wall of cabinets will be drawn first. Succeeding walls will be drawn by moving a clockwise direction. Only the new cabinets will need to be drawn if you are adding to existing cabinets.

Measure the length of the cabinets on the first wall from the end of the left side to the end on the right or, if the cabinets turn the corner on the right side, to the wall. (Since the floor plan is drawn at ¼ scale, be very cautious when measuring from one to the other to ensure that you do not miscalculate.) From the vertical line on the new sheet, which represents the left side of the cabinets, measure the length of the cabinets and draw a vertical line for the right side. Draw a series of horizontal lines using dimensions as in the illustration on page 32. The fur down (soffit) shown in this illustration is a blocked out space above the cabinets, since a shelf at this height would not be practical. This is optional, however, and will not need to be drawn if you wish to use full ceiling cabinets rather than furred down cabinets.

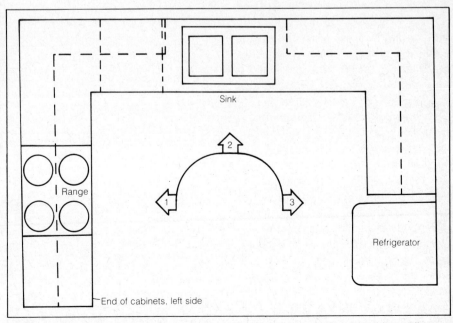

When drawing plan for layout of cabinets and appliances, start by drawing the cabinet wall to your left. Then move clockwise to draw all walls for which new work will be necessary.

The 4 inch backsplash is a general standard and is used on premanufactured countertops. If you are not using a premanufactured top you may consider having the backsplash installed to the bottom of the wall cabinets, in which case the line shown will not be necessary. Leave at least 16 inches from the countertop to the bottom of the cabinets when installing new cabinets. For those who are adding on to the present kitchen cabinets, you will need to check these measurements since there could be some differences. Use fur down or ceiling cabinets to match your existing cabinets.

If the cabinets turn the corner on the right side, block out as shown in the illustration, as shown, shading with diagonal lines. On the next elevation the block out will occur reversed on the left side.

Any doors or windows in the wall of the elevation you are drawing must be measured from the floor plan and located on the elevation with vertical lines. The wall cabinets should stop at 3 to 4 inches from each side of a window, and both wall and base cabinets should stop 3 to 4 inches from each side of a door. Now measure and place two vertical lines for the range, refrigerator, or dishwasher. Wall cabinets above the refrigerator should go no lower than 72 inches off the floor and no closer than 30 inches above a range or cooktop. Keep the range a minimum of 12 inches from the edge of the window so that the curtains will not be near the cooktop.

In the usable cabinet areas that remain draw in very light lines for the tops and bottoms of drawers and doors. Measure and draw in the sink. Since this area is needed for plumbing access there can be a "dummy" drawer and double doors which extend about 2 inches beyond either edge of the sink. On the remaining areas you may divide the doors and drawers to suit your needs. For smaller areas, such as between a wall and the range, you may be restricted in your design. For instance, if this width is only 30 inches, you can have a single door that is 26 inches wide or double doors that are 13 inches wide. When designing in larger areas you will have more freedom in the door and drawer arrangement. Try to keep the doors and drawers from becoming too wide; 28 inches is a reasonable maximum width. Leave a two-inch space between the cabinet door or double door and the end of the cabinets or another door, as on page 33, center. If you would like a series of drawers in the base cabinets, draw them in (you can use the dimensions in the illustration, which shows two different arrangements.) When the cabinet design is complete, darken and finalize the lines. Door designs for the cabinets do not need to be drawn in. Label the elevations. Since the elevations are only graphic representations of what you want, a minimum of lettering is required. The title of each elevation is based on the direction you would be facing if you were standing in the center of the kitchen looking at the wall of cabinets. So, if you were facing north the tile for that elevation would be "KITCHEN CABINETS — NORTH WALL." You can determine the general direction of north simply by locating the rising or setting sun.

A cross-section is required for the kitchen cabinets as well as for specialized areas and/or a linen closet.

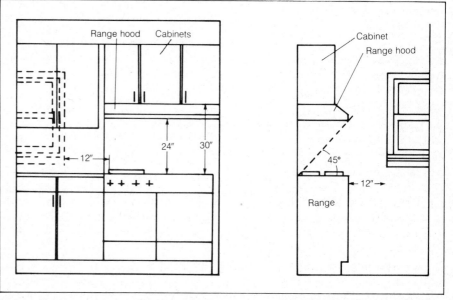

At right, for adequate headroom at the range the hood should not project beyond a 45 degree angle. At left, the 30 inch clearance may be reduced to 24 inches if the underside has protection equal to at least ¼ inch asbestos millboard covered with no less than 28 gauge sheet metal (.015 stainless steel, .024 aluminum, or .020 copper) or equivalent construction.

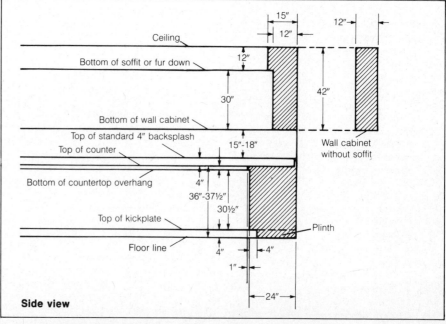

Shown are standard dimensions for kitchens with ceilings 8 feet high. The plinth height (usually 4 inches), may be adjusted to create a higher or lower counter. If you decide not to use a soffit, the wall cabinet can reach to the ceiling, or a railing can be added to the top of the cabinet to create a display shelf.

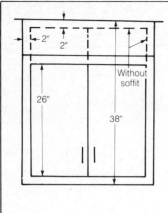

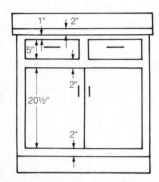

These are nominal dimensions to locate tops and bottoms of drawers and doors used for drawing purposes; actual dimensions should be worked out to fractions of an inch according to the cabinet you build or buy.

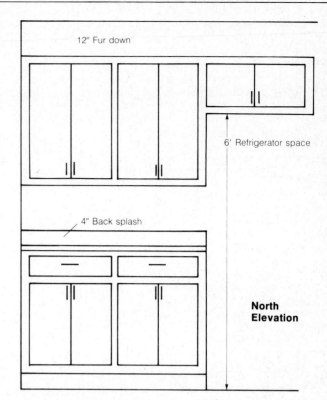

North Elevation

Title each elevation according to the direction you would face standing in the center of the kitchen looking at the cabinet wall.

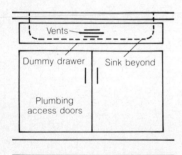

The cabinet below the sink may have a "dummy" drawer, usually vented, with wide doors for access to the plumbing underneath.

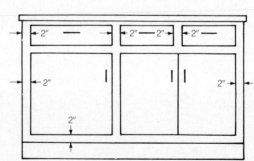

Leave a two-inch space on the sides of the drawers and doors when drawing them into the cabinet plans. Try to keep doors and drawers from becoming too wide; 28 inches is a reasonable maximum width.

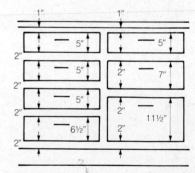

Shown are two typical arrangements for tiers of drawers, depending upon the types and sizes of the items to be stored.

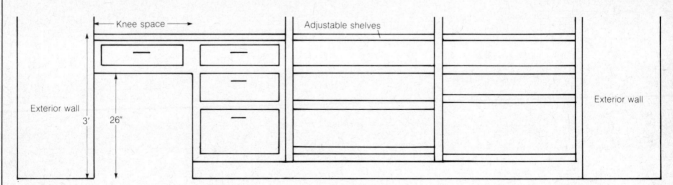

Vary the kitchen desk height depending upon the height of the drawer (if any) above the open knee space. Measure to ensure that the height of the knee space will be sufficient and comfortable for those in the household.

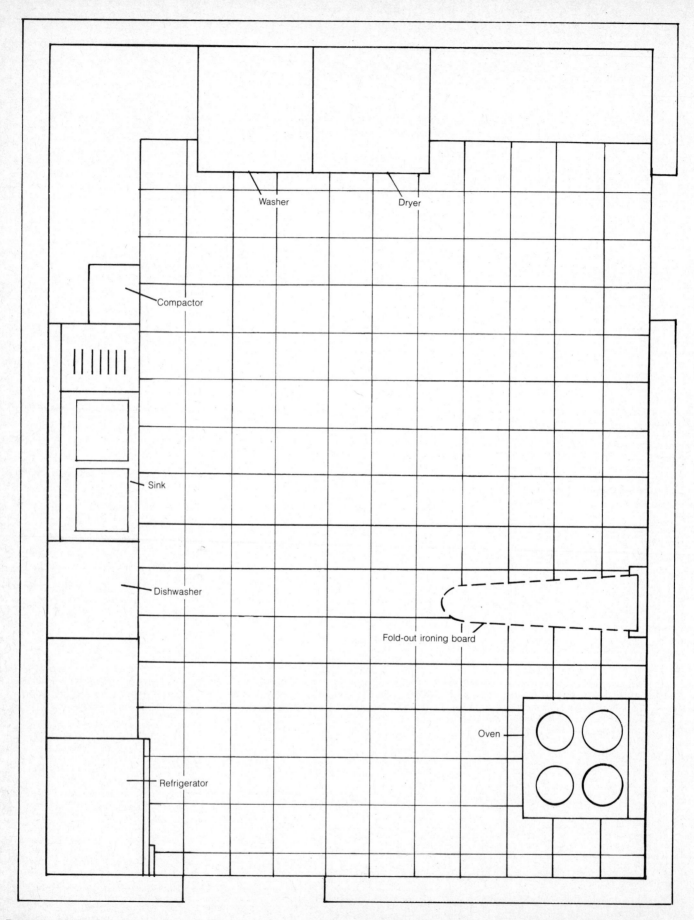

This well-laid-out kitchen is drawn to a scale of ½ inch equals 1 foot. The appliance sizes, based upon common sizes available, are: oven, dryer, washer, each 30"x30"; compactor, 15⅛"x12½"; refrigerator, 34½"x25½"; dishwasher, 24⅛"x25"; sink, 36"x25"; ironing board, 12"x54". If these dimensions match those of the appliances you plan to buy, make copies of this page and cut out the individual pieces, or trace the fixtures.

4
MATERIALS, PRODUCTS APPLIANCES

This kitchen, in a Victorian home, was recently renovated. The original pressed tin wall covering was retained and repainted. The gas range was rebuilt and a range hood added. A sheet metal cover was designed so the modern hood unit would blend with the period style of the room.

Good food can be produced with inadequate tools. More than one visitor to Paris has marveled at Cordon Bleu cooking acccomplished in cramped apartment-house kitchens with crotchety stoves and outdated equipment.

Mimi Sheraton, the authoritative New York *Times* food writer, says in her book of recipes and reminiscences, *From My Mother's Kitchen*, that all her mother's wonderful cooking "was done with the worst sort of utensils. Except for a few ancient, lethally sharp carbon-steel knives, my mother's kitchenware made a mockery of all recipes calling for well-insulated heavy pots and enameled interiors. Her pots were of the thinnest

aluminum, except for one or two that were thin enameled steel and for her cast-iron skillet. . . . The aluminum pots became so dented on the bottom that they would not stand upright when empty. None of this seemed to affect the excellence of her soups and stews, her cakes and pies."

Talent can overcome obstacles, but producing good meals with inferior equipment takes more work. Most of us are helped immeasurably by good tools.

COOKING UNITS

The choice of stoves ranges across a wide field. The cooking means and techniques you select affect the design and layout of

your kitchen just as much as the quality of life they help encourage. Work out a clear idea of what is available before making final decisions as to gas or electric units, or your final floor plan.

Gas vs. Electric

In deciding which fuel is best for you, consider that in recent decades electric ranges have sold at a somewhat better rate than gas stoves, in part because gas is not available everywhere. According to government and independent reports, both fuels provide about equal amounts of energy for cooking. Exactly how much energy any unit consumes may soon be able to be ascertained from attached tags stating energy data. Yet even if gas- and electric-powered units use similar amounts of energy in cooking, the cost of operating a gas stove can be half that of an electric one, although there are still some areas of relatively cheap electricity.

Ovens may be gas or electric, free-standing or encased in wall cabinets. They may also, of course, be incorporated within completely free-standing or drop-in-ranges. Electric ovens include conventional, convection, and microwave units. Both gas and electric ovens may be pyrolytic, self-cleaning at extremely high temperatures, or catalytic, continuously self-cleaning at normal baking temperatures. Both gas and electric manufacturers make wall ovens in single and double units of varying interior dimensions and as double units in combinations such as conventional/microwave or conventional/convection. Both microwave and convection ovens are available in small-appliance departments and at hardware stores as free-standing, counter-top units.

Gas. Gas top-of-stove burners enable minute adjustments of the flame. Even infinite-adjustment electric burners may seem inflexible in comparison. Gas burners can keep food at a simmer or any other level indefinitely because there is no on/off cycling. These are the primary reasons so many well-known cooks prefer gas cooktops.

Another advantage of gas is its speed — gas cooktops heat immediately and cool quickly once turned off. The control knobs for gas stoves are invariably at the front of the stove, making it unnecessary to reach over hot pans or heated elements. The flame of a gas stove is always visible, which results in fewer accidental burns because even children know that fire is hot.

Gas is more widely available than most people realize. In many places that do not have piped gas, bottled gas is delivered regularly.

Gas units, on the other hand, may not be as satisfactory as electric units. If the pilot light for a gas oven has been removed for conservation reasons, as is true of most new stoves, maintenance problems may occur. Pilots have been replaced by electrical ignition systems, but these rule out use of gas ovens during breaks in electrical service, brownouts, or when a family is on economical time-of-day electric service. (Top burners on gas stoves can be lit with a match when electric ignition fails.)

Self-cleaning ovens in gas stoves, with few exceptions, clean continuously. A special surface on the oven walls, which needs only wiping or rinsing, makes the catalytic system work. Continuous-clean ovens have been reported as less satisfactory than pyrolytic self-cleaning ovens. Pyrolytic self cleaning takes place with the oven turned to extremely high heat for a specified number of hours, during which the soil in the oven is reduced to ash. (Serious spillovers in either type need to be wiped up.) Yet pyrolytic ovens are said to use less energy overall because they are well insulated. However, continuous-clean catalytic ovens are less expensive than pyrolytic models.

Broilers. Gas broilers on freestanding ranges generally are low to the floor. Self cleaners often have waist-high broilers. Although household units are called broilers, they seldom are capable of temperatures high enough to really broil. A true broiler produces 35,000 BTU (British Thermal Units) per hour. Oven/broiler units cannot produce that much heat and actually braise/broil the food, which may toughen meat.

Waste King Universal makes a small broiler unit which can be built into a home

kitchen. This unit will generate 36,000 BTU's. It does require its own exhaust fan with a filter.

Electric. Model for model, gas and electric ranges are nearly equal in initial cost. Electric cooktops are easy to clean and can be disconnected for cleaning. Electric cooktops will maintain the heat to which they are set (though they will go through periodic on/off cycles) no matter how strong the wind from an open window, which could affect a gas flame. Electric ovens do an excellent job of maintaining heat and most people are satisfied with electric broiling.

The newest development in cooktops, such as magnetic induction cooking and smooth-top surfaces, are designed for electricity, not gas.

Gas and electric equipment can be purchased in component parts, rather than as free-standing stoves or ranges. This makes it possible to use a gas surface unit for stove-top cooking and an electric oven in a wall cabinet.

Burners and Alternatives

Surface Units. Surface cooking units, whether gas or electric, are top burners fitted into prepared openings on the countertop. These fit into work surface without objectionable seams, no matter what counter material is used.

Gas Drop-in Countertop Units. Gas surface units differ from one another only in detail — one maker's burner may be easier to clean than that of another, or may be designed with a different spillover bowl. Gas burners are made in two- or four-section units, which may be placed anywhere on a countertop where a gas connection can be provided. Some units come with a grill or a fifth burner. Other models offer a gas-fired broiler or barbecue.

Electric Drop-in Countertop Units. Electric surface units come in three main

Modern gas cooktops have features which make their cleaning and maintenance simpler. Here, all parts are removable, and the top surface lifts for quick wipe-up of spills.

types: conventional coil units, glass-top or smooth-surface units, and magnetic-induction surface units.

Conventional Electric-coil Units. They are by far the most widely used type of electric burner. They heat and cool much faster than they used to, although still not

The continuous-cleaning oven has eliminated one of the hardest cleaning problems in the kitchen. Except for major spills, these ovens keep their interior surfaces clean.

Stainless steel was once considered usable in industrial and hospital facilities only. The stainless cooktop and backsplash offer an unusual decorative feature.

A gas drop-in burner unit hooks up to the gas supply through a pre-cut opening in the countertop. The necessary heat-resistant backsplash is provided here by ceramic tile.

as quickly as gas. Some have what is called "infinite" variability, which means, according to their manufacturers, that users can adjust the supply of heat minutely, as with gas. Coil-type units come in six-inch and eight-inch diameter rings. Many people choose two of each for their countertops. The diameter size means more with electric burners than with gas because cooking on an electric ring with a pot smaller than the unit wastes electricity, while a pot larger than the unit will heat slowly. Special electric units such as pancake griddles and barbecue grills can also be built into countertops as surface units. Their wattage may differ from manufacturer to manufacturer; although higher wattage means higher energy consumption, it also indicates a faster-working burner.

Smooth-top Units. These were the newest innovation until magnetic induction cooktops were introduced. The smooth white tops look like part of the countertop until they are in use, then they take on a slightly yellowish cast. If you had never seen a smooth-top before and entered a kitchen where one had been installed, you might think that no cooking facilities existed, so completely can they blend into a counter's surface. They are handsome, and look as though they would be the easiest stove top to clean, a factor that is surely part of their appeal.

However, the units may be more difficult to clean than other burners. The smooth-top retains heat for forty-five minutes to an hour after being turned off.

In that time spillovers can bake in, making the residue difficult to remove. The smooth-top surface can also become stained. To avoid stains, special ceramic cooktop cleansers must be used promptly and regularly. Stains also can interfere with heating capabilities.

On many of the units only certain flat-bottomed cookware will work. Others take any utensils. If the bottom of the cookware is soiled, the cooking surface may be marred. Because smooth tops don't show heat, members of the family can easily be burned. So can pots and pans, if left on the unit. This can happen even after a burner is turned off, since they lose heat slowly. All smooth-top units now have lights to show when the burners are on. Some smooth-top units heat more slowly than conventional coils. Their initial cost continues to be substantially higher than for conventional coil units.

Magnetic-induction Surface-cooking Units. New and different, these need no new cooking methods, according to manufacturers. One maker says that electric energy is magnetically transferred from below the surface into the cooking uten-

sil. Heat is "induced" into the cookware, according to their brochure, resulting in more efficient, cleaner cooking.

The system allows a single burner to be placed almost anywhere on a countertop, whereas conventional coils, smooth surface, and gas units come in sets of two. A magnetic-induction burner looks like a ceramic square, and may be plain or decorated. They may be grouped in a long row, staggered on a diagonal, or arranged nearly any way on a countertop that pleases users. Some versions look like conventional glass top burners.

Magnetic-induction burners convert energy to heat only when a pan is set on them. The burner never becomes as hot as a conventional burner. Makers claim the system does not overheat the kitchen, an asset during hot weather. Because the burner does not get hot, it is easier to clean, since spillovers and drips can be wiped away quickly.

Certain types of stainless steel and cast iron utensils must be used on magnetic-tops. Aluminum, copper, or glass cookware will not allow the necessary transfer of energy from the magnetic electric unit embedded in the burner which must pass through the pot to the food. Magnetic surface units cost more than other types of surface burners on the market.

Ovens

The main features to consider, after making a choice between gas and electric, are the size of the oven's interior, whether you need one or two ovens, and what attachments are practical for your family. Most standard ovens, for instance, will hold a 20-pound turkey. But if you regularly roast larger ones, or simmer huge casseroles, or turn out half a dozen loaves of bread at a time, you will want to investigate more spacious ovens.

Timers can be one of the most practical of oven attachments. Some can be set to turn ovens on and off at predetermined times. Some can also be set to keep food warm after the oven turns off. Other optional attachments on conventional ovens include rotisseries, meat temperature probes, and more.

One important feature to look for is a glass oven door. It allows you to keep watch on the progress of a dish without opening the oven. However, some of the popular doors made of black glass can so obscure vision as to make them virtually

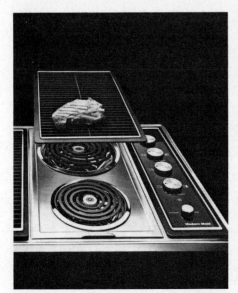

Modern Maid Manufacturers a series of interchangeable accessories. All fit into its basic cooktop, which features downdraft venting.

Glass doors on these built-in ovens ensure success (and save energy) by enabling the cook to watch a dish without opening the door.

worthless. Even some doors of purportedly clear glass have a wire mesh embedded in them that can also seriously interfere with visibility.

Convection Ovens. Introduced only a few years ago, convection ovens now are widely used. They include a small concealed interior fan that blows heated air all around the oven interior. Because the air circulates, convection ovens bake and roast somewhat more rapidly than conventional ones. Their manufacturers also suggest that food bakes at temperatures 25 to 50 degrees lower than in conventional ovens. Combined, the two factors can save some energy.

A convection oven never gets hot outside, so it transfers little heat into the kitchen. It does not need venting, and rarely smokes. Free-standing, self-cleaning models made with a stainless steel exterior, tray, and grill are easy to clean. Almost nothing sticks to the stainless steel, which washes easily with soapy water. The walls require only an occasional wipe.

Manufacturers of convection ovens say they broil as well as bake and roast. However, some testers maintain that convection ovens "mimic broiling" when preheated and used at their highest settings. Meat, fish, and fowl do not need turning when broiled in these ovens, but they will not be quite as crispy and brown as they would be if made in a conventional broiler. Extra time will enable roasts to brown nicely.

Microwave Ovens. Microwave ovens have been around for decades in some restaurants. In the last ten years they have become home appliances. They can cook incredibly quickly. Roasts that might normally take 20 to 30 minutes a pound can be cooked in 8 or 10 minutes a pound.

However, food cooked in a microwave oven often demands a certain amount of coddling. Roasts usually have to be turned at least once in contrast to conventional ovens and convection ovens. Baked meat, fish, and fowl usually need to be covered during part of the cooking time to prevent over-cooking. Microwave cooking can demand more attention than other methods. However, as microwave users point out, the lessened cooking time often means that other kitchen chores can be accomplished between microwave dish turnings.

Microwave ovens require utensils made of specified materials. Aluminum (unless specified by the manufacturer), stainless steel, copper, cast iron, and enamelware are unsuitable. Glass ovenware, Corning's pyroceram cookware, and certain plastics newly developed for microwave cookery are the main utensils.

Many ceramics, porcelain, and pottery can be used in microwave ovens. Some foods do not brown in a microwave oven unless cooked in "browning pan" or under a "browning element" which can be turned on to brown food.

Cooking with a microwave oven takes some relearning, and microwave-radiation speculation has caused much comment. But many users seem satisfied with microwave units.

Foods do not cook in microwave ovens by means of the heat from a fire, as they do in all other methods. This is part of the reason for the radiation arguments. Actually microwaves cook by friction, which causes heat. The water molecules in food vibrate and rub against each other when struck by the microwaves. The rubbing causes heat, which is transferred through the food, since the microwaves only penetrate two inches, and the food is cooked. If your microwave leaks energy, any adjacent material containing water may also "cook".

Testing the Seal. The seal on a microwave oven can, and should be, tested every 6 to 12 months. A simple home test requires only a small fluorescent tube. Take a glass measuring cup or bowl and put the fluorescent tube into it. Set the cup into the oven. Place a cup of water in the oven, and turn the oven on. You will

If counterspace is at a premium, a microwave can be installed in a raised cabinet. Back ventilation space must be provided for the fan.

A special cabinet, designed to match the kitchen cupboards, can be made for a microwave so that it becomes a part of the kitchen.

Some manufacturers offer built-in units that combine microwave and conventional oven units. Separate units may also be built in.

notice that while the oven is on the tube will glow. Now take the tube out but leave the cup of water in the oven (because you should never operate the oven with nothing in it) and turn it on. Keeping the length of the tube flush to the door edge, run the tube around the edges of the door. If there is a leak, the tube will glow, even if only faintly. Inexpensive testing devices are also on the market.

Complete Ranges

Complete stoves, or ranges, come in three forms: freestanding, slide-in, and drop-in. The first, of course, stands on its own legs. The latter two can be aligned with countertops. The slide-in stove has its own base, while the drop-in is usually housed in a base cabinet or supported by the countertop.

The ranges are made with any and all of the variables already described for component parts. The free-standing range can be placed anywhere in the kitchen. Slide-in models are essentially free-standing stoves without side panels. This allows them to be set into place in a run of cabinets, with a neat fit. Drop-in units do not have legs, and their base cabinets are made with the same kick space as all the other cabinets in the kitchen.

When you buy any range, make certain that the top burners are spaced far enough apart to allow use of several large pots at the same time, without crowding and without one or another of them being pushed off center. Spacing can be particularly important if you sometimes entertain large groups or cook for a dozen or more. Canning and freezing also demand large utensils.

Commercial Ranges. Commercial ranges appeal to some families because they have more and better-spaced burners than stoves designed for home use. The smallest commercial ranges have six burners and can fit into a modest space. Large restaurant stoves with twelve burners would fit only in huge kitchens and thus are not practical for most families.

Commercial ranges are extremely well made, with superior insulation in their ovens. Many come with sizable stove-top griddles. Their sturdy appearance appeals to many kitchen designers and to serious cooks, who are their greatest fans. They can easily last a lifetime. Their heavy-duty burners can deliver more heat more quickly than those on the usual kitchen stove. But restaurant ranges do not have self-cleaning ovens, although some have porcelain-finished interiors that wash easily. They do not come in colors to match your decor, but are usually finished in stainless steel, matte black, grey or sometimes copper. Gadgets as clocks, timers, glass doors, meat probes, and down-venting are omitted.

The advantage in purchasing a professional range is its cast-iron cooking surfaces. These permit use of pots and pans of varying shapes and sizes. The heat-diffusion characteristics of the solid top outperform those of a conventional range, making the professional model ideal for low-intensity, prolonged cooking.

Wood Stoves. Wood cook stoves came into general use in this country in the 19th century and then virtually disappeared beginning in the 1920s, when gas and then electric ranges became cheaper and more widely available. Although rural electrification finally was completed immediately after World War II, wood stoves — often in combination with gas or electric — were still manufactured in the early 1960s, until demand fell off. Now energy concerns have brought about a resurgence of cooking with wood, with two models offered in the current Sears catalogue. Wood and even coal cookstoves are offered by many other companies. They are more practical in cooler climates because they do heat up the kitchen.

The revival of the manufacture and use of wood stoves in the late 1970s and early 1980s occurred because the price of oil and electricity greatly increased in cost. Many homes with heating costs which formerly seemed nominal were suddenly transformed into expensive fuel gobblers. Some householders switched to wood to save money. Wood stoves also are used both to heat homes and to supplement solar or conventional heat systems.

If you put a wood stove in your kitchen, find one designed for cooking as well as for heating. Wood cookstoves are not difficult to use after the first few tries. Instead of adjusting surface heat by the turn of a knob, you move the pot to a cooler place. Some people feel that it is harder to cook on a wood stove.

There are other problems with wood stoves. Someone has to keep the woodbox filled with logs and kindling of the right size, shape, and quality. There must be a place outdoors or in a woodshed to stack wood. You must remove the ashes. An excellent chimney must be provided if a wood stove is not to be a fire hazard, and pipes must be connected with care. Any

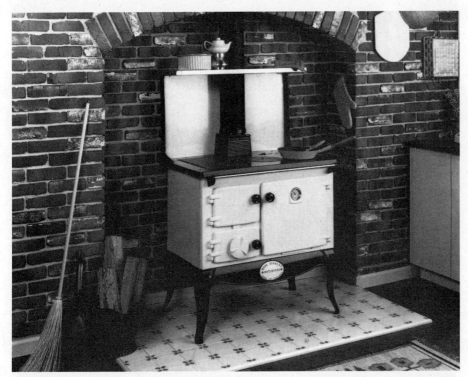

As energy becomes more expensive, many people turn to wood for heating and cooking. This wood stove is a modern unit. It is better designed than older stoves, with more insulation and better efficiency. However, it requires careful installation to avoid risk of fire or injury.

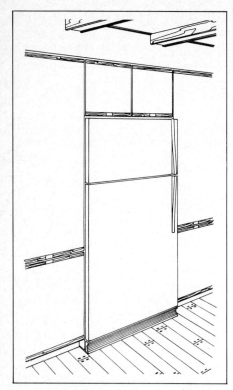

If storage is at a minimum, you can surround a free-standing refrigerator with flush cabinetry, leaving space behind the cabinets.

Enclosing this side-by-side with cabinetry provides an extra wall surface, which you can cover with cork and use for messages.

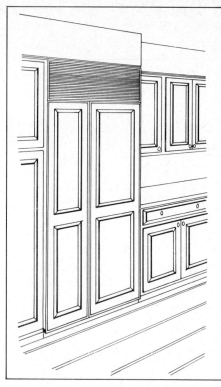

The custom wood grain panels on this built-in side-by-side refrigerator match those of the kitchen cabinets in both grain and trim style.

chimney requires periodic sweeping and inspection for creosote, the wood residue that can result in chimney fires. It is almost impossible to make woodstove ovens perform as reliably as gas and electric ovens, though most have thermostats that indicate the temperature. The ovens often are smaller than modern ones. In addition, the stoves do not come with hoods or vent units. Few families today rely solely on a wood-fired cookstove. Most households supplement them with one or two gas or electric components.

REFRIGERATORS AND FREEZERS
The size and style of refrigerator and freezer you choose depend on the size of your household, pocketbook, cooking, and shopping habits.

Refrigerators are larger and bulkier than sinks and stoves. They are the only kitchen basic that has not been standardized to the 24-inch depth of base cabinets or to a cabinet-matching height. With a few exceptions, refrigerators stick out, although many suggestions within this book show you how to disguise their girth. Chest freezers that open from the top can occupy four feet or more of wall space and front-opening upright freezers can be as large or larger than your refrigerator. Few kitchen designers are

happy when they are required to include free-standing freezers within the confines of the kitchen because of the space they consume. Where yours is kept depends on the wall space in the kitchen, the size of the freezer you need, and the alternative space that might be co-opted elsewhere.

Size
To estimate your requirements, allow eight to ten cubic feet of refrigerator capacity for the first two adults in a household, then add one cubic foot for each additional member. A family of four, then, would buy a refrigerator with a capacity of ten to twelve cubic feet. One guideline proposes that you multiply the number of people in your household by 2½. This, they say, will result in a reliable estimate of freezer requirements. The same family of four would own a freezer of about ten cubic feet. In this case, however, the freezer capacity in the refrigerator should be subtracted from the freezer estimate. If your refrigerator has a two-cubic-foot freezer capacity, you would do well with a compact eight-cubic-foot freezer.

Careful comparisons are necessary. Some manufacturers' statements are misleading. Some refrigerators-freezers are claimed to be almost a third larger than

they actually are. The disparities can be attributed only in part to nonconsideration of unusable areas such as "dead space" around crispers or bins. However, since all the companies use the same rating system, the figures are consistent and comparisons can be made.

Guides to capacity are all right as far as they go, but if you freeze produce from the garden, you will need a larger freezer than the rule-of-thumb allows. This holds true, also, if you regularly buy large quantities of food on special or sides of beef or other meats in wholesale quantity, or frequently cook up batches of food ahead of time, or entertain a great deal. The same sort of personal evaluation is called for on refrigerators. Your satisfaction, or lack of it, with the capacity of your present refrigerator may lead you to buy a smaller or larger one.

Everyone should be aware, when making a selection, that the fuller a refrigerator or freezer is kept, the less it costs to run. Empty refrigerators actually use more energy than those which are well stocked. This offers a compelling reason not to buy a refrigerator or freezer too large for your household or for the amount of food you normally keep at hand.

Energy Efficiency Factors. The amounts of energy used by refrigerators

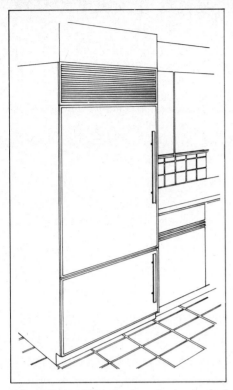

This built-in refrigerator has its mechanical equipment behind the grill on top, allowing the unit to be only 24 inches deep.

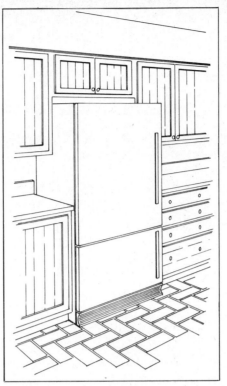

A refrigerator with a freezer on the bottom, such as this free-standing one, puts high-use areas at levels easy to see and to reach.

and freezers have been rated. Energy Efficiency Factors (EEF) employ a set of numbers with which all of us will have to become familiar. In rating a refrigerator, the EEF divides its cubic feet by the number of kilowatt hours used daily. The fewer the hours, the better the rating. The ratings can vary widely.

If electricity costs you 3.8 cents per kwh and your appliance uses, as an example, 160 kwh monthly, it costs $6.08 a month to run. If your part of the country is now faced with electric charges rising to 10 cents per kwh, however, the same refrigerator-freezer will cost you $16.00 a month to operate. Some manufacturers make units of 14 to 25 cubic feet which use between 50 and 115 kilowatts. These are, to be sure, only estimated averages. Costs also depend on size, the frequency with which a refrigerator or freezer is opened and how long it is kept ajar each time, how much food is stored in it, the quality of its insulation and design, the climate in which it works, and the temperature of the room in which it is kept. One point is certain: any freezer will use more fuel if it defrosts automatically. However, improvements in self-defrosting techniques and insulation have lessened the differences. Upright freezers consume more energy than the chest type

because so much more cold air escapes each time the door is opened.

Built-in Look. You can find refrigerators, refrigerator-freezers, and freezers which give the appearance of being completely built in. Sub-Zero makes a line of such appliances, currently the only one available. The usual home refrigerator cannot be placed directly against the wall, for space must be allowed at the back for air flow. The same is true at the refrigerator's top. This design-engineering problem has been solved. Visually, the "built-ins" are satisfying because they do not sport the trim, logos, and other attachments which make for cluttered design. As you might expect, these refrigerators and freezers are priced higher than comparable models.

Features to Look For. Keep in mind good design features when you shop for a refrigerator or freezer. Smooth, seamless interiors are easier to keep clean than those interrupted by seams or obstructions. Glass shelves are much easier to wash than wire grids, but they are more fragile. If the shelves on the interior of the door are removable, they will be much simpler to clean.

Controls near the front are accessible without removing bottles or other containers. Make sure the refrigerator you

buy can hold tall bottles and upright storage. Door shelves should have room for taller jars and bottles too. Make certain some of the interior shelves are adjustable.

Ice-makers built into freezer may become a maintenance problem. They add to energy costs. An ice-maker in the refrigerator can produce ice cubes for easy storage in any freezer.

Where to Keep a Separate Freezer. Professional kitchen designers usually prefer separate freezers in the basement or an adjoining room or vestibule, just as they would rather keep laundry facilities out of the kitchen. A freezer in the kitchen, however, can be convenient for unpacking the week's groceries, preparing a meal, cooking or baking ahead. A big freezer can dominate a kitchen and ruin a pleasing plan, but for some homes there may be no choice. If you want and need a freezer, work on your design to see how you can work one in. A compact, under-counter model can work where space is limited. A large two-door refrigerator-freezer may also fill your needs.

SINKS, COUNTERS, UNDERCOUNTER APPLIANCES
Sinks
You can find sinks in many sizes and of many materials: stainless steel, porcelain enameled steel, cast iron or ceramics.

Stainless steel comes in 18 and 20 gauge. Because it is heavier, the 18 gauge is best for larger sinks and those with garbage disposers. Stainless steel also differs in grades, depending on the proportion of nickel and chrome it contains. Those with a higher proportion of chrome are easier to care for and tend to improve their finish with age. Try to find a sink with Type 302 AISI stainless steel. Although some owners complain of spotting, stainless steel continues to be the most popular choice for sinks, and offers the widest variety of bowl sizes and sink configurations.

Cast iron and pressed steel sinks have finishes of baked porcelain enamel. The cast iron is heavier and is less likely to chip than pressed steel. Cast iron is quieter than stainless or pressed steel when water runs on it, or when appliances like a disposer are operating. Cast iron and pressed steel come in a variety of colors to fit with appliance colors.

Corian is one of the newest and most expensive materials to be used for sinks. A sink and countertop of Corian permit good integration of lines and smooth design. Other sinks are colored to go with colored ceramic tiles for integrated design.

Sink Bowls. Sinks made of each material come in single, double, or triple-bowl models. Two-bowl sinks may have both made the same size, or one smaller than the other, or one shallower than the other. Three-bowl sinks usually have the smallest in the center, with the other two equal in size. Some kitchens may profitably include another sink at a second location, for a wet bar, for freezing and canning convenience, for a quick wash-up near the back door.

Where Does the Sink Belong? For at least a generation the most frequently recommended position for a kitchen sink has been under a window. Originally, the thinking was that the person doing the dishes could thereby enjoy the outdoors while washing the dishes — or, if young children were playing outside, while keeping an eye on them. A window location remains a good one for a sink. But a dishwasher often takes care of dirty dishes and utensils.

If the sink is placed below a window and the outlook is pleasant, the simplest window treatment is probably the best. You might eliminate curtains or blinds for daytime use altogether. If the view is unpleasant, you might use glass shelves to fill the space with plants. Use the window to display your bottle collection or other objects of colored glass, which always look best against light. Folding shutters or curtains also can be useful in veiling a view.

Where light from the window is diminished by buildings or trees, plants on shelves can thrive with the help of mercury vapor light fixtures (which require special ceramic sockets) or fluorescent tubes, some of which are specially designed for plant growth. Both types may be hidden in coves above a window or on either side. (See Chapter 9 on lighting for more details.)

The window over the sink might be the place for a window greenhouse if it receives sufficient natural light. A number of firms offer these greenhouses. They also can be made by those handy with tools, as shown in Chapter 6. There is no place in the house more convenient for watering houseplants than directly over the kitchen sink, so even if you forego more elaborate treatments, keep a pot or two on the sill.

A variant window, practical only when a kitchen is totally re-built or renovated, is the fixed panel of insulated glass which runs behind the sink and continues along the wall behind the length of the countertop, forming a clear backsplash. This double glazing can fill the space between wall cabinets and countertop for an entire wall. The section of wall above wall cabinets can also be used for fixed glass when there is sufficient height.

Faucets. Faucets may come as part of your sink or there may be openings for faucets and a spray spigot. Actually, most modern sinks have one faucet that mixes hot and cold water, some working with a single lever, others with double faucet handles. High spouts that can facilitate dishwashing and filling tall vases and pitchers are available. So-called hospital handles can be specified by those who want to be able to turn on water when both hands are full. Consumers also have a choice between faucets with and without washers. Faucets are also available which conserve water.

Appliances Near the Sink

Water Filter. Water filters, whether free-standing, top-of-the sink, or built-in models, are designed to purify drinking water so it will look and taste better. Some claim to filter out impurities hazardous to health. Unfortunately, some water filters, despite claims, do very little of anything. Filters for clarifying cloudy or silt-laden water come with a cellulose element which can be replaced as necessary. Filters with replaceable carbon elements remove chlorine and other additives that affect taste or odor. Filters attached to the cold water line at the sink differ from filters connected with the main water intake, which soften hard water, remove corroding iron, or neutralize acidic water — all conditions that shorten the life of pipes and water-related equipment.

When buying your water conditioner, first recognize that there is no single water conditioning unit which will handle all water problems. Have your water analyzed to discover its drawbacks — consult a reputable water-conditioning specialist. Some states perform such analytical laboratory services free or at a nominal charge to residents.

The window by this two-bowl sink gives more than adequate natural light for daytime work.

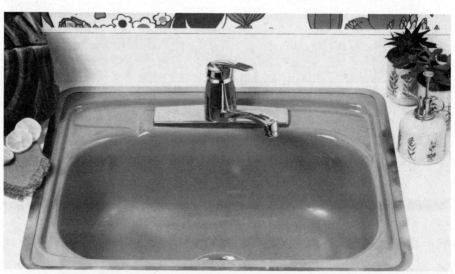

A single-bowl sink provides enough space to rinse vegetables or wash large utensils such as roasters. A short backsplash topped with wallpaper calls for an easily-cleaned vinyl.

Tankless Hot Water. Everyone is familiar with hot water tanks. They heat and store hot water. They are the second largest consumers of energy in the home, with central heating first. Some savings can be made by wrapping the tank in extra insulation and doing the same for exposed hot-water pipes in unheated basements.

More thrifty are the tankless water heaters used in England, Germany, Italy and other European countries. These compact units, installed near the sink, do not store water. They heat water instantly with a strong and speedy heating coil when tap is turned. Energy reportedly is saved because hot water does not have to travel through lengthy lines and because no tank is necessary to keep water constantly (and wastefully) hot. Two manufacturers, and possibly more, now make tankless hot-water heaters in North America — Thorn Company, distributed by General Mail Corporation, 25 Valley Drive, Greenwich, Conn. 06830, and Instant Flow, made by Chronomite Labs, 21011 South Figueroa Street, Carson, California 90745. These may be used to replace your hot water tank or as a supplement to an existing tank.

Instant Hot Water. Instant hot water is supplied by miniature hot water tanks installed under the kitchen sink. They hold one or two quarts of water at a bubbling 190 degrees, whereas your regular hot-water tank is set at 120 to 140 degrees. Some of the better units such as In-Sink-Erator have proven to be the most efficient in providing 190 degree water, even more efficient than boiling on a stove.

Garbage Disposers. A garbage disposer installed under the kitchen sink is a convenience at relatively modest initial cost. But its one-half horsepower or stronger motor does consume energy, whereas garbage also can be converted into compost to provide energy for lawns or houseplants. Most of the garbage put down a disposer is organic and decomposes quickly — as opposed to many detergents, which add to the pollution problem.

Some communities require disposers, while others ban them. Garbage disposers may add some to pollution in streams and rivers, a serious concern in many places. This can be an incentive for composting. Trash cannot go into a garbage disposer, so families still must dispose of paper, cans, and bottles.

Garbage Compactors. Compactors can save on human energy by cutting down on steps to and numbers of outside garbage cans — or to the dump, if you live in a rural area. It is estimated that three out of four trips to the sidewalk, or wherever you keep your garbage cans, can be eliminated by compactors. Motors of compactors operated 90 seconds 2 to 6 times a day contribute to electricity bills. Addition of this unit will raise the cost of a kitchen renovation by about $300.00.

In states requiring a deposit on cans and bottles, a compactor might cost you more money. Some communities collect aluminum cans and other waste products in conservation efforts, or incinerate them to provide energy.

If you decide to include a compactor, carefully consider where it should be placed. If built into the kitchen, it will occupy base-cabinet storage space. A free-standing compactor in a rear entryway or garage may be preferable, if room permits.

Exhaust Vents and Fans. Most kitchens require some kind of venting to draw oven grease, heat, odors, and smoke out of the kitchen. Since top-of-stove cooking can also produce any or all of these, kitchen exhaust fans are the usual answer.

There are ducted and unducted exhaust fans. Ducted exhaust fans carry kitchen air outdoors through a vent pipe. The stronger the fan pulling the air out and the fewer the twists and turns of the vent pipe, the more effective the venting will be. Ductless vents do not reach the outside. Rather, air is pulled by the fan through air filters, which attempt to remove impurities before returning it. But since ductless exhaust vents are much less successful than ducted vents, they are used only when there is no other choice.

The shape of this small island reinforces the line of the countertop with its corner sink.

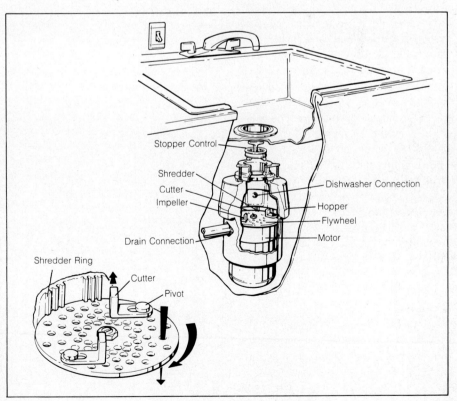

The flywheel spins at about 1725 rpm. Its centrifugal force throws the food against the shredder ring in the disposal wall, where the cutters and the ring grind food into a liquid mass.

Both ducted and ductless fan vents are incorporated into hoods for stoves, top burners, or ovens made by many manufacturers, or they may be purchased separately. The hoods may be of metal, or they may be made of wood. The latter are frequently made by kitchen cabinet manufacturers to match the other cabinet work in the kitchen. Small sizes are made to fit under wall cabinets, large ones to fill the wall over a stove. Fans set directly into the wall above and behind the stove on an outside wall will carry off quantities of fumes and grease, whether or not a hood is provided. Wall fans provide the least expensive venting method.

Four manufacturers have introduced hoodless, ducted venting: Jenn-Air, Thermador, Amana and Modern Maid. Their tops include such grease-and-smoke generators as stove-top barbecue and rotisserie units, yet the exhaust systems (the two systems differ somewhat) are strong enough to pull air down and out of the house.

Vents rid the kitchen of accumulated cooking residues, but also of heated air during the heating season. They can also send cool air-conditioned air outside in summer. Exhaust fans should not be kept running for hours at a time at any season.

If natural ventilation is poor, a two-way window fan that pulls in fresh air and exhausts stale air can help. The old-fashioned ceiling fan is now being reproduced, too, and some owners say that it simulates natural air movement successfully. Ceiling fans come with installation instructions; directions will vary according to the model. Keep in mind, however, that for sufficient support the fan must hang from the bottom of a joist, and requires cutting into the ceiling.

If you can design in cross-ventilation, you will benefit. But avoid placing a stove too close to a window, and never put it under one, though such a location might seem ideal. If you use gas, wind can blow the flame out. With an electric stove, a window can be a hazard if you reach across a stove to open or close it.

Dishwashers

Few people need to be convinced that dishwashers are among the blessings of modern technology. Even though dishwashers consume energy in the form of hot water and electricity, a dishwasher carefully used may actually use less energy than the handwashing of dishes.

(When you do wash dishes by hand, however, always fill the sink with hot, soapy water and rinse by turning the tap on briefly or by dipping dishes in a second sink filled with clean hot water. Never waste energy by washing dishes under running water.)

Types Available. The two types of dishwashers for the home are those permanently installed and portable models. The latter, called "convertibles" by at least two major manufacturers, may indeed be converted to a permanent position alongside the sink. If you already own a portable in good condition, make it part of your remodeling plan to include its installation in a fixed position. But if you plan to buy a new dishwasher, make sure to design the kitchen with sufficient space allotted for an installed model. Under-counter models are invariably more convenient to load and unload, and fre-

The supports for the hood above a built-in gas or electric barbecue prevent a cross-flow of air, increasing the hood fan's effectiveness.

A fan rather than a hood was built into the tile-trimmed cabinet above a built-in barbecue, with an extension of the wall's stucco texture.

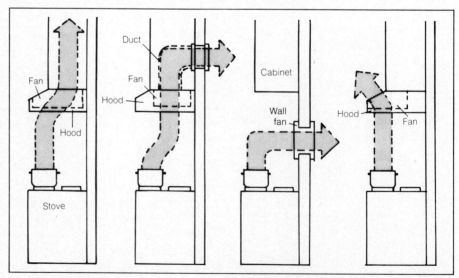

(From left to right) Ducted hoods vent cooking residue through soffit or up and back through a duct in the wall. Wall fans draw air out of the kitchen directly through the outside wall. Least efficient, ductless hoods filter out grease and smoke but return heated air.

quently the mechanism may be superior to that of the portables. Where space is scant, the undersink model made by General Electric may be the solution. It can be installed under a special six-inch deep single-bowl sink mounted in a 1½-inch thick countertop, so that the sink and dishwasher will then occupy a space only 24 inches wide. If paired with a special food waste disposer, the two will take up only 36 inches. Standard dishwashers are 34½ inches high, 24 inches wide, and 24-plus inches deep. Portables with work tops are 36 inches high.

Energy Considerations. By now all dishwasher manufacturers have incorporated some energy-saving features. Many machines allow users to select options using less hot water. Some, such as KitchenAid, automatically heat water entering the machine to 150 degrees. This permits homeowners to turn their hot water heaters down; for example to an energy-saving 120°, and still have efficient and sanitary dishwashing. (Despite some claims by other makers, the standard 150° is not sufficiently germicidal to make much difference when certain contagious diseases are present.) In addition to their standard dishwashers, Waste King manufactures a dishwasher trade named the "Steam Machine." It bathes dishes in a "gentle steam mist" followed by a water jetting action to help remove food particles. Another innovation in one of their Steam Machine models allows users to delay operation for up to nine hours after loading. This permits the machine to go into action while owners are asleep, away from home or, most significant, when lower off-peak electric rates are in effect.

Cycles and Options. Most dishwashers have so many cycle choices that their fronts, with lights flashing on and off, can look like airplane control panels. But many of the options are worthwhile. A "rinse-and-hold" cycle, nearly universal, allows a small household to pre-rinse a small load, before soil becomes encrusted, while waiting to accumulate a full load.

There are also "soak-and-scrub" (KitchenAid) or "Potscrubber" (General Electric) cycles. These use extra hot water to remove the extra soil, although no machine can remove baked-in or burned-in food, which responds best to soaking. The soak-and-scrub cycle in the KitchenAid, for instance, uses more than

14 gallons of hot water, while the normal wash cycle of the same machine consumes 12 gallons, and the "light wash" uses only 8 gallons, the same as the rinse-and-hold. Even more frugal is the fast wash/no dry option, which also uses only 8 gallons to complete a full load. (Other makers claim substantially lower water consumption, cycle by cycle.) Hotpoint is one of the manufacturers that has a china/crystal, in which a slower speed and lower water pressure are said to protect delicate items.

New dishwashers have "no dry" pushbuttons. According to some investigators the energy conserved in foregoing the drying cycle is too minute to matter, while others maintain that it can save as much as 10% of the total electricity used. When the machine is set at "no dry," heat already in it will dry most dishes without the boost of added heat in a drying cycle, but some pieces will inevitably have to be wiped by hand.

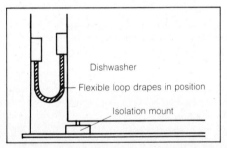

To avoid noisy vibration that comes with rigid connections on heavy-duty appliances, install flexible Greenfield or BX cable looped in position as shown here.

This ducted hood has a metal finish. Others come in wood grain patterns to match the grain and trim patterns of kitchen cabinets.

Makers of dishwashers usually insist in their advertising that the need to pre-rinse dishes by hand is a thing of the past. Consumers should remember, however, that dishwashers are not food waste disposers. Excess food has to be scraped off plates with a rubber spatula, the side of a knife, or a paper towel no matter what type of dishwasher is used. Remaining food residue can be taken care of by such devices as the "self-clean filtering system" included in the General Electric dishwashers. According to the company, the system "catches food particles and holds them in a chamber beneath the tub until they are washed down the drain. Larger particles are cut to size by the soft food disposer. No messy filter to clean." Remodelers should be reminded nonetheless that as recently as May, 1980, the Federal Trade Commission hauled one of the largest makers into court for advertising that their machine eliminated the need to rinse or scrape plates. The F.T.C. or-

Wood-grain panel over a built-in dishwasher provides design continuity for the row base cabinets and appliances.

This modern-style hood cycles air through charcoal filters to eliminate grease and fumes. It slides under the cabinet when not in use.

dered them to get "competent and reliable tests" before issuing performance claims on major home appliances.

Racks. Rack arrangement is an equally important factor in the operation of your machine. Some racks are adjustable, not necessarily an advantage, with the helpfulness of this supplement depending upon its design and the materials of which it is made. Some racks have grids that allow users to place almost anything anywhere — glasses on top or bottom, plates wherever there is room, and so on. Others make it impossible to fit glassware on the bottom rack or plates on the top, and for many families this rigidity becomes an inconvenience. Generally speaking, the most flexible grid will prove the most useful.

Labeling Appliances for Energy Consumption

Exactly how much energy a particular unit consumes is now spelled out for the consumer. The Federal Trade Commission's new appliance labeling rule has been in effect since May 19, 1980, although appliances manufactured before that date need not comply. Based on the requirements of the 1975 Energy Policy and Conservation Act, the labels are mandatory on refrigerators, refrigerator/freezers, freezers, clothes washers, dishwashers, and water heaters.

The label on each appliance must include an estimate of its annual energy consumption. This is based on the average cost of electricity across the country, currently just less than five cents per kilowatt hour. In order to figure out whether the cost of electricity in your area is higher or lower, divide your total monthly or bimonthly bill by the number of kilowatt hours for which you have been charged. The answer represents your cost per kilowatt hour. (On appliances that depend upon heated water, the label compares gas and electric charges for heating water.)

The labels also include an estimate of the range of energy consumption for similar appliances made by other manufacturers, although the competition is not identified by name. (Walk down the aisle of any well-stocked store, however, and you will quickly discover the brand that is most energy efficient.) Finally, the cost of running each appliance will be compared for a range of energy rates — currently

between two and twelve cents an hour nationally.

Countertop Materials

The market offers a lot of choices, some of which are new; others have been around for a long time.

Plastic Laminates. The most popular material for countertops today, familiar products are sold under trade names such as Formica and Micarta, but plastic laminates are made by many fabricators under other trade names as well. Pastels have long dominated the market, and continue to be available along with such well-known patterns as wood grain, and Fifties revivals such as marbleized designs. New solid colors and geometric designs in lac-

quered finishes have recently been introduced by Formica in strong, dark colors. Whether the gloss will show glass rings and fingerprints is still unknown. Plastic laminates also are made in textures that simulate linen and marble. One real wood veneer is available encased in clear plastic laminate; this is far more attractive but more costly than the simulation.

Plastic laminates are relatively simple for professionals or homeowners to install. Their smooth surfaces wash easily. They are heat resistant, although very hot pots set onto plastic laminate can burn it. So, too, can cigarettes rolling out from ashtrays. It can be scratched or marred by knives — one good reason not to use it as a cutting surface. These plastic laminates

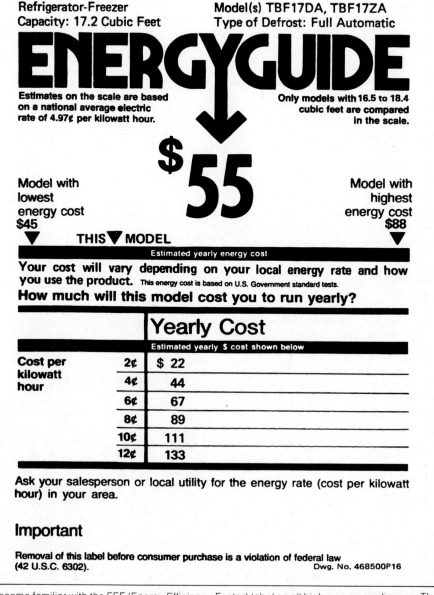

Become familiar with the EEF (Energy Efficiency Factor) label on all high-energy appliances. The label gives the yearly cost and the base rate for that figure. Included also are charts comparing similar models and additional base rates so you can compute costs in your area.

are manufactured in several different prices and quality levels, so make sure you know what you are getting for the price you pay.

Ceramic Tile. Made from clay, it is shaped, baked, and glazed. Unglazed tile is available, but is not recommended for countertops. Handmade and mass-produced tiles are to be had in a broad range of sizes, colors, shapes, qualities, and prices. One of the oldest materials made by man, ceramic tile can last, literally, for thousands of years. It is usually lustrous, smooth, easy to wipe off. It cannot be burned by hot pots or cigarettes. Both domestic and imported tiles can be magnificently decorative for countertops, backsplashes, walls, or as display inserts.

Ceramic tile is set into a mastic or a cement-like mortar that holds the tiles in place. Grout used to be available only in off-white, forming a visible grid a fraction of an inch wide between tiles. Users of ceramic tile countertops complained that the grout soiled quickly, turning a dirtier gray. The grout also absorbs water. However, grout sealers are now available. A grout spray sealant, used every other week, renders the joints impervious to water and dirt. Colored grouts allow purchasers to color match their tiles. Epoxylike grouts avoid the absorption, color, and soiling drawbacks, but take a little more skill to handle successfully.

Ceramic tile is more expensive than plastic laminate, if being installed by a professional. If applied by the homeowner its cost is only slightly higher than plastic laminate. If you drop a dish or glass on a tile counter it may break, which is not true of more resilient materials such as plastic laminate. Ceramic tile will chip, crack, or even break if hit with sufficient force.

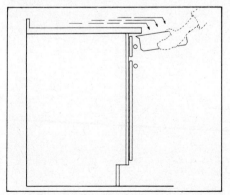

To simplify cleaning and enable bowls to catch materials scraped into them from a countertop, allow for at least an inch overhang.

Stainless Steel. A practical worktop for a whole run of countertop or for a section, stainless steel also works on either side of a stove or adjoining a stainless steel sink. Stainless steel is not really "stainless," however. It does show water spots, and it looks its pristine best only after it has been washed, wiped, and dried. Large stretches of stainless on a work surface may look a little too institutional for you, which is probably a reason it is not used as widely as it might be. Keep in mind that your knives will become dull and your arm will ache if you use stainless for a cutting board.

Cultured Marble. A new material, it is made by combining marble fragments with a plastic resin. It looks similar to marble in color and texture. Unlike real marble, it resists stains or etching from acids, and it is far less likely to crack from sudden blows. However, it is not generally used for kitchen countertops, and is hard to repair.

Synthetic Marble. Similar to marble in appearance, it is made of a synthetic material, methacrylate, and contains no marble. It comes in ¼, ½ and ¾ inch thicknesses and can be cut like wood. Some reports say that it resists moisture, heat, stains, and cracks better than marble, while others maintain that it is not as durable as marble. It can be cut with a power saw and shaped with a router like marble. Yet, like marble, Corian (the trade name) can be scratched. It can easily be repaired by sanding or buffing.

Marble. Quarried, polished, it is sold in tones of gray or black, whites with much or little veining, browns, greens or pinks. Marble requires waxing and polishing to maintain its appearance, but even then porosity will soon cause it to be marred if used as a kitchen countertop. Marble scratches easily, is difficult to repair, can be cracked, but will never burn. Many knowledgeable pastry bakers insist that it is the finest surface for rolling dough because of its smoothness and coolness. If this is one of your concerns, consider using a marble slab as your baking center.

Slate and Granite. Quarried from the earth, their colors are natural earth tones, ranging from blacks and grays to pinks and reds, with some greens and blues. If there is a quarry near you, find a stonemason who will cut to order an entire granite countertop in one piece. Such a solid,

seamless piece of stone will be extremely heavy, so figure out first how you will transport it and set it on top of the base cabinets. Granite cannot be hurt by moisture or heat, nor does it stain, once properly finished. It is more expensive than slate, which can be scratched and cracked easily. Granite can take a high polish; slate cannot. Slate is thinner and lighter and is usually sold by the box in assorted mixed or solid colors cut into rectangles. Larger slabs can be purchased at quarries.

Copper. Infrequently used, copper can glow beautifully, when it is highly polished — which it requires regularly because oxidation turns it green. Heat can do it no harm. A long stretch of copper should be insulated underneath (with a wood base) against noise, as should similar lengths of stainless steel.

Butcher Block. Used for a portion of a countertop more often than for an entire length, butcher block should be thick, which means that it will be heavy. Base cabinets should be strong. The term "butcher block" refers to an end-grain hardwood laminated under pressure. (If the wood is sealed with anything other than oil sealant it is no longer real butcher block, but rather a wood countertop, as discussed later.)

Unsealed, butcher blocks are porous. Some cooks maintain that they are impossible to clean and that they harbor germs. Unsealed butcher block mars easily and immediately, but it can be scrubbed and sanded endlessly to renew its finish.

The octagonal ceramic tile in this kitchen is used as a unifying element, covering the floor, countertop and built-in dining shelf. The latter two require special protective sealers.

Wood Countertops. Made of soft or hard wood, they can be sealed with tough, urethane varnish in a clear glossy or matte finish. They can be stained any wood tone and then varnished with urethane for a handsome warm looking surface that is inexpensive. A wood countertop may scorch or burn; it also can be scratched, but it is more easily repaired by an amateur than any other countertop material. Wood countertops are especially effective when the wall and base cabinets are also made of clear-finished wood.

Cabinets

Stock vs. Custom Cabinets. Stock cabinets are, literally, in stock wherever they are sold. They are made in standard sizes.

The quality of stock cabinets may be fair, good, or excellent, depending on the manufacturer and the price. Materials may be solid wood, or wood and particleboard, or wood and masonite. They may be made of hard or soft wood, carefully jointed and doweled, or they may be nailed and glued together. Stock cabinets also come in steel and in several types of plastic, either in part or entirely. The quality of cabinets made from these materials varies.

Because custom cabinets are made to order, delivery may take from 4 to 16 weeks. The delivery delay rarely causes a problem inasmuch as kitchen planning and shopping for equipment takes time.

Custom cabinets almost always are delivered completely finished, like fine furniture, whereas stock cabinets may be finished by the do-it-yourselfer.

European Custom Cabinets. Imported kitchen cabinets are widely available, coming mainly from Germany and Italy. Poggenpohl and Allmilmo are two of the best known names. Most of the imports are highly styled and beautifully made, either in wood or plastic laminates.

Carpenter-built Cabinets. You or your spouse may prefer to create your own cabinets for the kitchen. A basic design and plan for building a cabinet is given in a later chapter.

Unfinished Cabinets. A modest amount of money can be saved by buying unfinished stock cabinets and then staining or painting them yourself. A bit more can be saved by knockdown cabinets, which are shipped flat to lower the costs of packing and delivery. These savings are passed on to the customer. Knockdowns are often unfinished, as well. If you want a country-style finish in stain, wax or oil, instead of painted cabinets, unfinished or homemade cabinets are a good choice.

Cabinet Accessories. One of the greatest changes in modern kitchen cabinets in recent years is their fitted and accessorized interiors.

Many of the newer fittings originated with quality European manufacturers, although by now virtually every American maker offers similar devices. Among them, are base cabinets made as sets of drawers, which may all be the same size or graduated in depth. Some base cabinets have doors that open to shelves which pull out like drawers. Any of these may be fitted with dividers for large or small items, especially such difficult-to-store items as lids, trays, and cookie sheets. Another innovation is the use of shallow interior shelves set back to allow space for shelves of equal size on the door of the unit. This technique does not add shelf space, but it increases convenience and accessibility.

Chopping, Slicing, Pastry Boards

Butcher Block. Chopping against wood is excellent because wood resiliency keeps the wrist from tiring quickly and avoids marring of kitchen knives. The finest modern butcher block for chopping is made from end-grain maple which is laminated electronically.

Separate, free-standing butcher blocks on legs are widely available. They are available in graduated sizes, are not at all cheap, and look good in the kitchen which has sufficient room for them.

Butcher block cutting boards are also available, as are pull-out cutting boards set into countertops. Backsplashes to match butcher-block countertops are also made to order.

Slicing Boards. These are used for slicing on an everyday basis. A slicing board does not take the pounding a butcher block can withstand. A wood slicing board is, in most cases, made of ordinary pine. It may be built-in as a section of countertop or as a pull-out that slides from under the countertop. A paddle-shaped wood slicing board can be picked up in almost any hardware store.

Nonwood slicing boards come in two very satisfactory materials. Corning's "ceramic" slicing surfaces are sold in white only, though they are made in various sizes. A piece of appropriate size may be used as a section of countertop. In addition to its fine qualities as a slicing (but not chopping) board, it is impervious to heat, making it desirable next to a stove. Plastic boards also are available.

Ready-made rubber boards are made with a groove around the circumference to collect juices. They also can be made to order as an entire run of countertop or as a section.

Bins that slide into the base cabinet increase your storage area. The open-basket style is a lightweight bin that slides easily. Its contents are easily visible.

This restored Victorian kitchen has a wood countertop. The surface was sealed with marine varnish for durability and easy care.

5
PERSONALIZED DESIGN

Style is the word used to sum up how all the elements in a room combine to make it uniquely its owner's. One person chooses a particular color scheme; another selects wood surfaces and plants. A third wants another arrangement altogether. Since every component in your kitchen is an aspect of style, from the type of cabinets you select to the plants on your windowsill, you should keep two basics in mind if too few or too many choices prove confusing.

Do not choose any item merely because someone tells you it is the latest thing or because it is in style. Fashion is a poor basis for selecting kitchen fixtures and appliances. Years ago, well-known designer Elizabeth Howes coined the phrase "Fashion is spinach." By that she meant all the here-today, gone-tomorrow cosmetic changes and fluctuations promoted to convince consumers they needed the latest product off the assembly line. Such promotion is closely related to planned obsolescence and is not in the spirit of the 1980s. The best style for you is what pleases and works best for you and your family, not the one that pleases the manufacturer who sells the product. In fact, sometimes the oldest, least fashionable item may suit your purposes exactly.

COLOR USE
Do try to settle on a color scheme soon after you have worked out a basic design plan. Take into account that most appliances are available in white and a limited range of colors, often pale pastels or muddy tones like avocado green or mustard yellow. Since these are the colors manufacturers think the public wants, these are the colors offered — and the consumer must select from them. Similarly, colors in accessories ranging from dish towels and can openers to plastic storage baskets can be equally limited, although these are often made in strong primary colors. Therefore, it can be nearly impossible to make a match. One

Red trim in this kitchen creates a strikingly bold contrast to the white cabinets and counters.

solution is to include white in your scheme by buying appliances in standard white finishes and using color on the walls, floors, countertops, and accessories. The consumer has another option in planning, provided by a number of appliance manufacturers who offer fixtures which simulate or match wood-toned finishes on custom or stock cabinets. For those who want a dash of strong color in at least one permanent fixture, a bright porcelain-enameled sink may be the answer, for these come in a range of fresh colors.

There are a few truisms about color that everyone knows but that some of us tend to forget in the stress of work on a project. Color can expand or contract a room. Cabinets with a dark finish can make a kitchen seem darker and smaller than it is. On the other hand, light walls and cabinets, by reflecting light off their surfaces, actually make the room lighter. Strong contrasts, such as light cabinets

and dark wallpaper, take up more space visually than do modified color and value relationships. White cabinets with red trim on all the moldings look bright and shipshape and will appeal to many. For others, however, the red trim will be too strong a contrast. On the other hand, red accessories, perhaps combined with a glossy red sink, might provide the necessary sparkle in an otherwise white kitchen.

Paint — Finding Colors You Like
Although it may be hard to find appliances or toasters or wallpapers or dishes in exactly the colors you want, paint is sold in so many varieties of color, hue, and tone that just about any shade you want can be ferreted out at a well supplied paint store. In addition, most retail paint shops will mix colors to order. Once you realize the number of choices available, you can select from color schemes that range from simple to complex.

Color Schemes

A color scheme need not be based on two or three colors. Some marvelous kitchens have been done in one color only, with variety supplied by the gleam of stainless steel or copper — the texture of tile or marble. Although using one shade of color might seem the simplest way to work, it can be the most difficult way to put together a striking kitchen.

The primary colors — red, yellow, and blue — almost always work, though not all three together. You can choose any two, use more of one than the other, or add a dash of white, and the effect is usually one of cheerful simplicity — surely a desirable quality in any kitchen.

On the more complex level, color schemes can be based on monochromatic colors, related colors, or complementary colors. With a monochromatic scheme, one might only use varying shades of pink, or of blue, or keep everything within the tan and brown range. Related colors may be composed, for example, of all the tones of autumn leaves, going from closely associated browns though burnt oranges to warm golds. One kitchen scheme could be based on the related colors of spring greens, lightened with touches of pure yellow. A complementary color scheme uses opposites on the color wheel, such as red and green or blue and yellow. White can be a successful component of any color scheme and can also serve as a key second color, as in a blue and white or yellow and white design. The addition of white to any color lightens its value, so that white added to red produces pinks; the color strength then depends upon the proportion of pure red to white. Remember this point when devising complementary or monochromatic schemes. Once you have established your color scheme, note that different intensities of the same color will serve to vary and fortify the effect.

TEXTURES AND SURFACE MATERIALS

In terms of color, natural substances, such as wood in cabinets and flooring, brick or slate on walls or floors, tend to be neutral and unassertive. Colors can work in conjunction with these materials, even though they have intrinsic colors of their own. (These alternatives, incidentally, tend to show less dirt and fewer fingerprints.) Such substances, however, con-

tribute to your kitchen even more in terms of texture than as color elements.

There will be differences of texture and surface qualities in most kitchens whether they are planned or not. A vinyl flooring may have the texture of brick or terrazzo. A plastic laminate countertop has a shine quite different from that of a stainless steel sink. The gleam of appliances contrasts with the linen texture of a washable wallpaper. Window curtains may be sheer or opaque, the plants on the sill soft and lacy or stiff and succulent. It would be difficult to achieve a single-textured kitchen — and a pointless exercise as well. Some amateurs, however, go to the other extreme. They use a brick wall behind the stove, a patterned wallpaper, strong-grained wood cabinets, marbleized flooring, beamed ceilings, confetti-patterned plastic laminate countertops, intricate moldings and hardware, a wall featuring natural stone — all in one room! Too many textures and patterns are far worse than too few. A guide to the use of texture holds that if you are using one texture which calls attention to itself, make it your key. With this as your central

feature, tone down or avoid other eye-catching textural elements.

Strong textures which frequently dominate are stone (both the real thing and manmade copies), brick (real and manmade), multicolored slate, and decorative tile. Other patterns and forceful contrasts that probably should be allowed to make their own statements without competition include: highly patterned wallpapers, floor coverings, or countertops; architectural features such as arches; stark contrasts, such as a midnight-blue, highly polished floor in an all-white kitchen. Dominant, oversize or complex light fixtures should not have to compete, either. Attention-getters look best in an otherwise simple kitchen.

VARIATIONS ON A THEME

Three similar kitchen layouts on pages 52-3 show how details can change a room's look. All three have the similar appliances and cabinets located in much the same way. All have desk areas (kitchen offices), double sinks and double ovens, separate in-counter burners and broiler grills.

The floor cabinet along this angled wall creates a modified U-shaped work area. On the right, the glassed-in overhanging cabinet sits at an angle to provide access to space usually lost.

An added dual-purpose wall created both a fireplace and a wall for a galley kitchen. Rough planking and beams lowered the existing ceiling.

Rustic natural textures unify this room, combining smooth quarry floor tile with a rugged brick fireplace and wall, rough beams, and a stucco ceiling.

Kitchen #1 uses extremely simple cabinet doors, without moldings and with hidden pulls. The hood over the island top-burners is straight-lined, in keeping with the simplicity of the lines elsewhere. Both the floor and the wall tiles behind the barbecue grill are almost square and regularly aligned. Over the desk at the far right a closed cabinet has plain shelves above it, a handy place for cookbooks.

Kitchen #1 is the most modern, contemporary of the three, although as we suggested earlier, even kitchens with period or stylistic labels like French Provincial or Colonial are essentially modern. Kitchen #1 can afford the strongest colors or the greatest contrasts because its unassertive cabinets and design allow the contrasts to stand out. It probably would also be the easiest of the three to maintain, all other things being equal, because the room is free of moldings, door handles, and decorative bumps and hollows which catch dust, grime, grease, and spills.

Kitchen #2 features simple moldings on its cabinets. The corners on its center island have been sliced off at an angle, a treatment that can reduce knocks and bangs while adding a decorative variation. The hood above the island has become a major feature, and the ceiling has beams.

Beamed ceilings are usually included to reinforce the atmosphere or as a point from which to hang a collection of baskets or pans or plants. Otherwise, this feature might be eliminated in this kitchen, since the arched fireplace effect over the barbecue grill will probably steal the show, depending on the lighting and the colors used. Brick trim emphasizes the arch's curve, which is echoed by the smaller arch over the double ovens. The tiles behind the barbecue grill have been set at an angle to form a diamond pattern. Walls are stucco, adding another texture.

Notice some of the other differences between Kitchen #1 and #2. Kitchen #2 has a broom closet to the left of the double ovens, unlike Kitchen #1. (The broom-closet type doors in Kitchen #2 might, however, actually hide a fold-out ironing board, a shallow spice rack, a fold-out hospitality center, or even a fold-out snack table.) You can also see that Kitchen #2 divides the space over the built-in desk into bookshelves and an enclosed, glass-doored cupboard. The floor tiles are arranged in a herringbone pattern.

Kitchen #3 offers some of the details most of us think of as Early American. The cabinet doors are similar in appearance to simple, vertical planks, and the

handles of doors and drawers are adapted from 18th century cast iron. The change in the refrigerator door reflects this scheme. Brick, also associated with Colonial kitchens, has been used extensively on the oven and barbecue walls. Although tile has been used on the wall behind the barbecue, in this case brick would work as well, in terms of texture. However, unless brick is specially finished or glazed, it cannot be wiped clean like ceramic tile. Conversely, tile could have been used instead of brick to emphasize the arch as well as to back the grill. Glassed doors close off the entire cabinet above the kitchen office.

The features in the island for Kitchen #3 do not resemble those in other two kitchens. A small snack bar drops down from counter to table height, utilizing space which might otherwise be wasted.

While examining these kitchens and thinking about ways to incorporate some of their features into your design, note that essentially identical units manufactured by the same company make up all three kitchens. Finish and trim vary, but the cabinets are actually the same.

You can duplicate any one of the many variations, or you may employ totally different final touches. The desk area, for instance, could be the site of a hospitality

Complete renovation led to an unusual kitchen, with its corner stove and greenhouse window.

BEFORE

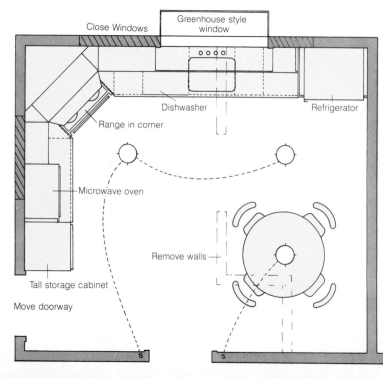

Wall shelves

Sink

← To dining room

Refrigerator   Closet

AFTER

Close Windows   Greenhouse style window

Range in corner

Dishwasher   Refrigerator

Microwave oven

Remove walls

Tall storage cabinet

Move doorway

center, just as another family might prefer a baking or preserving center to a separate barbecue grill. Kitchen #2 gives up cabinet space for the arch feature, while Kitchen #1 has the largest number of cabinets. In any of the three, one or all of the wall cabinets could be made without any doors, or the doors could be made of clear or opaque glass.

The window could become a window greenhouse or could be fitted with interior glass shelves. (The latter are available by mail from Buzza. Similar devices can be made at home.) Instead of a kitchen office, the space could be given to a set of well-lighted plant shelves. Artificially lighted plants might also fill what is now the barbecue center, if this were preferred. Instead of a center island, an old-fashioned farm table, with drawers and perhaps a tiled top, could double as an eating and working surface. The top burners now on the island could then replace the barbecue grill. As another possible modification, the refrigerator might replace the desk. A bank of new windows then could be placed on one or both sides of the present window.

The colors, shapes, and designs of the small appliances you choose to leave out on counters or shelves affect the room's appearance, as do the dish towels, drainer or the small rug you may use in front of the sink or near the back door. Envision pots and pans hung over the countertop burners or the grill. Brightly colored enamel-on-steel utensils would look quite different from aluminum, cast-iron cookware or copperware.

DINING IN THE KITCHEN

Nothing rivals the convenience of serving and eating meals near where they are prepared. This is why eat-in kitchens always have been and always will be highly valued. Even if your home is expansive enough to allow space for second and even third dining spots — perhaps a separate dining room or a living room "L" — the most popular eating area is the kitchen itself.

Families with big kitchens have no trouble finding sufficient space for dining. Their only problem lies in selecting the best location within whatever plan they have devised. Remodelers with small kitchens can consider alternatives, based upon this book, for adding eating facilities into their kitchen plans.

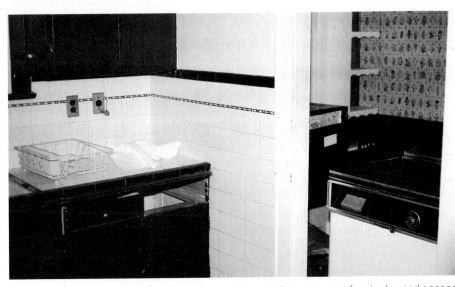

The doorway on the right side of the kitchen led to a small storage area for staples and canned goods. Because of its inconvenience, this room did not see much use, and the space was wasted.

Before remodeling, walls on each side of the narrow kitchen boxed in a small storeroom and a dining room. Limited space, insufficient light, and institutional decor resulted in an unpleasant atmosphere.

Once the cabinets, sink and paneling were removed from the outer walls, the wall separating the storage room and the kitchen was knocked out to create added work and eating areas.

The two existing windows were closed off and a single greenhouse window placed in the center of the new room. New wiring was added to provide fluorescent lighting above the sink area.

The completed kitchen has a well-lighted, expanded work counter on both sides of the sink. A built-in dishwasher is conveniently placed. Neither steps nor space are wasted.

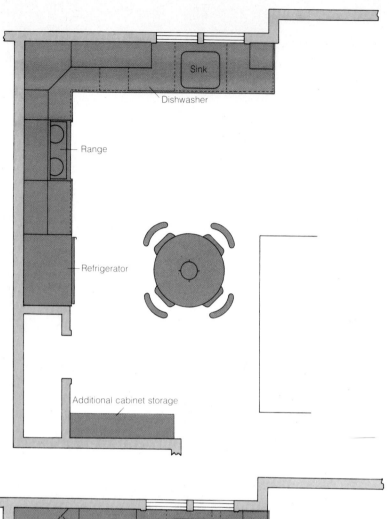

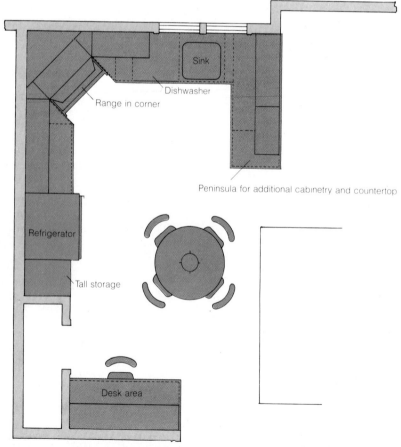

A planning desk and work and storage areas were added without affecting traffic flow.

Space Requirements

Before you can design the type of eating area you want, you must calculate the amount of floor space you require. It's astonishing how much space must be allowed for table, chairs, and the people who are to occupy them. If adults are to have sufficient room to sit down or get up from a table gracefully, they will each need about three feet between the table and any wall or base cabinet. Yet another foot, at a minimum, is necessary behind the chair for the passage of anyone serving or clearing the table. Built-in benches, when immovable, do not need as much room for clearance; when they are fixed to a wall or other unit, no space need be provided at the rear.

One way to estimate space allotment per person is to calculate by means of square feet. About 12 to 15 square feet per person is a good allowance of floor space. A couple will be generously served by 24 to 30 square feet, a figure which includes table, chairs, and space for passage. A family of four will double the figure to 48 to 60 square feet, and so on.

About two linear feet per person at the table should be the rule if each is to have elbow room. Figure round tables somewhat differently: one of three-foot diameter will seat four and one of four feet will seat six.

Whether at table or counter, leg room also is a comfort factor. A person of average size seated in a straight chair needs approximately 20 inches of leg room under the table. On a higher stool at a higher counter, only 14 inches of leg room need be provided because of the angle of the legs, but a very high stool calls for a footrest or rail.

Space Savers

Snack Bars at Islands, Peninsulas, and Counters. A snack bar is a popular space conserver. Such bars can stand at the usual 36-inch counter height, if you allow sufficient leg room and use a 24-inch high stool or chair instead of one of the normal height, 18 inches. Base cabinets then could not be used under the counter at which people are to sit, although if the eating counter were a fold-out flap, it would be possible.

If you design a peninsula or island which utilizes one side as an eating space and devotes the other to a sink or stove, you will need to separate them in some way. This can be done by raising or lowering the dining side of the unit, or by building a low divider, perhaps a foot high, between the two. If the snack bar is lowered to table height, ordinary chairs will suffice. If it is raised, 24-inch or 27-inch bar chairs or stool will be necessary. Sometimes revolving stools which turn higher and lower, like old-time piano stools, can be particularly suitable if there are young children in the household.

Whatever type or height of dining counter is constructed, you must allow a space about two feet wide for each seated person, giving consideration to leg room. Counters that are not deep or long enough for eating can have hinged drop-leaves added to them and the same is true of islands or peninsulas. If a long section is added, supports will be necessary underneath.

One negative aspect of a snack bar is that, with few exceptions, everyone is seated facing in the same direction — a situation scarcely conducive to conversation. Dining at a bar may be fine for pick-up meals and for breakfast, when people feel less sociable, but evening meals should provide a time and place for the people who live together to relax and talk. Eating bars that face blank walls can be the most deadly of all, so if you include one, try to orient it facing into the kitchen or out a window.

Tables Attached to Base Cabinets. Sometimes the best way to conserve space and still have a table around which the family can gather in the kitchen is to design one that becomes a permanent, fixed extension of a counter, island, or peninsula. You can create a diversity of designs, depending upon the arrangement of your kitchen. A pie-shaped wedge, a semi-circle, or a full circle might be needed. Be extremely cautious about invented shapes, however. Free-forms can be pitfalls; geometrics are better.

Built-in Tables and Benches. A built-in table with one or more of its seating benches or edges against a wall pares down square footage demands. Depending upon the kitchen plan, the back of a counter, island, or peninsula, or a wall, can be situated behind one side. Seating units can also be constructed with backs high enough to create walls of their own.

Built-in tables supported on one side can require fewer legs than regular types. Benches also can be cantilevered out from

a wall, eliminating legs completely, or they can have one or more legs as auxiliary or total support. Benches can also be built like boxes, solid to the floor with notched heel-space. If the seats are

hinged so they will lift up, you will gain extra storage space.

Built-in benches or banquettes can be comfortably cushioned, with mattress-style pads, or the tops can be upholstered

A U-shaped counter runs on three sides of this kitchen as extra work area and to preserve the view. The counter at the window is 21 inches deep. A 3-inch space is left open at the back for window maintenance access.

The counter is 3½ inches thick and is faced with a decorative laminate strip to match the wallpaper.

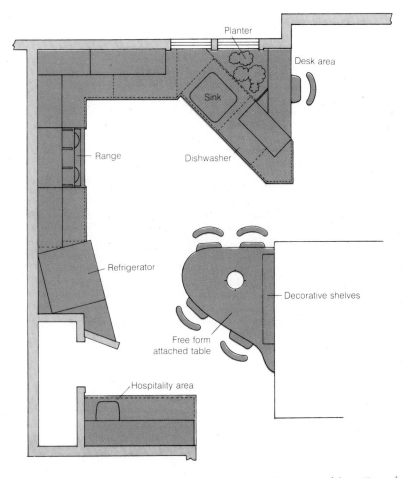

The rounded triangular shape of this built-in table is a softer repeat of the pattern of the sink and dishwasher peninsula near it. The curve allows a better traffic pattern.

like any other piece of furniture. It is best to cover them with a wipe-off material, such as Herculon, or zipper the cushions so that a washable fabric can be quickly removed. And there is no need to make benches backless. In fact, sitting on a chair with back support rather than on a backless bench or stool is more comfortable for most adults. On the other hand, backless benches extend the visual impression of space.

Fold-out or Pull-out Table. The least space-hungry type of table is the wall or counter drop-leaf. It is most suitable in small kitchens, although as a supplement in large kitchens it can add to the width of an island or peninsula dining counter. (Sometimes such drop leaves are part of the standard line of custom or stock cabinet makers.) Factory-made wall-hung folding tables are available from several sources. Among them is the

Hirsch Company, which makes the Hide-a-Table with a melamine surface simulating butcher block. When open, it measures 36x20 inches. When folded flat against the wall it is 40 inches high and 2½ inches deep. One firm, Sico, Inc., makes a table called "Floating Fold" in several sizes. It is finished in impermeable materials.

Other companies make similar tables, as do the firms which fabricate kitchen cabinets. If you cannot find the exact size, shape, and finish you are looking for, building a fold-out drop-leaf, or pull-out wall or counter-hung table, is a relatively easy project for a home carpenter.

Tables Which Move, Expand, and Diminish. Folding tables, (standard card tables), when used for dining, can be annoying to put up and take down regularly. A crowded home may have no place where one can be stowed away easily. Other designs for folding tables do exist, however, and these do meet the storage problems. The standard 19th century card table had a top which folded back to half its size. When not in use it usually stood against a wall as a side table. With casters, it had only to be wheeled into place and opened when it was time to put it to use. The hollow space under its turntable top stored small items — place mats, or a cloth and napkins. Surprisingly, old models are often available in antique shops at comparatively modest prices; modern versions are now being manufactured also. These or similar tables can solve space problems for families of four or fewer. Wall space requirements are approximately 36 inches wide and 18 inches deep when closed, and 36 inches square when opened.

A very good range of contemporary gateleg and dropleaf tables are currently being merchandised. Two types are typical, both less than a foot wide when closed. One is a gateleg folding table with a unique virtue: its center support is also a storage compartment into which all four of its matching folding chairs can fit. When open it measures 34x64 inches, a size which would be only slightly crowded for as many as eight and at which six people could regularly dine very pleasantly. Another strong point is that it rolls on casters, a commonplace of the 19th century now being widely re-adopted. The second table is a more common gateleg style that opens to 36x54

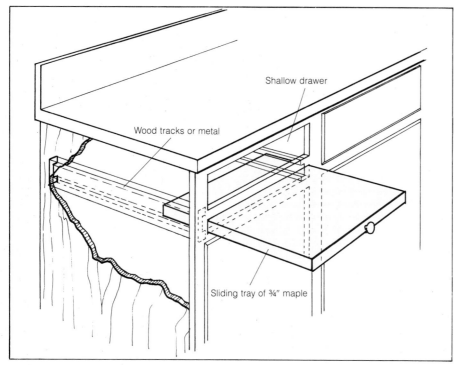

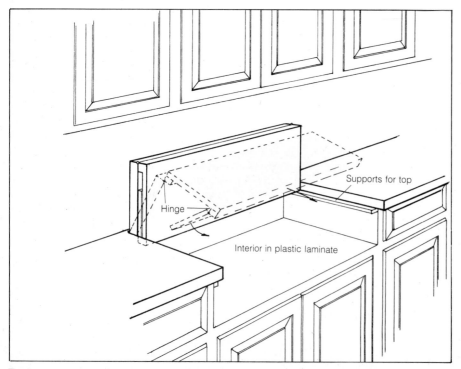

To give a lower work surface in a kitchen, use a pull out shelf or a counter that will lift and fold out of the way. In either case, you will lose all or part of adjacent drawer space.

inches. (As in this example, extensions attached to the ends of any table lead to far less leg straddling for those seated than at tables that open by means of leaves inserted into a movable center opening.) These tables are sold by such chains as Workbench and Brazil Contempo.

Space-Saving Seating. Certain types of stools stack, and since these are particularly handy when space is at a premium, it is worth searching them out. Some chairs also stack, so that between meals two, three, or four of them may be stacked to occupy the same floor space as only one. Folding chairs are another staple, but pulling them in and out of a closet can be inconvenient and too often the house which is short on dining space is also pressed for closet space. The right sort of folding chair, however, can be unobtrusive and even look handsome folded and hung on a wall near the table. The Shakers hung their simple wood chairs on the wall, not so much to save space as to ease room cleaning. Few modern homes have sufficient height and wall space to follow their example, but if you do, attach a strip of molding a foot or so below the ceiling to hold dowel pegs spaced at regular intervals. Hang each chair on two or three dowels.

Finally, if there is no other solution, think about places in nearby rooms where chairs could be placed without making the house look like a furniture store. Perhaps one chair could double as a desk chair or grade the front hall. Even young children can be taught to carry chairs in to meals; adults, of course, should find it no problem.

Trays and Wagons

Most people clear the table one or two plates at a time, though practically every household has at least one good-sized tray. But small, wheeled tables are even better than trays. These are sometimes called tea wagons, cocktail servers, or (in England) trolleys, and they have been around for generations. You can buy a new one, find an old one, or build a wheeled push-table for yourself. Once you do, you will find it an asset in setting and clearing any table not within arm's reach. Whether making or buying a wheeled cart, keep in mind that its finish will be in constant contact with food and alcohol. Double tiers will double its usability.

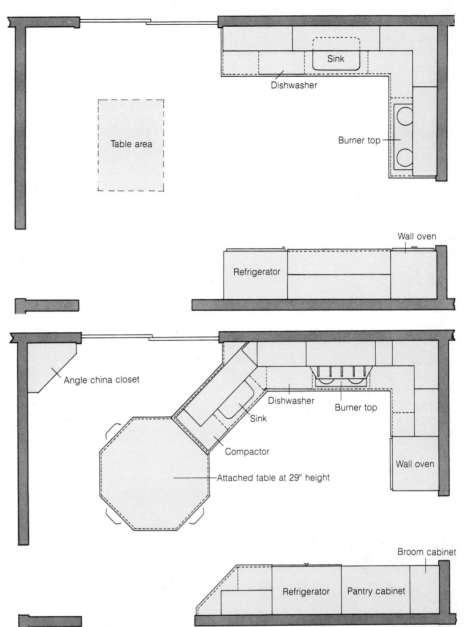

The original kitchen layout provided all the basics, but used little of the space. A new layout utilizes the space better, groups appliances more efficiently and gives more storage and work space. The octagonal table attaches to the sink cabinet for quick after-meal cleanups.

A permanent home can be provided for a wheeled push-table under a countertop. You can build one, or have it built to order, with a drawer door front matching that of your other cabinets. The handle of the drawer serves as a pull so it can be rolled out. When parked under the counter it will look built-in and be hidden.

CREATIVE KITCHEN WINDOWS

Additional windows, increasing the light and airiness, are almost certain to add to the attractiveness of your kitchen. However, before you carve out extra openings, recognize that some exposures are more desirable than others. South light is desirable, provided there is some sort of overhang or awning which prevents the sun's entry during the hot season. Outdoor plantings which create summer-shade, such as deciduous trees or vines, will also serve. East light brightens the morning kitchen yet is rarely hot. Western exposures are usually undesirable — in summer the direct rays of the late afternoon sun can keep a house uncomfortably hot until far into the night, or they can make air-conditioners work too hard. Nevertheless, if a western window is your only possibility, use overhangs, sun-stopping blinds, insulated curtains or shutters, and appropriate outdoor plantings. North light is favored by artists because it is sunless and even, and thus does not throw bright spots and shadows onto their work. It casts a light which lacks the drama of other exposures, although kitchen design and colors can compensate effectively. North windows may also permit entry of too much cold air into houses located in severe climates. Thus, the choice of window exposure depends on the climate in your part of the country, the directions in which outside walls of your kitchen face, the prevailing summer breezes and winter winds, as well as the design of your kitchen.

Climate Control

Climate and exposure are important because glass of any type insulates poorly. For this reason, either double glazing or windows with well-fitted storms or other devices are mandatory in any energy and cost-conscious household. Some manufacturers are now offering triple-glazed windows, which boost the insulating value and reduce heat or air-conditioning loss. Since more heat is lost at night than during the day, some sort of movable insulation will prevent air warmed by the sun or by your heating system from exiting via uncovered glass once it is dark outside. There are many ways of achieving an insulating closure, from drapes lined with an insulating material to window "quilts" to movable shutters or flaps. One excellent book written on the subject is *Movable Interior Insulation* by Rodale Press.

You can usually seal double-hung windows more successfully against air filtration than is possible with casement or awning types. If awning windows are made on sliding hinges so that the top slides down as the glass is pushed out, an awning window can open a totally horizontal position. This allows for a more complete opening and air passage than any other type of window.

Fixed glass has the capability of being thoroughly sealed, but too much fixed glass prevents good air circulation. Unfortunately, many readymade commercial units are made with far too few movable openings. One can rely upon air conditioning, but a better solution today is to add windows that open and close above, below, or alongside fixed glass. Another possibility is to put together one's own bays, bows, and picture windows. For picture windows, the large panes of safety-tempered insulating glass designed

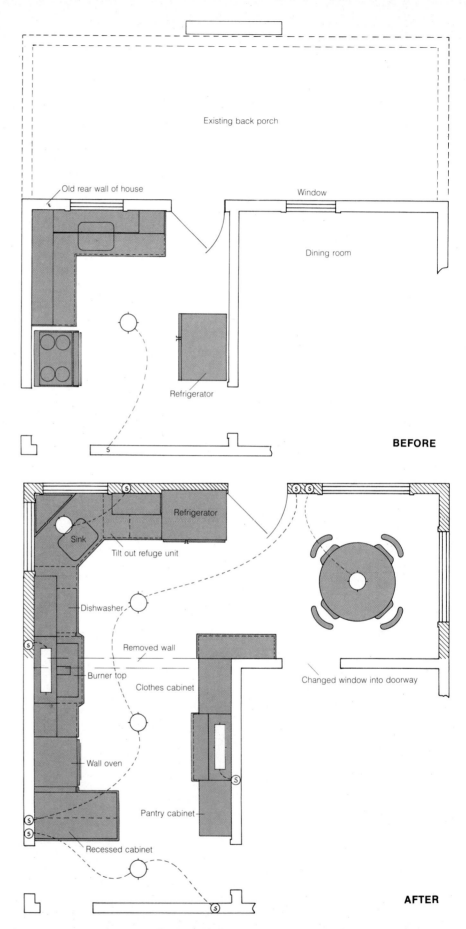

Expansion into an existing back porch turned a tiny, cramped kitchen into a comfortable, useful working and eating space. Four adequate-sized windows give excellent light.

A large sunny window behind a sink is a perfect place for an herb garden. This tiled window greenhouse offers both space to hang plants and recessed flats to start plants.

The corner windows in this kitchen give natural light to the room. The windows overlook the back yard with a pleasant view. The area also provides space for plants.

A back porch offered space for a kitchen addition. The existing roof and floor of the porch were kept in the remodeling. The roof line was adapted for an extended roof over the new back entry door. New windows at the corners and glass in the door supply the room with light.

to replace aluminum sliding-glass doors are a good choice. The glass can be ordered directly from the factory at a charge lower than for picture windows. Aluminum sliding doors themselves are a poor alternative. The aluminum transmits heat and cold and the doors can never be well sealed against air leaks. Many people find them a security problem. Carpenter-built or home-built, wood-framed, sliding doors are more satisfactory in the long run. (For instructions on how to prepare a wall to accept a window, and how to enlarge an existing window, see Chapter 8.)

Clerestory, Bays, and Picture Windows

Windows particularly suited to creative kitchen design are the clerestory, the bay or bow, and the picture window.

Clerestories. The clerestory (clearstory) is a high window, usually above eye level, which admits light and, if it is movable, air as well. A clerestory can run as a long horizontal strip above wall cabinets (instead of a soffit) when there is sufficient height above cabinets hung on an outside wall. Clerestories have several strong points: they free wall space below them, they ensure privacy, and they may be fixed or movable or a combination of the two. Many types are manufactured, but a bargain it particularly pays to know about is an awning vent manufactured by the Anderson Window Company. It is 32 inches long and comes in three sizes with heights from 15 to 24 inches. The awning vent opens and closes, and the glass can be removed for washing. The units are sold with screens, but at this writing are offered with single glazing only, which makes them less attractive in cold climates. Although these are intended by their manufacturer as basement vents (which perhaps accounts for their modest price), a series can be extraordinarily effective in the kitchen.

Bay Windows. Any angular wall or projection from a house front that is filled with windows is called a bay window. If the projection is curved, it may also be called a bow window. If such a projection is on an upper floor only and not on the story below, it is properly termed an oriel window. These windows provide light (and perhaps air) from three directions, yet they occupy only one wall. Few spots are more pleasant for a dining table than one pulled up to a bay or bow window. A

A pass-through gives access for serving and allows light into a dark room.

An enlarged window has been converted to a pass-through between the kitchen and an added dining room. Large windows in the new room contribute needed light to the kitchen.

Picture windows affect the appearance of the outside and the inside of your home. Although this one looks out on a lovely enclosed patio, it still adds natural light to the kitchen.

bay or bow can go from floor to ceiling or have the same height as any other window in the house. When bays terminate at usual sill height, they allow for a relatively deep sill shelf which you can finish as desired. If fitted with a tin liner and lip, you can set potted plants on it. The pots should rest on saucers or a layer of pebbles. Water poured to just below the top of the pebbles keeps the atmosphere humidified. You can also make a sill into a comfortable and charming windowseat by building a plywood unit and upholstering the space or covering it with large pillows.

Bay windows are factory-made in kits in sizes from five to nine feet long for all three sections. In these kits the center panel most often comes as only fixed glass. The smaller side panels on either side usually have movable, double-hung sash windows. The bay window shape is a widened triangle.

Bow windows, with their rounded form, are more expensive, but they also come in sizes up to fourteen feet. As with bays, they are available in one-foot increments from five feet on. Both bays and bows are made by numerous manufacturers. Visit dealers and look through catalogues to become familiar with your options.

There is another means of obtaining a bay window: It can be built by a carpenter from any three or more windows. A home-designed bay window will have another advantage over one designed commercially: the center panel can be de-

A skylight offers a natural light source for a kitchen that is largely enclosed, or with exterior walls used for cabinet storage. Even in winter, the skylight gives an open feeling.

signed to open and close just as the side panels do.

Picture Windows. Picture windows have come in for adverse comment in the past because many of them framed an unattractive view, or the only way a family living behind one could duck perpetual display was to pull the blinds. If this describes your situation, clerestories may be the wiser choice.

The advantage of a large picture window is that it lets in enviable amounts of light. However, it also loses heat in winter and gains it in summer unless, once again, it is caulked and weatherstripped adequately. Storm windows also help. Because a picture window has fixed glass and cannot be used for ventilation, place movable windows above, below, or even alongside fixed picture windows. Awning vents can serve this purpose.

Skylights

Factories turn out all types these days, and almost any type permits patches of sky and light into your kitchen. But the manufactured ones are costly, and some of them are not particularly attractive. See Chapter 8 for installation instruction.

Odd Shapes and Translucent Glass

If you want to frame a special view, admit light to an odd corner, or follow a design concept of your own, you can make or have made almost any shape, or size of window. You can cut fixed windows into circles, diagonals, narrow vertical or horizontal slits, pie-shaped wedges, or whatever other shape fits the plan.

While glass in windows is usually clear, at times you may prefer opaque glass — to avoid an unsightly view or to give privacy. Window glass can also be made from pebbled, ribbed, colored, or frosted glass, all of which permit light to pass but through which little can be seen. In some schemes an interesting piece of new or antique stained glass might make an effective fixed window.

A small window was replaced by an attractive set of glass doors that open onto the patio.

This kitchen was especially designed for a large family. The wall counter and the center island are spaced so that many people can work at once.

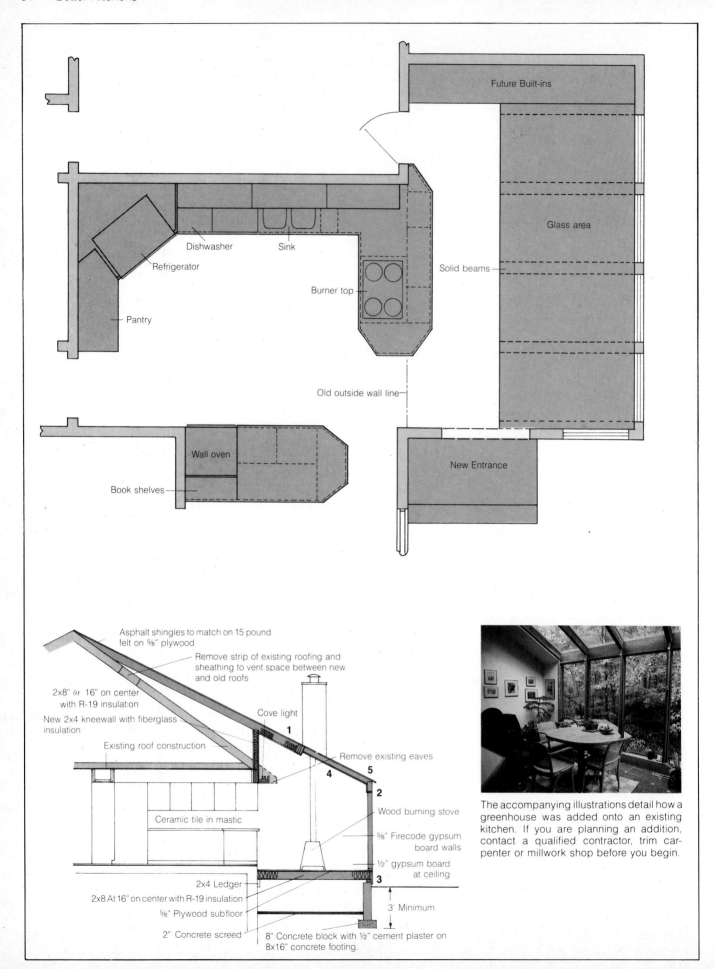

Future Built-ins

Glass area

Dishwasher

Sink

Refrigerator

Solid beams

Burner top

Pantry

Old outside wall line

Wall oven

New Entrance

Book shelves

Asphalt shingles to match on 15 pound
felt on ⅝" plywood

Remove strip of existing roofing and
sheathing to vent space between new
and old roofs

2x8" @ 16" on center
with R-19 insulation

New 2x4 kneewall with fiberglass
insulation

Existing roof construction

Cove light

1

Remove existing eaves

4   5

2

Ceramic tile in mastic

Wood burning stove

⅝" Firecode gypsum
board walls

½" gypsum board
at ceiling

2x4 Ledger

3

2x8 At 16" on center with R-19 insulation

3' Minimum

⅝" Plywood subfloor

2" Concrete screed

8" Concrete block with ½" cement plaster on
8x16" concrete footing.

The accompanying illustrations detail how a
greenhouse was added onto an existing
kitchen. If you are planning an addition,
contact a qualified contractor, trim carpenter or millwork shop before you begin.

Window Greenhouses

Window greenhouses can wonderfully enhance or enlarge space. They are sold as readymade units and in kit form to be put together by the homeowner. Home carpenters easily can build them from scratch. You can fill one with flowering plants or greenery all year round or use it to grow such edibles as parsley, lettuce, and even tomatoes during the winter. In spring you can give your outdoor garden a jump on the season by starting seeds in a window greenhouse. Size is, again, flexible — yours can fit into a window or a small sash window.

Window greenhouses work best in windows with southern exposures, although sufficient light can come from eastern or western exposures if there are no obstructions that cast shadows, such as trees or other buildings. While it is true that several categories of excellent houseplants thrive in north light, that direction would be a poor choice for a window greenhouse.

Far more light reaches plants living in a window greenhouse than on a windowsill because light comes in from three sides plus the top. Far less light, however, will work its way through a full greenhouse into the kitchen, since the plants themselves obstruct it. Because of the greenhouse's interior window — its inside "door" — the window will no longer be as satisfactory a source of ventilation, even if vents or a lift-up roof are included (one or the other should be). If you don't want to give up an entire window's worth of light, you can select the half-window, covered, window-box type of greenhouse. This design interferes less with sunlight, although of course it contains fewer plants. Decisions regarding any window greenhouse have to be weighed against your kitchen's other needs.

A window greenhouse can also affect the temperature of your kitchen. You can remove the interior window to give the kitchen direct access to the greenery or retain it to function as one layer of double glazing. In the latter case, plants would not benefit from household heat in winter, but in a south-facing, well-insulated window greenhouse with appropriate plants, this might be no problem. Some south-facing window greenhouses, with their interior windows removed, actually help warm the house. If your kitchen has an infrequently used outside door, it too is a likely candidate for removal and transformation into a "window" greenhouse.

Several manufacturers sell window greenhouses, either as already-built units or as kits for the home carpenter. See the appendix for a list of sources.

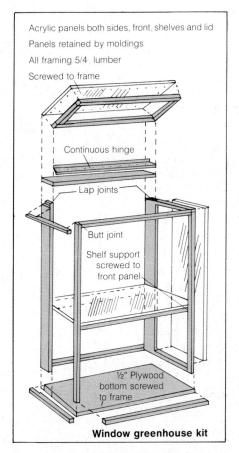

Acrylic panels both sides, front, shelves and lid
Panels retained by moldings
All framing 5/4 lumber
Screwed to frame
Continuous hinge
Lap joints
Butt joint
Shelf support screwed to front panel
½" Plywood bottom screwed to frame

Window greenhouse kit

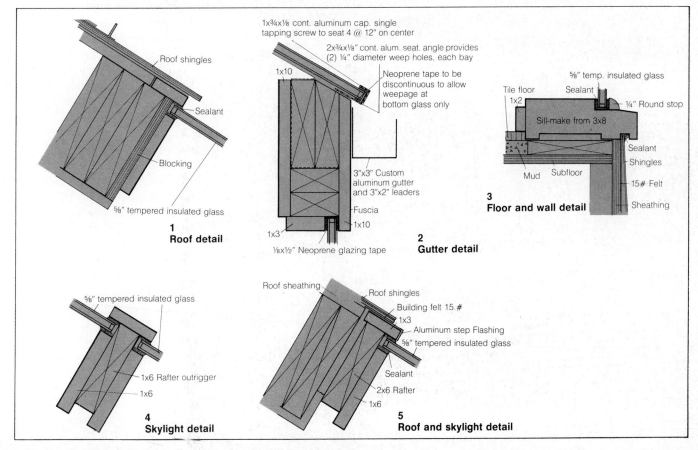

1 Roof detail
Roof shingles
Sealant
Blocking
⅝" tempered insulated glass

2 Gutter detail
1x¾x⅛ cont. aluminum cap. single tapping screw to seat 4 @ 12" on center
2x¾x⅛" cont. alum. seat angle provides (2) ¼" diameter weep holes, each bay
Neoprene tape to be discontinuous to allow weepage at bottom glass only
1x10
3"x3" Custom aluminum gutter and 3"x2" leaders
Fuscia
1x10
1x3
⅛x½" Neoprene glazing tape

3 Floor and wall detail
⅝" temp. insulated glass
Tile floor
1x2
Sealant
¼" Round stop
Sill-make from 3x8
Sealant
Shingles
Mud
Subfloor
15# Felt
Sheathing

4 Skylight detail
⅝" tempered insulated glass
1x6 Rafter outrigger
1x6

5 Roof and skylight detail
Roof sheathing
Roof shingles
Building felt 15.#
1x3
Aluminum step Flashing
⅝" tempered insulated glass
Sealant
2x6 Rafter
1x6

6
ALTERNATIVES TO COMPLETE REMODELING

Given the cost and time required to remodel a kitchen, you would be wise to consider less expensive alternatives to a major and complete remodeling. This is especially true if the basic layout of your kitchen pleases you. After your analysis, you may discover that recycling components and renewing areas or facilities will give the most desirable results.

Most kitchen problems fall into patterns, and many can be met by means other than a complete remodeling. Some kitchens feel cramped or seem to be too dark. This may be because there is not enough light or the decor may have dark tones. The kitchen appliances may be too old or insufficient for a family's present needs. Cabinets present a host of prob-

lems, from doors whose paint is worn and dull to drawers that either will not open or fall to the floor when extended. Last — and most aggravating to the person who spends the most time in the kitchen — is lack of necessary counter or storage space. Careful kitchen analysis will reveal your particular complaints. The answers to them will help you decide whether you need to tear out and add new features, or if you can have the kitchen you want by following a much simpler course of action.

INCREASING USABLE LIGHT
Artificial Light
First examine the artificial lighting in your kitchen. If the room seems well-

lighted during the day but too dark in the evening, you may be relying too heavily upon a single central fixture. If so, it should not be hard to add additional fixtures. If the problems lie with the location rather than the number of fixtures, you can rearrange and supplement them to better serve your needs and your floor plan. Chapter 9, "Lighting and Wiring," suggests improvements you can incorporate.

Natural Light
Sometimes a kitchen receives too little natural light because plants, shrubs, eaves or walls block incoming light. Check outside for obstructions: plantings can be cut back and trees moved or trimmed if they block light at kitchen windows. The problem may be a structural one — a porch or an overhang may be blocking sunlight. In these cases, alteration or removal are more complex and costly. You may wish to consider using more artificial light or adding a skylight or clerestory, rather than removing or altering the cause of the problem.

Another solution is to enlarge the existing window. For instructions on how to replace and enlarge a window, see Chapter 9.

Color Scheme. What seems to be inadequate lighting may in actuality be an illusion created by the color scheme of your kitchen. Dark walls and floors absorb light and cause the physical space of the kitchen to appear smaller than it actually is. So does a ceiling that is not painted white, since white reflects light down into a room better than any other color. If your cabinet finish is either a dark paint or wood grain, the available light will be reduced. A wallpaper that features large designs results in a room that feels smaller; small patterns look farther away and make a room seem larger.

You can solve color scheme problems fairly simply. You can recover a floor, or you can repaint or refinish walls, ceilings and cabinets. The result will be a room

This kitchen received cosmetic, not structural, changes. Its new look results from refinished cabinets and tiled countertop and backsplash, complemented by attractive accessories.

that takes advantage of all the light it receives and appears even larger than it actually is. Refinishing cabinets will be discussed later in this chapter. Instructions for replacement of floors and wall and ceiling finishes can be found in Chapters 7 and 8.

Wall Removal. As with the color scheme, the size of a room can make it seem dark. If that is the case with your kitchen, the solution may be to remove either all or part of a wall that separates the kitchen from a dining, family or living room. Removing half a wall will bring in extra light from the adjoining room, as well as provide additional counter space that you can use for any number of purposes. (See Chapters 3, 4 and 5 for suggestions about islands and counters.) In addition, the extended visual line of the ceiling will make the room appear larger, even though its size has not changed. If you take out an entire wall, of course, you will dramatically expand your sense of space and light. For instructions on wall removal, see Chapter 8.

INADEQUATE APPLIANCES, SINKS, COUNTERS
Appliances

Repair and Renewal. Kitchen appliances, according to industry sources, have a life expectancy of 10 to 15 years. Many individuals, however, own appliances that have served a great deal longer. Appliances can lead 9 lives when they are well maintained and repaired promptly.

To grow herbs or plants on your counters, add special fluorescents under the wall cabinets.

Partial wall removal adds needed light and a handy pass-through to a sunken dining room.

Light blue and white enamel accents the geometrics of cabinets and countertops. A matching floral wallpaper softens and lines and completes this satisfying, low-cost remodeling project.

One major structural change was made here: an existing window was enlarged to become the focus of the kitchen. Paint and wallpaper enhance the window at little additional cost.

Sometimes the best way to revive old appliances is to hide them. Panels match the cabinets to disguise the refrigerator and dishwasher, creating the appearance of "built-ins."

No major structural change was made, but an island work area and a retiled countertop resulted in a completely new look.

The tone of this kitchen is augmented by the addition of a commercial range. Its size, color and unornamented lines reinforce the businesslike, utilitarian style of the room.

Refrigerator parts, for instance, are widely available, allowing an old mechanism to be renewed indefinitely. Surface burners on an electric stove can be replaced with very little cash outlay and effort. Gas burners rarely need replacement, but should be cleaned out regularly. To obtain information on repairing both stoves and refrigerators, contact a local product representative or write to the manufacturer.

If you want a new look for an old appliance, without the expense of replacing it, paint it with a spray epoxy paint — available from large department stores, and hardware and paint stores. Be reasonably careful when you apply the spray. In fact, if at all possible, try to do the painting out-of-doors. If you work inside, do be sure that you have adequate circulation so you do not breathe in the propellant or the fine spray paint. Carefully cover all other surfaces upon which the spray might fall; lay a tarp or drop cloth over the floor and cabinets. Use drop cloths on sinks and countertops. Then scrub the appliance thoroughly. Sand the surface, especially rough spots and loose enamel. Follow the manufacturer's directions on how to use the apparatus provided, and you should have an attractive "new" appliance.

If you decide to switch from gas to electrical equipment it is not necessary to shift everything else in the kitchen. The biggest consideration will be whether or not the utilities you will need are already available in your house. If you have a gas dryer, a line can be extended to the kitchen. If not, you will have to add the service you need, be it a gas line or a new 220 volt electrical connection. Be sure to check local codes.

Wall Ovens. When a wall oven needs to be replaced, the job is obviously much easier if the new one is the same size as the old. But a competent home carpenter can modify the opening if the dimensions differ. A double wall oven can replace a single wall oven by a partial reworking of a part of the wall-oven cabinet and perhaps a portion of countertop. A wall oven can be moved from one location to another. Then you can transform the cabinet that once held the oven into a broom closet, an ironing board cupboard, pantry, or even a hospitality center. When a double oven is to replace a single oven, the height of the new unit usually is fairly easy to handle. However, enlarging the width beyond the inside dimensions of the cabinet sides involves major work, often beyond the scope of the average homeowner. Provided the opening can be enlarged sufficiently, the first step is to remove the old oven.

Removing an Electric Oven. Disconnect power to the unit by turning off either the fuse or circuit breaker that controls its power. With the power off, back out the fastening screws until the oven is loose in the cabinet. Slide the oven out of its cavity onto a platform of plywood placed on a couple of sawhorses placed in front of the cabinet. Disconnect the electric wires from either the oven terminal box or, if it is equipped with a pigtail wire as most are, from the connection box at the end of the pigtail. When installing a new electric oven, always check that the existing line and fuses are heavy enough to handle the new oven (see Chapter 9). When making the new connections, always use large enough wire connectors. Tape connections; make sure all connections are tight and secure.

Removing a Gas Oven. To remove a gas unit, find a shut-off as close to the oven as possible. If there is none, you may have to shut off the entire gas supply at the main. This, of course, means having to relight pilots in the furnace, water heater, gas dryer (some) immediately after you turn the gas on again. With the gas turned off, remove the oven from the cavity in much the same way as the electric unit. When replacing the unit, it is best to install a convenient shut-off valve and a new flex connector to ease installation replacement, or repair at a later date.

Modifying the Opening. Once the oven is out, use a yellow carpenter's pencil to mark the recommended cut-out size of the new oven onto the face of the cabinet, starting at the suggested height above the floor. If, by good luck, the recommended opening falls close to either the top or bottom of the existing opening, you may be able to simplify your job by only having to rework either the top or bottom section instead of both. If it is close, you can deviate from the manufacturers' recommended measurements by a few inches without seriously affecting the efficiency of the unit.

Once you have determined the location of the new oven and assessed the degree of cabinet work needed, it is time to begin the modifications. Remove the cabinet

doors from the section or sections that require reworking. Use a finetooth saw to cut out the existing rails; you may be able to reuse them in the new location. If not, create new support rails of the same material as the existing cabinet, and install them in the desired location. (See illus.) With the rails in place, cut and fit new shelf bottoms into the sections as required. Support any shelf carrying the weight of the oven. Once the new openings are set you will have to cut down the cabinet doors to fit. First, cut the door to the overall size you will need, allowing for door style. If it is a lip door, leave material for the lip. Then undercut the door to create the lip. Add the hinges and reinstall the doors. Slide the oven into place in front of the cabinet. Make the necessary connections; then secure the unit in place.

Hoods. If you are face-lifting your cooking area, you may wish to install a hood over the stove or to replace the one you have. See Chapter 9 for replacement instructions.

Sinks

There can be any number of problems with the sink area in a kitchen. Perhaps the one in your kitchen requires only new

faucets. When choosing a brand, remember that parts for nationally known brands are more readily available when the faucets need repair.

However, you may decide that you need a new sink. The old one may not have as many sections as you would like — or it may have more than you want. The finish may be marred. Years of use may have worn away the enamel surface so that it now is stained and impossible to clean. The old and new sinks may be the same size; if they are not, you will have the situation discussed below in "Replacing Cooktops."

The range hood in this kitchen is a major design feature, chosen to match the cabinetry.

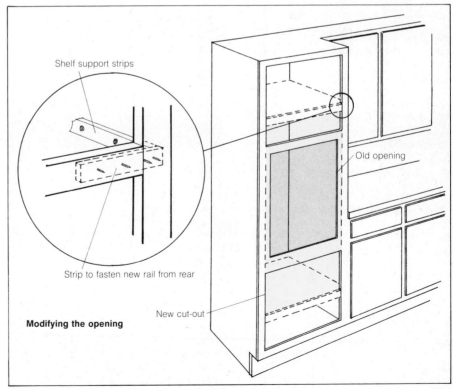

Shelf support strips

Strip to fasten new rail from rear

Old opening

New cut-out

Modifying the opening

If the cabinet walls are at least ⅜ inch thick, fasten shelf supports for the lower oven shelf with ½ inch to ¾ inch screws. (For a cabinet with thinner walls, build a 2x4 frame from floor to oven level.) Attach rail to front to support, flush with finished cabinet wall. Insert ½ inch plywood lower shelf. Fasten shelf supports; then attach rail.

Around the Sink. Sometimes what one wants is to replace the sink and update with a new sink area. The addition of a garbage disposal unit or a hot water dispenser can fulfill such a desire. Maybe what you really need is a dishwasher, surely one of the most helpful of 20th century inventions, particularly in families of more than two or three and in households that often have guests for meals. If you already own a portable, you can create space adjacent to the sink to house a built-in dishwasher without disturbing more than one base cabinet. The convenience of a built-in dishwasher more than makes up for the lost shelf space, and you can get that back by installing shelves or cabinets where you kept the portable.

Replacing Built-in Cooking Units. You can easily replace a countertop cooking unit. If you are fortunate, the old and new units will be the same size. When the new unit is larger than the old one, you will need to enlarge the opening. The ease or difficulty of this job depends upon the material out of which the countertop is made. Corian can be cut and sanded with ordinary woodworking tools. Plastic laminate is usually applied over plywood, particleboard, hardboard, or old laminate; therefore, it can be cut and altered with ease. Ceramic tile can be cut, but you may damage it in doing so. (Instructions for removing tile are given in "Replacing One Tile", later.) One way to get around the problem is to install a new counter surface of plastic laminate over the entire top. To do this you leave the tile in position and either lay a ready-made countertop over it, or add an underlayment over it and cement the plastic laminate to the underlayment (See Chapter 10.) If your countertop is marble, your best course is to hire professionals to cut through the surface.

If the new unit is smaller than the old, or if you decide to place the new unit in another area, you will need a new section of countertop. You can replace the entire run if you so desire, but it is not necessary to do so. At the same time, you will find it almost impossible to add countertop that exactly matches the original. Also, you will be unable to avoid visible seams between the old and new sections. A better strategy is to use a different material in the area of the old cooking unit, one which in color and feeling complements the rest of the kitchen. For instance, you can insert a section of tile, butcher block, or Corian. The rest of the counter can remain as it is.

Ceramic Tile Counters

Replacing Just One Tile. Score an "X" on the face of the tile using a glass cutter. Bear down as hard as you can on the cutter, and then throw the glass cutter away; it will be ruined.

With a hammer, tap the "Xed" spot lightly. This will break the tile into four sections. With a putty knife or scraper, pry out the broken pieces of tile. Clean the grout from the surrounding edges of tile and remove as much dried tile adhesive from the wall as you can. You can level it fairly well with a putty knife or scraper.

Test the new tile for fit. Then put a walnut-sized amount of ceramic tile adhesive on all four corners of the tile. Press the tile in the void and align and space the joints to match the joints of the other tiles.

Let the job set a couple of days, and then mix up a fairly stiff batch of ceramic tile grout. Press the mixture into the joints around the tile. The best way to do this is with your index finger. When the joints are full, wash away any fresh grout on the tiles. Then, with a clean index finger, smooth the freshly grouted joints so they have a concave shape. Again, wipe away any excess grout or haze on the tiles. Let the job set for a week. Clean the area with regular ceramic tile cleaner, and spray with a silicone sealer.

Regrouting Ceramic Tile Joints. If you decide to regrout a whole counter, wall, or floor, note that the colored grout now on the market hides grime better than the white grout used in most homes.

Create a tool to dig the grout out of the joints: drive a 10d finishing nail through a piece of 1x3 near the end of the scrap. Use this to remove the grout from the joints. This takes patience; the work goes very slowly.

Drop-in burners create a clean, finished line on a newly installed, bright ceramic countertop with matching backsplash.

An old island becomes brighter, and easier to clean, with the application of ceramic tile to several of its surfaces.

To update a cooktop, install drop-in modules. Available in gas and electric, these versatile units let you switch easily and quickly from a set of burners to a barbecue or pancake griddle.

As you work, brush out the joints with the whisk broom and clean up this debris with a vacuum cleaner. It is important to keep the work clean. If you do not, you will track the grout all over the house.

When the joints are clean, mix up a small amount of grout. Spread this mixture over a small area of tile, using a damp sponge to distribute the grout and force the grout into the joints. When the joints are filled in this small area, wipe away any excess grout and move on to another small area.

Now go back to the first section you grouted. With a container of water, dip your index finger in the water and smooth the grout in the joints. Do not use too much water. "Damp" is good enough. Your finger will produce a concave joint, which is ideal.

Let the job set overnight. Go back with a damp sponge and wipe the haze off the tile. Keep using clean water as you go.

Give the grout time to harden — about a week — wetting the grout down twice a day to harden it. Then go over the tiles with tile cleaner and seal the tile with regular nonyellowing tile finish or a silicone spray.

Color-coordinated design tiles were included in this reworked ceramic countertop and backsplash, resulting in a unique work area.

Easy-to-install pregrouted sheets of small ceramic tile refinished this island.

For replacement or addition of an entire counter, see Chapter 10.

Plastic Laminate Counters

You can cut out damaged portions and replace with butcher block or a glass top, as mentioned under "Cooking Units."

DEALING WITH CABINETS

Complaints about kitchen cabinets fall into two general groups: those about the exterior finish and hardware and those

This kitchen did not need to be completely remodeled, but its color scheme was uninviting. Work and storage areas were small and dark.

To prepare the frames for the laminate, they were stripped and sanded to remove the old finish and smooth any mars and nicks.

about the interior workings and storage capacity. The ultimate solution, especially for wall cabinets, is to remove the old ones and hang new. However, you should consider other alternatives before you go, checkbook in hand, hunting new cabinets.

Exterior Appearance

There are any number of reasons for changing the exterior appearance of your cabinets. You may wish to lighten the

The old cabinet doors were to be replaced with new formica doors. The cabinet frames would be recovered with matching plastic laminate.

Laminate comes in large sheets that are easily cut with a shears. Adhesive is applied to the frame and to laminate before alignment.

An extra rear cabinet and overhanging top expanded the island. Installation of a bay window and additional lighting increased the available light. Paint and wallpaper completed the project.

Color visually unifies a kitchen and dining room. Soffits, open shelves and cabinetry are painted blue to contrast with white countertop and walls.

Although counter space is ample, insufficient lighting and dark decor compound the inconvenient, elongated work triangle.

To pass dishes and food to the dining area, one had to reach over double burner units on the kitchen side of the peninsula.

Installation of recessed ceiling fixtures and white ceramic tile solved the lighting problems. Note use of special Mexican tiles.

Kitchen and dining areas were joined by removal of the peninsula. Cabinet frames were stripped and new doors were finished to match.

overall color scheme of the room. The original finish may be worn or scratched. Or you may just want a change.

Paint. The easiest way to change your cabinets is to paint over the old surface. You can choose colors that are lighter, darker, or even the same as the ones you have now. Metal cabinets and those made of wood that were painted originally are the least complicated to repaint because their surfaces accept paint readily. In some cases you can apply new paint over the old. If the old paint is chipped or loose, however, the paint should be sanded or even stripped before repainting. Cabinets covered with plastic laminate such as Formica have finishes that are too smooth to accept paint readily. These cabinets must be handled in other ways.

Refinishing. Painted wood cabinets can also be stripped and then refinished with stain and polyurethane varnish. The degree of satisfaction you feel about the final product will depend in part on the quality of the wood that you find once you remove the old paint. The cabinets may have been constructed from what is called "paint grade" lumber, which means that the grains of the different pieces were not matched. However, the staining process can attractively disguise or minimize the differences in the panels.

Tools and Materials List: old newspapers; old rags; scraper — 3″ flat blade; rubber gloves; 2 brushes — 2″ width (one for applying varnish remover, one for applying new varnish; finish remover; lacquer thinner; fine sandpaper; stain; varnish; steel wool (grade 1 or 2).

Refinishing divides into two stages. The first is removal of the old paint and varnish. The second is the application of the stain and new varnish. The success of the latter stage relies heavily upon careful work during the first.

Stripping. The objective of the stripping process is to remove all paint and varnish down to the bare wood. You will use varnish remover for this. First, remove the doors and drawers. Take off all knobs, pulls and, if necessary, hinges. Spread newspapers in a well-ventilated location. Varnish remover usually is toxic and flammable. If possible, work outdoors. You will have fewer worries about the mess and less danger from fumes.

Use rubber gloves. Lay the doors as flat as possible so that the remover will not run off before it has done its job. Cover one side of the door with a generous coat of remover. Let this penetrate for 5 to 10 minutes before scraping away the sludge-like residue of dissolving paint and varnish. As you work, keep your scraper at a very shallow angle against the wood. Exercise care during this step so that you do not gouge the wood surface. Use the steel wool to clear away the residue in any trim areas and around the hinges. You probably will have to repeat this entire process two or three times, depending upon the remover and the old finish. Once you have worked down to the

BEFORE
This kitchen's original work triangle wasted both space and steps. The amount of floor space between the countertop near the refrigerator and the burners and ovens required too many steps. Because the burners were not close to any work area, their location made the pass-through between the kitchen and dining room virtually useless.

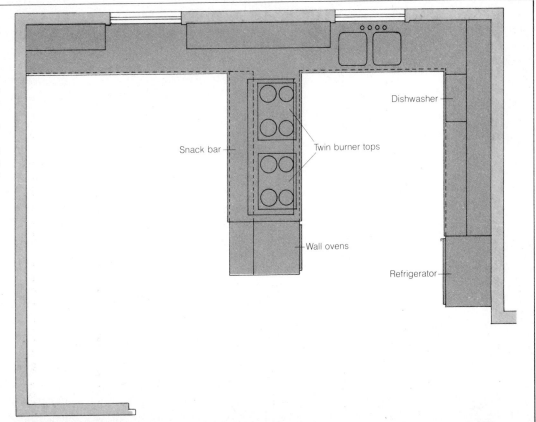

AFTER
In the redesigned kitchen a deepened countertop has increased the work area by the sink, but the main change is the island that replaces the peninsula. The added grill and new cooktop on the island reflect the needs of the family and update the cooking facilities. The island's size provides a meal preparation area. The refrigerator's new position places it conveniently near both cooking and eating areas.

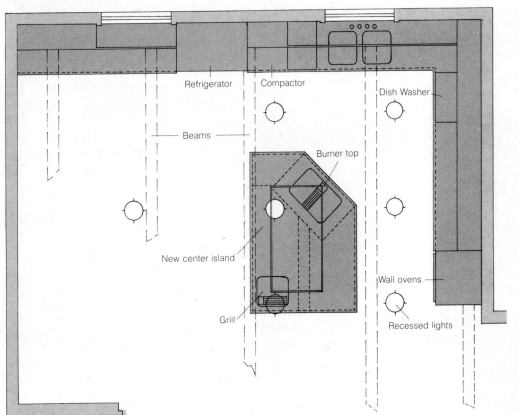

wood on the first side, turn the door over and start all over again.

Follow the same steps for drawer fronts. The cabinet frames will present more difficulties since they are vertical surfaces. Be sure that the layer of newspaper on the floor and the countertop is more than ample, since the remover inevitably will drip. Work with the windows kept open; running a fan is not a bad idea, either.

Once you think you have thoroughly removed all paint and varnish from the cabinets, give the surfaces one more scraping, and follow with an application of lacquer thinner (soak rags in lacquer thinner and wipe). Once the surfaces are thoroughly dry, sand the wood to an even surface. No matter whether you work with an electric sander (usually on the built-in framework, not the doors and drawers) or the woodblock-and-paper technique, use a lot of elbow grease. Casual sanding will result in a surface that will not accept the stain evenly.

Staining. Your cabinets are now ready to stain. However, if you would rather keep the natural color of the wood surface, you can simply varnish the cabinets. Instructions for that appear below.

Although paint is designed to seal the surfaces to which it is applied, stain merely colors the surface and highlights the wood's grain and texture. You can control the amount of color that the wood absorbs by the number of times you apply stain to the surface, as well as by the color of the stain purchased.

Stir the stain well. Then, using the old rags or cheesecloth, cover the surface thoroughly and heavily. Apply an even heavy coat with long, smooth strokes. Otherwise the staining may look streaked. Wait for 10 to 15 minutes to be sure that you get a good "take." Then wipe off the stain with a clean, absorbent cloth.

Do not apply another coat for at least an hour. The wood should have a chance to dry and absorb the first coat. The second coat does not have to be applied with as heavy a hand as the first one. As you apply it, note the color that the wood is acquiring. If you are satisfied with the tone, you will not repeat the staining process a third time. Let the second coat set for 10 minutes; wipe off any excess.

If you desire even more color, apply a third coat. This should be the last one, in a very light layer until you reach the tone you wish. You should not have to remove any excess when you have finished.

Wait at least another 24 hours before adding the varnish. You can use either high gloss or satin varnish. Either kind is appropriate, although satin varnish will not show fingerprints as readily as will the high gloss. If you choose a polyurethane varnish, it will dry more quickly and better resist scratches and moisture.

Sealer Coat. For a seal on the wood — which stain alone will not provide — apply two or three coats of varnish. Always be sure that each coat has dried thoroughly before the next is applied. The manufacturer's directions will tell you the average drying time for a coat, as well as whether you need to sand the surface of one coat before you apply another.

Replacing Doors. If you are satisfied with the size and location of the doors currently in your kitchen, but the doors are in bad condition, the answer may be to replace the doors only. New doors come in a variety of finishes and styles, but for replacement purposes they are usually bought unfinished. In most instances, you would have to strip existing built-in cabinetry and restain it to match any stain that comes on new doors. It is easier to buy unfinished doors and stain them to go with the old cabinet framework.

However, doors (and drawers) need not match cabinets. An emphatic two-tone treatment, with a strong contrast to avoid the appearance of accident, can be achieved with paint. The cabinets and existing framework may, of course, always be painted to match.

Resurfacing Doors and Drawers. Although marred or outmoded plastic-laminate-covered doors cannot be painted, they (or even old wood doors) can be surfaced with new laminate. You could do this yourself to existing, absolutely flat surfaces only. It is not feasible for recessed panel doors or those with moldings. First, sand nicks and scars so they do not show through. Apply new plastic laminate, following basics given in Chapter 10. For cabinet frames, doors and drawers, you will need only 1/32-inch-thick laminate.

A commercial process for refinishing is often available at reasonable prices. All the old finish is stripped. Then the exposed surfaces are covered with a type of plastic laminate. The choice of finishes is impressive; recent offerings include metallics, wood grains, slate, patterns and colors, textures, and marble.

Substituting Shelves for Cabinets. Rather than replacing doors you can remove the doors to the wall cabinets and use them as open units. Sometimes removing the wall cabinets entirely and replacing them with shelves can be the best and least costly solution. Shelves can be constructed of moderate quality pine or veneered plywood. They can be finished with polyurethane varnish, gloss or semi-gloss paint or stain and sealer.

Hardware. New hardware can improve both the appearance and function of cabinets. Before you choose the set you wish to use, look through *Sweet's Catalogue* in your local public or college library. This resource lists all manufactured products, and in it you will discover more products in each category than you even dreamed possible. Once you know of their existence you can write to the manufacturer for the names of local outlets. The catch is that manufacturers sometimes take so long to answer this kind of query that you may be long finished with your project by the time you get a response.

Some of the best hardware is available only at sources other than the local hardware store. Big cities usually have one or two stores that specialize in a variety of pulls, knobs, hinges, and handles. If you are interested in high-quality period reproduction or contemporary hardware, write to the firms listed in the appendix. Any fee charged for a catalog usually is applied to the item's purchase price if you decide to order.

When you replace hardware, you will face the problem of the screw holes in the cabinet doors and drawers. If the new

To build in an appliance, enclose the base cabinet with wallboard. Apply doors and paneling (not yet added as shown) to match.

This Victorian home was carefully restored: ceramic backsplash and pressed tin wall were cleaned and then the wall was enameled.

Open shelves designed for storage and display are in keeping with this rustic kitchen's beams, wall/floor materials, cabinet styling.

The dominant theme in this restyled kitchen is informal and modern, as indicated by the translucent bamboo curtain. Rather than enclosed cabinets, which are more expensive, shelves are used to store cooking and serving pieces and to display their colors and textures.

A tall, narrow sliding cabinet contains shallow shelves for spices. Stained glass inserts over the sink match windows in the kitchen.

Due to the intricacy of the ornate woodwork in the original cabinets in this kitchen, they were stripped and repainted rather than refinished.

hardware has the same center — that is, identical fastener openings — your job will be simplified. Even if the new hardware has dissimilar openings, it often has enough backplate to cover the original marks. If, however, the new hardware will not cover the old opening, you must try to repair or patch the old door with a plug. If the hole is small enough, fill with wood putty, sand and finish to match.

Cabinet door hinges also come spring loaded, eliminating the need for a catch. Measure for the correct size but, to be on the safe side, buy only one pair. Try it out on one of your cabinets.

Interior Workings and Storage Capacity

Drawers. Drawers that stick can be repaired. First, look for the source of trouble. It may be that a loose nail is sticking out, in which case you need only hammer it back in. Frequently, however, the sides of the drawer have begun to work apart. If so, you must re-glue the drawer with a plastic resin adhesive, applying it to all the joints. Then (because it does not immediately dry thoroughly) use a belt clamp to tie the drawer together tightly, holding the sides in place until the glue dries.

It may be that the drawer guides are worn and need replacement, which is another frequent cause of stubborn, sticking drawers. If your drawers have side guides, there is generally no choice other than to have them repaired. You can substitute ready-made metal glides, but they often occupy more space than the drawer case can accept. If the drawer has a single wooden center guide underneath, however, a modern metal center guide can replace it. These come in many different sizes. Measure the old guide and buy a new one to match. Remove the old guide, and then fit the inner channel of the metal guide to the bottom of the drawer. Then fit the outer channel of the new center guide to the cabinet. Replace the drawer in the opening and test its fit. If it is riding too low, push shims under the outer channel to raise it. Test the drawer again. If it rides too high, consider planing it to fit. When the fit is satisfactory, rub the surface of any wood part that slides against another with paraffin.

Some drawers have been made without any guides at all. These drawers often must be held when opened, to prevent them from falling. If this is the case, frequently you can add a raised center slat under the drawer, and either insert a center guide as described in the preceding paragraph, or dado a slot in which the slat will fit. You can add a dado only if there still will be at least a ¼ inch thickness in the drawer bottom.

Storage Capacity. If it is the interiors of your base cabinets that trouble you, kitchenware departments and good hardware stores now sell many items that can be of immense help. Many types of specialized storage bins, usually made of plastic-coated metal, have been designed.

Creating a Sliding Shelf. If your single-shelved, deep-base cabinets turn into vast storehouses, a simple remedy is the pull-out center shelf. Remove the cabinet's present shelf. Measure the distance between the inside wall of the cabinet and also the distance from the back to the inside of the front frame. Then determine the distance between the front stiles (vertical rails).

Most modern side track runners take up about ½ inch in width. Attach furring strips as indicated, running from front to back. Use tracks rated at 50 lbs. or more for larger sliding trays.

Construct the sliding shelf much as you would build a flat, wide drawer (covered in Chapter 10). Use at least ¼ inch plywood or thicker for the floor. The sides should be of ⅜ to ⅝ inch plywood to strengthen the shelf and accommodate track fasteners. When laying out the size, allow for the combined width of the side runners. Build the shelf as shown. Then mount the runners to the previously installed side supports and to the shelf. Another shelf tray can be added to the base of the cabinet in the same way.

UNSATISFACTORY WORK AREA
Outmoded Electrical System
New types of electrical appliances are constantly put on the market, and if you buy only a small fraction of them, the existing wall outlets are too few. You can add new outlets without extensive alteration, as explained in Chapter 9.

Insufficient Work Space
The hardest inadequacy to solve without thorough renovation is inadequate work space. But there are a few techniques that can help even if they do not entirely solve the problem. First, remove every single object now occupying countertop space. Once counters are cleared, you may discover that what you need is storage facilities for odds and ends, rather than countertop work space. Next, see if there is a corner either in or near the kitchen where you might be able to keep a portable work table. One such table is made by Taylor Woodcraft and designed as a food-processor center. It has a removable cutting board, a stainless steel basin, a knife holder, a utensil drawer, a vegetable basket that hangs under the countertop, a holder for food processor blades, dish-towel pegs, a bottom shelf, and casters that can be locked for stability. The dimensions of the Taylor table are 36 inches

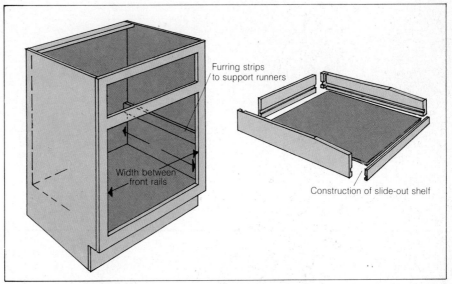

Furring strips to support runners

Width between front rails

Construction of slide-out shelf

To construct sliding shelf, attach furring strips to the side walls to support runners. Cut shelf to fit between front rails of the cabinet, leaving room for runners. Use tongue-and-groove method to add sides and back to shelf. Angle the two shelf sides to ease access to contents.

wide, 24 inches deep, and 26 inches high. Similar tables, on casters for easy movement, from other makers are sold in many outlets, or such tables can be made by the moderately skilled home carpenter.

In many homes the dish drainer occupies a couple of feet of countertop space on one side of the sink, whether there are dishes in it or not. You can free that space by buying a folding wooden drainer and setting it aside, or by hanging it on two cup hooks screwed onto the door of the base cabinet adjacent to the sink.

The floor space in this square kitchen was ample but inefficiently utilized. The remodeling itself involved little structural change. The cabinets were replaced. Since counter space was lost when the stove was built in, a large island with attached eating area was part of the new plan.

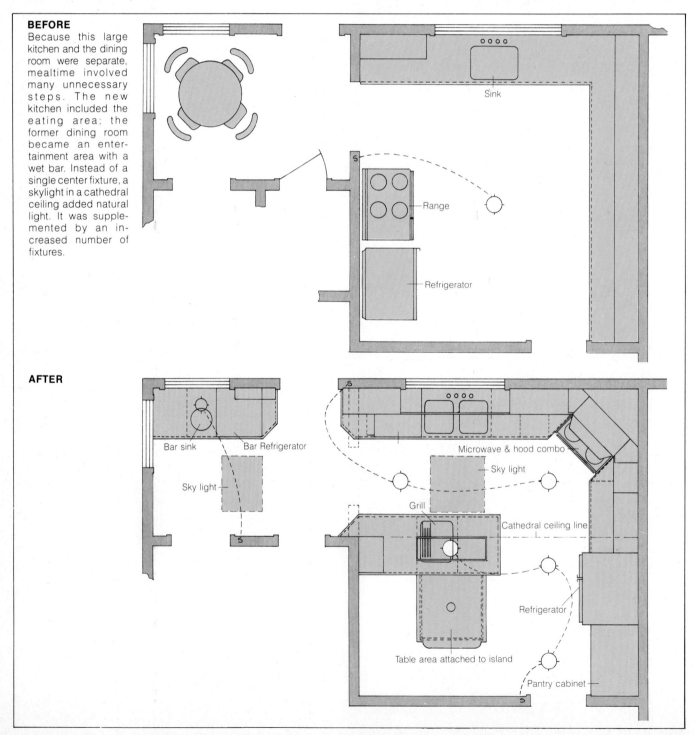

BEFORE
Because this large kitchen and the dining room were separate, mealtime involved many unnecessary steps. The new kitchen included the eating area; the former dining room became an entertainment area with a wet bar. Instead of a single center fixture, a skylight in a cathedral ceiling added natural light. It was supplemented by an increased number of fixtures.

Sink

Range

Refrigerator

AFTER

Bar sink   Bar Refrigerator

Sky light

Microwave & hood combo

Sky light

Grill

Cathedral ceiling line

Refrigerator

Table area attached to island

Pantry cabinet

7
LOOKING
AT FLOORS

The first half of this chapter describes the wide variety of flooring materials available. The last sections give installation instructions.

CHOOSING MATERIALS

Kitchen and dining area floors can be covered with wood, asphalt tile, vinyl asphalt tile or vinyl, rubber, cork, kitchen carpeting, stone or slate, ceramic tile or quarry tile, concrete with epoxy resin or brick. Some of these, in turn, may be finished with other materials. Wood, for example, may be sealed with polyurethane after being painted or stained. One material may be set into another, as when tile is made to adhere to a plywood subfloor.

Floor coverings are generally divided into resilient flooring, which have some elasticity or bounce, and hard flooring — surfaces with no flex whatsoever.

There is a large selection of flooring that may be installed by the homeowner. Most manufacturers have their own systems of installation, so that the directions that follow can only generalize on the overall procedure. Every step may not be applicable to every situation or material. The product you buy will usually include directions for nonprofessional installation. Since every producer wants new consumer business, improvements in both the product and its simplicity of installation are being constantly introduced.

Resilient Flooring

Wood. Wood is a flooring material which has been traditionally used throughout American homes. Although it increasingly faces competition with the newer, manmade materials, wood is still a frequent floor-covering choice for many homeowners.

Wood has the advantage of long life, structural strength, and warm tone. When finished with a top-quality polyurethane, it is impervious to penetration by water

Tan grout not only provides contrast and pattern, but seldom shows soil on tiled floors.

A wood floor that appears to have a natural, aged color and texture can help create a rustic-kitchen look.

and other liquids. It can be finished in any wood tone desired or stained in the color of your choice. Much of the wood flooring available today comes prefinished in an assortment of shades.

You may already have a wood floor in the kitchen and want to keep it. If the wood floor is in good enough condition, you may only have to remove any old linoleum or other floor covering over the wood in order to refinish the wood floor. If the existing wood floor is in too poor a condition to be repaired or resurfaced (a rare case), you can still choose wood as your floor covering. You can lay new floor-tiles or blocks (parquet) or you can nail down or glue on plank wood floors, both of which can be purchased ready-made for this purpose. In a new kitchen — an extension or wing, for instance, or a new house — you can lay a new floor of wood over the subfloor.

You may choose to stain the wood floor and finish with a polyurethane finish or you can choose one of the following, attractive variations.

Stenciled Wood. Painted floors, which for a period of time were considered unfashionable, are enjoying a revival today. They are especially effective in kitchens with country themes. You can create an impression of a rug or develop an all-over pattern with stencils, as well as surface textures using various paint techniques which are compatible with stenciling.

You can either purchase a kit which will allow you to stencil an attractive design suited to your kitchen, or you can create your own stencil design. Kits are available from one of the firms listed in the appendices. Most kits are easy to use and come complete with instructions. Some firms charge a nominal fee for their illustrated brochures and price lists.

Floor preparation for stenciling may require a complete refinishing, especially if the floor is old. If your surface is relatively new, you may be able to apply the stenciling after a careful scrubbing, a light sanding and mopping, or general cleaning.

Stenciling may be applied to plain wood floors; however, in most cases, stenciling is applied over a coat of base paint. If you wish to create the effect of a rug, you may paint a section of your floor with a base coat, after determining the desired location and marking the area

Wood floors offer rich color and texture. For instructions on how to refinish, see the end of this chapter.

Set up stencil materials on a small tray so you need not keep going back to your work table.

Paint is built up slowly because the color is more beautiful if it is slightly translucent.

Wood is ideal for floor stenciling, but it may also work successfully on concrete, brick quarry tile. Stenciling on resilient tile is not recommended.

Floor scumbling can offer a simulation of the texture of an old floor cloth.

Stippling a broad expanse of floor takes longer than scumbling, but is equally attractive.

either by following the lines of the floorboards or snapping a chalkline.

Your base coat should be of a high-quality floor paint which will be compatible with acrylic paints used for the stenciling. If your floor has been freshly stripped, you probably will need to apply two coats of your base color.

Circular areas also can be created. For a circular area, tack one end of a string to the center of the area to be painted and attach a piece of chalk at the other end. The length of the string should be exactly one-half of the desired diameter of the circle. Keeping the string taut, scribe the circle.

Textures. If the base coat looks too intense in color or resembles a vast, featureless expanse which the final stenciling will not break up, you can create a visual texture in several ways. You may spatter the surface with a slightly contrasting shade or tint of the same hue as the base coat, or you may use a slightly different color. The base coat must be totally dry before the texture coat is added. Before starting, cover your walls with paper extending from the floor to a height of three or four feet. Dip a paint brush about one-half inch into your paint and remove most of the paint by scraping the brush against the side of your paint can as you pull out the brush. Holding the brush parallel to the floor, pull your wrist back and then snap it down smartly. Small droplets of paint will fly off the bristles onto the floor. Practice this before you try it on your floor, until you get the feel and range of the wrist action. Begin at a point opposite your exit; spatter the floor evenly.

You may also create textures by stippling or scumbling. Stippling can be done with a brush or a sponge. With a brush, dip only the very ends of the bristles in paint, wipe off most of the paint on the edge of the can, and apply by gently tapping the floor with the ends of the bristles. Hold the brush at right angles to the floor. This will be a time-consuming process, but it enables you to control the pattern exactly.

The process is faster with a sponge, but the pattern then is determined by the pattern of the sponge. Buy a large *natural* sponge for this process. Dip the sponge in paint and wring it out well. Blot the floor surface with the sponge. Rotate the sponge to vary the pattern laid down. Wring the sponge well each time you dip

it into the paint. This will avoid heavy splotches of paint.

The fastest form of texturing may be scumbling. For this you dip a large piece (at least 3 feet square) of rough-textured natural fabric into the paint. Wring it out well. Fold the fabric into a bundle and roll it across the floor. Do not apply pressure; just let the paint and the cloth surface create the pattern. It will change each time you rewet and reroll the cloth. If you are not familiar with the technique, lay a long piece of brown kraft paper on the floor and scumble on that until you are confident of your skill.

After you have painted the base coat and applied whatever texture you desire, you may begin stenciling. You will need acrylic paint, stencils and stencil brushes. You may design your own stencils or purchase ready-made traditional stencils. It is advisable, if you are covering a large area, to have several duplicate stencils. Determine the location of your pattern and tape down your stencils with masking tape. Apply the paint with a stencil brush, lightly dipped in paint. Use a straight up-and-down stroke similar to the brush-stippling technique. If you instead brush back and forth, paint will be forced under the edge of your stencil and result in a ragged edge. Wait until the paint has dried before removing the stencil.

If your chosen pattern requires two or more different stencil patterns or colors applied one over the other, complete one stencil pattern and one color before starting a new color. Make sure the paint has dried between applications. Seal with urethane varnish.

If you are very exacting in applying the stencils and paint, you should have an attractive and unique floor treatment that will last a long time.

Your Own Stencils. If you are going to make your own stencils, you should buy stencil board or stencil paper. Either of these should be available at any art supply store. If you cannot find this special material, use a bristol or tag board. However, this material will not hold up as well or as long, and it will be worth your while to find the proper material.

Design your pattern and trace it onto the stencil board. Cut out the pattern with an Exacto knife or other razor knife. The blade must be very sharp and will need changing to maintain a clean, sharp cut. If your design is complicated, you may have

to cut a series of stencils for a complete pattern. Do not cut out so much of the material that there is no stability to the stencil. Even if it does not fall apart, it may pull out of alignment and your patterns will not match.

Cut several stencils, tracing the pattern from the original design rather than cutting from one stencil to make another. This keeps all stencils identical, and will allow you to position several stencils in a row, tape them in place, apply the paint, and let it dry. This procedure prevents any one stencil from becoming overloaded with paint. You can move the first stencil as soon as the paint is dry. Follow this "leap-frog" arrangement around or across your floor.

Floor Cloths on Wood Floors. Long before the invention of linoleum, 18th and 19th century Americans used floor cloths, which were made from canvas or similar materials painted in colorful designs. Even elegant homes used floor cloths under the tables and chairs in dining rooms.

You can have a floor cloth made to order in a traditional or custom design through a firm called Floorcloths, Incorporated. Their work is striking and unusual. These floor cloths also are practical, although at prices beginning at ten dollars a square foot they can be considered a luxury

Grooves carved down the centers of hardwood block tiles create an unusual floor design.

One of the advantages of using resilient sheet vinyl is that if it is slightly undercut, it can be stretched. If cut a little too large, it will contract to eliminate wrinkles.

item. The cost is due to the hand-painted process, requiring skilled craftspeople.

Asphalt Tile. Asphalt tile is probably the least favored of the manmade tiles for kitchen use because it resists marks poorly, has a limited color range, and offers only a dull finish. However, it wears well and is less expensive than other tiles.

Vinyl Asphalt Tile. Somewhat more costly than asphalt, vinyl asphalt is asphalt with a thin covering of vinyl. This coating makes it longer wearing and more resistant to scuffs and stains than asphalt tiles.

Vinyl. Vinyl is currently the most popular choice for kitchen flooring. It wears very well, needs only an occasional waxing or polishing, and cleans readily. In addition, it comes in a variety of colors and patterns to suit your design needs.

Vinyl, however, does have disadvantages. It can be dented easily when subjected to certain pressures, such as shoes or the legs of a table or chair. The stilleto heels which women wore in the 1960s gave vinyl floors an undesirable pattern of small indentations. Many vinyl surfaces also scratch or tear fairly easily. A heavy refrigerator, pulled without great care, could tear a vinyl floor. Certain areas of the kitchen floor, such as the spot where a dining chair is pulled in and out regularly, are likely to show wear.

Vinyl flooring is available in sheets or in tiles. While the tiles are simpler for the homeowner to install than the sheets, they also are usually more expensive per square foot. Unless you plan to install the floor yourself, always check the installed price of the design you prefer before making your decision. The cost of purchasing and installing underlayment, if over a

Since resilient sheet flooring comes in 12-foot widths, the completed job usually will have no seams. Here it is going over old vinyl.

Press a guide — a metal straightedge or carpenter's square — firmly along the baseline. Then cut away excess flooring with a knife.

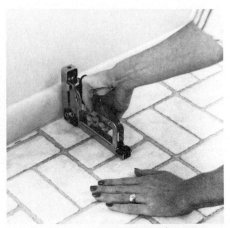

Fasten at edges using a staple gun, or use cement in areas where a staple gun can't reach or there is no molding to cover staples.

concrete or a bare joist floor, should be kept in mind when estimating the cost of any type of floor covering. Unlike the tiles, sheet vinyl comes in a "cushioned" grade, with an extra layer to add greater resiliency and comfort. The depth and the effectiveness of the cushioned layer vary according to the quality and the manufacturer.

The largest American manufacturer of vinyl floor covering, Armstrong, now has a line called "Interflex," which is aimed at the do-it-yourself market. "Interflex" is a cushioned flooring in sheet form that is extremely pliable, and easier for the amateur to install than other sheet vinyls. Furthermore, because it does not require cementing all over for installation, floor preparation is simplified.

In spite of some obvious advantages of sheet vinyl, tiles remain the usual choice of homeowners for self-installation. Instructions for laying this tile (and other types) appear in the second portion of this chapter.

Rubber. Rubber is known for its quietness and its superior resiliency. Like vinyl, it is available in sheets or tiles and comes in a wide range of colors. It is especially appropriate over concrete subfloors, although it can be used on top of wood and other subfloors as well. Rubber has a tendency to be slippery when wet; however, textured finishes are available to overcome this drawback. Rubber is expensive, and perhaps for that reason has never been popular for the home.

Kitchen Carpeting. Kitchen carpeting was more popular when it was first promoted than it is today, but it still offers certain advantages. Of all the available types of floor coverings, it is probably the most resilient. It is softer and warmer than other flooring, and it gives a look of luxury, even though (if self-installed) it may be one of the least expensive new floor coverings. Because it is made of synthetic materials and backed by waterproof latex or foam, kitchen carpeting is washable. In addition, the rich surface texture of carpeting disguises mildly uneven floors without requiring new underlayment.

Before you choose kitchen carpeting, however, consider some of its disadvantages. Because it is highly resilient kitchen carpeting is vulnerable to wear, and thus is relatively short-lived. Although it is washable, carpeting is not as easily kept as clean and sanitary as smooth flooring. Bacteria may be a risk. Because it is more absorbent than other types of floor coverings, it is more susceptible to stains.

If you decide to purchase kitchen carpeting as a floor covering for your kitchen, do not buy outdoor carpeting. These two types of carpeting are not identical. The backing of kitchen carpeting is waterproof, but the backing in outdoor carpeting permits the passage of water. This is an asset outdoors, but not in the kitchen.

Hard (Nonresilient) Floors
Stone or Slate. Depending upon such variables as quality and availability, stone and slate may be inexpensive or costly. Even if you find these materials to be more expensive than other floor coverings, do not dismiss them solely on price. Stone or slate will never wear out and will almost always look good. Unlike other types of flooring, these materials probably will never need to be replaced, making your initial investment your final one.

When a floor provides the dominant pattern in a room, the walls and cabinets should not have competing patterns. Walls can pick up the flooring colors for color coordination.

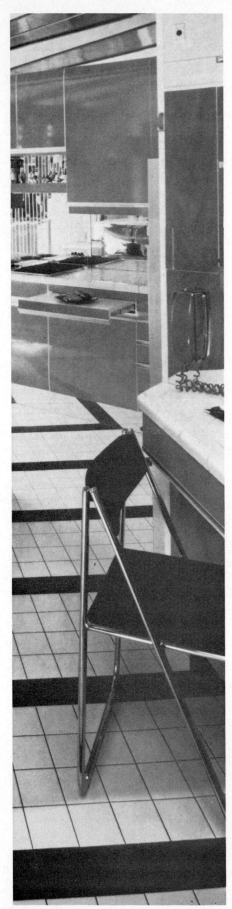

There are a few disadvantages to using stone or slate. Like ceramic tile and brick flooring, stone is a very hard material. It is thus more tiring to walk on and stand on than resilient flooring. You can minimize this effect, however, by placing small rugs or straw mats in heavily traveled areas. If you should drop anything fragile on this type of floor, it is likely to break. Since stones or slate are laid in heavy mortar, and are themselves weighty materials, the floor underneath must carry a significantly heavy load, except in houses where the kitchen rests on a cement slab. Therefore, you will usually find it is necessary to reinforce the floor from below with double the usual number of joists. (Joists are the boards, usually 2x8s, to which the subflooring is nailed. They are spaced at 12-, 16-, or 24-inch intervals.)

You may find stones or slate lying about in the fields, free for the picking, depending upon which part of the country you live in. In other areas you may use slate which is offered packaged in boxed assortments from any lumberyards and home centers.

If you choose to purchase boxed slate, decide on just one of the colors in which the slate is quarried (a shade of gray, green or red). Try to have the colors and textures as similar as possible, while al-

lowing for the variations inherent to all natural materials. Avoid the multi-toned collections in cartons, which are the most readily available. These are distracting to the eye when combined with the random-sized rectangular shapes into which slate is usually cut, and the zigzag mortar lines. You may have to insist that your dealer special-order the type of slate you want.

Ceramic Tile and Quarry Tile. Real ceramic tile is becoming a more frequent choice for kitchen floors. Quarry tile, which has quarry shale added to the clay base of which ceramic is made, is not as common a choice. Many people consider ceramic tile floorings a luxury, without realizing that some ceramic and quarry tiles are actually competitive in price with resilient flooring. Like slate or stone, ceramic and quarry tile are extremely durable. A flooring composed of either of these two materials will wear forever. There are some disadvantages to using ceramic or quarry tile as your kitchen floor, but most of these can be overcome. New grout sealers now prevent what used to be a problem with dirty grout between tiles, and grouts also come color-keyed to either make them inconspicuous or to add a new design dimension. Ceramic tile floors tend to be tiring to walk on and stand on; they can be noisy when hard shoes are worn. However, vinyl-bonded

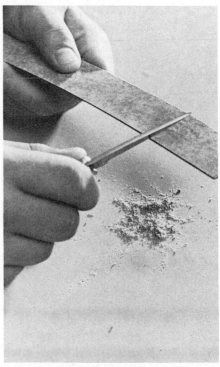

Strips of dark tile contrast with the light floor for an interesting pattern. The dark grout adds to the floor design and hides dirt.

To remove a damaged vinyl tile, use a scraper or putty knife; then chip and scrape off all of the adhesive underneath.

To fill small holes in resilient tiles, make a "sawdust" from scrap resilient tile. Mix with white glue and press in the mixture.

tile now on the market is somewhat resilient and, therefore, quieter and more comfortable.

Ceramic tiles are available in a large assortment of both imported and American-made styles. Tile sizes range anywhere from tiny mosaic bits to square foot slabs or larger. Ceramic tile is manufactured in brick shapes, hexagons, and in other complicated, decorative forms, designed to fit neatly together.

Ceramic and quarry tiles are best suited for a concrete subfloor, although you may lay them over any firm base. All types except glazed ceramic tile (the most popular for kitchen use) should be sealed for kitchen applications.

Concrete with Epoxy Resin. Epoxy resin or epoxy-urethane coatings are unfamiliar to homeowners, although designers of industrial installations are familiar with them and frequently use them. This material is an excellent choice for covering an existing concrete floor because the plasticized liquid hardens into a tough, smooth finish which resists penetration by liquids and wear. You may purchase epoxy resin either in a one-pot solution, which comes ready for use, or in a two-pot solution, which you will need to mix before applying. The main disadvantage to covering your floor with concrete and epoxy resin is that the concrete, while

To remove an entire vinyl tile floor, use an ice scraper or flat tiling spade. Do not gouge underlayment while scraping off adhesive.

it wears indefinitely like other hard floorings, may place a strain on the legs of its users.

If you choose to cover a new cement floor with epoxy resin, or an epoxy-urethane coating, do not apply the material until at least one month after the concrete has been poured. You will generally have to apply two coats; each will take about six hours to dry.

Brick. Although brick was a traditional kitchen flooring material in Europe and in areas of this country in centuries past, it is not commonly used for this purpose today. New, real brick is expensive and professional installation is costly. If, however, you can gain access to a good supply of used brick and you are willing to go through the time-consuming effort of installing it yourself, you may find that a brick kitchen floor is within your budget. A brick floor requires either extremely strong joist support or application over a concrete slab. If this is not feasible in your kitchen, you might consider splitting the brick so it is only one half or one third the usual thickness — and weight.

INSTALLATION METHODS

If the existing flooring is in good condition, you can lay your new flooring right on top of your old floor — provided that your old floor is either wood, old inlaid linoleum, asbestos, vinyl, rubber tile, concrete or plywood flooring.

Some existing flooring materials, such as rotogravure (printed vinyl or linoleum), may have a finish that repels most adhesives. Try the new all-purpose latex adhesives before deciding that a new overlayment of subflooring is necessary. If you want to lay ceramic tile over existing ceramic tile, there are adhesives that allow you to do this by making a special bond between the old and the new ceramic tile, after roughening the old surface.

There is one disadvantage to laying a new flooring directly over an old one. Placing a new floor on top of the old one raises the floor level noticeably. This can create problems around doorways (see "Thresholds," later this chapter).

If the existing floor is in poor condition, it may still be possible for you to lay a new floor over it without removing the old floor first. Try the following repairs before you decide to remove the old flooring or to lay an underlayment.

New Floors Over Old

Floors Which Sag Badly. These may require major work below the kitchen floor level such as jacking it up from underneath, adding extra joists on one or more new posts, or a new girder. You can try the first method yourself, but the other two require professional assistance.

Use a metal jackpost, sandwiching it between two pieces of 2x12. Put one piece on the floor; place the other spanning the joists. The 2x12s help distribute the pressure from the jack. Give the jack a quarter of a turn once a week, until the floor is level. It may take many weeks to get the floor level. Leave the jackpost in place and check for level on an annual basis. If the floor goes out of level again, again give the jack quarter turns until the floor is level. If the floor spans a wide area, you may have to install several jackposts to boost the sag. Jackposts are inexpensive.

Some codes require that the adjustable jackposts be set or buried in 6 to 8 inches of concrete as a permanent repair, or that you weld the screw of the jackpost at the point where the floor is level.

Another method replaces the jackpost with metal Lally columns after the floor is level. Two Lally columns should be used to support a 4x8 inch beam, which in turn bridges and supports the sagging joists. If Lally columns will be used, a concrete pad should be positioned under each column. A pad 24 inches square by 12 inches thick usually is standard.

Floors With Minor Irregularities. For holes in old linoleum, vinyl or cork, patch with appropriate fillers. For bubbles in linoleum, vinyl, or similar material:

(1) use a utility knife to slice a rectangle around the outermost edges of the bubble;

(2) lift the piece out;

(3) spread a latex adhesive over the subfloor on the opening;

(4) replace the piece which you have removed;

(5) press the piece down firmly and wipe away any excessive adhesive; if the piece you have removed has stretched and is too large to fit the opening, shape the hole which you have cut, so you can replace the piece you have removed;

(6) place a stack of heavy books over the fresh patch and allow it to dry for several hours.

Removing and Preparing Old Flooring

Removing Resilient Tile. If your existing tile floor has many bubbles or is quite warped, or if there is some other condition which makes it unsuitable as a base for a new flooring, you will have to remove the old tiles before laying the new flooring.

Remove the baseboard, trim or coving. Using an ice-scraper or a flat tiling spade, pry and chip under each tile until each one is pried completely from the floor. To aid loosening tile, you might try a hot iron, using a sheetcloth to prevent melting or scorching. After you have pried the tiles off the floor, clear away any dirt and gummed-up adhesive. Fill any cracks, splits, or holes in the subfloor with floor patching material such as Flash Patch. If the subfloor is wood, rent a floor scraper with a medium-grit abrasive and go over the entire floor.

Subfloor materials. If your old wood floor has uneven boards, or high or low spots caused by shrinking and weathering, it is best to cover it with a new subfloor before applying your new flooring material. Even wood floors that show no visible damage may warp eventually, causing floor boards to become visible under the new floor.

Hardboard. Masonite is the best known trade name for hardboard, although there are many other manufacturers. It is made from real wood which has been ground, mixed into a batter, and pressed into sheets, usually four by eight feet. Hardboard can be either tempered (treated to withstand moisture) or standard. Both standard and tempered are available in ⅛-, ³/₁₆-, ¼-, and ⁵/₁₆-inch thicknessess. Many manufacturers of floor tiles also make hardboard and specify their own brand as underlayment. It is a good idea to follow the producer's specifications for installation.

Particleboard (or Chipboard). Particleboard or chipboard is used primarily for wall and roof sheathing, although it is sometimes used as a subfloor.

Plywood. Although some knowledgeable home repair specialists say that hardboard or particleboard can be used successfully as an underlayment, others insist that plywood is the only sufficiently stable material. Plywood is the strongest and the most expensive of the alternatives.

Plywood is sold in about a dozen grades for interior and exterior use. Subflooring must have a smooth finish. Boards with open or unfilled knots should not be used. The lowest recommended grade is ⅜ inch B-D Interior, and for kitchens ½ inch Exterior is recommended. The thicker the plywood, the better it will cover a disfigured floor.

Laying a New Subfloor. If you have removed any old tile, you may nail the underlayment to the old subfloor. If you have decided to keep your old tile or floor, you can nail new subflooring directly to the old flooring. Repair any squeaks or loose boards in an existing wood floor before adding the new subfloor. Have an adequate supply of screw-nails or underlayment nails on hand. These are rust-proof and ringed with grooves so that they will not work their way out of the new subfloor. The basic steps are:

(1) lay out the 4x8 panels (without adhesive) on your kitchen floor — stagger the seams and joints, rather than aligning them;

(2) make any necessary adjustment cuts in the panels toward the center of the room — there is more elbow room for working. Trim in the center of the room rather than working close to the wall;

(3) using screw-nails or underlayment nails, nail panels to the old subfloor or old flooring, spacing nails two to three inches apart — slightly countersink nails;

(4) when you have finished nailing, patch nail holes; let dry;

(5) lightly sand seams and the nail

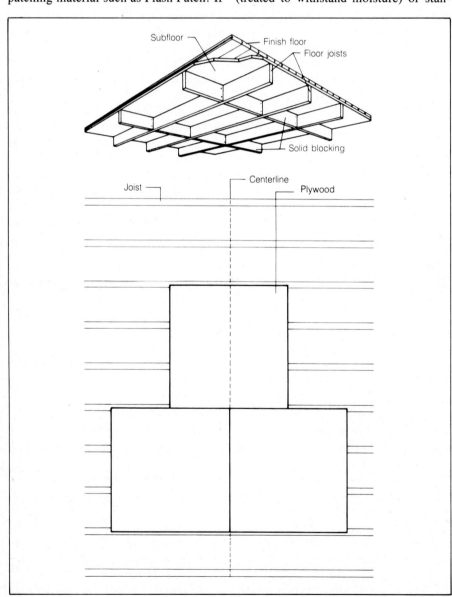

Align the center of the first sheet of the plywood underlayment with the center of the room, placing the edge on the center of a joist. Stagger placement to avoid meeting of 4 corners.

holes if applying resilient flooring other than carpeting. This ensures they will not show through.

Installing Resilient Tile

Since dye lots can vary, work from several cartons of tile at a time. This will ensure a uniform appearance. If you have stored the tiles in cold weather in an unheated garage or shed, let them sit at room temperature before you begin to work with them.

Step 1: Making the Chalkline. Before laying new tiles, you will have to lay out guidelines for them on the floor. With the aid of a measuring stick or yardstick, find the center of each pair of facing walls. Snap a chalkline on the floor between each pair of facing walls where you have approximately pinpointed the center of the room. When you have finished, the kitchen should be divided into equal quarters.

How to Snap a Chalkline. Tack nail small brads on the floor at the center of facing walls and stretch chalkline taut between them. Pull the line up near the center and let go. The line will strike the floor and leave a chalk mark.

Step 2: Adjustments. After you have made the initial chalkline, try a test run with the new tiles. Lay rows of tiles alongside each of the chalklines, working from the center to the walls. If the last tile in any row is less than one-half its width away from the wall, you will have to decide if you want to move your chalkline. A small fraction of tile close to the wall can look awkward and unprofessional. If you decide to move your chalkline, do so by the width of half a tile. Snap a new chalkline, and rub out the old one. Try laying out your tiles in both directions once again. The last tile in any row should now be one-half its width or more away from the wall.

Step 3: Making the Chalkline Permanent. When you are certain that your chalkline is exactly where it should be, you can trace the chalk with a heavy ink line, if you wish, using a marking pen. If the process of laying the tile extends over several days or if people keep walking in and out, the permanent line will prevent your having to repeat the entire process.

Step 4: Laying Out the Tile. Some tiles have patterns or grains that you should consider when you lay them out. Marbleized tile and similar designs are traditionally placed with each tile at a 90° angle to the next one, as in a checkerboard pattern. Some tiles have arrows on the back to indicate which direction you are to place them in. If the pattern is complicated you might want to lay out the tiles in the correct arrangement and then number them.

Step 5: Spreading the Adhesive. Spread adhesive (if not using self-stick) in only a small portion of your quarter at a time. Although some adhesives remain usable for up to three hours, others dry very quickly. Otherwise you may find that you do not have enough time to lay the tile exactly as you like.

Use a notched trowel for spreading the adhesive. This will give ridges that help the bond. Keep the thickness of the adhe-

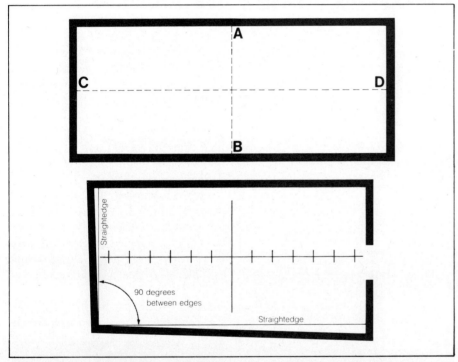

Use a long metal tape measure to find length of each wall. Mark the centers (ABCD). Cut string about a foot longer than room width (AB). Rub string with chalk. Drive small nails into the floor at A and at B. Tie chalked string tightly to each nail, with no slack. Pluck the string smartly, snapping it against the floor. Repeat at CD; the intersection marks the floor center. For out-of-square rooms, use straightedges to realign; less tiles will need to be cut.

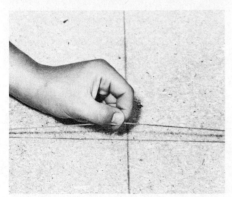

For tile layout, snap first chalkline and adjust as necessary to minimize cut tiles. Then snap the second chalkline.

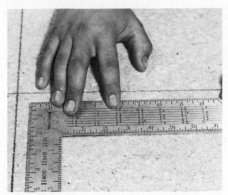

At the intersection of the two chalklines, check for square using a framing square. If not square, resnap the lines.

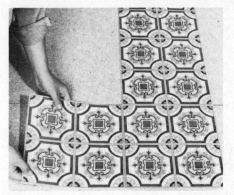

For a dry run, lay a row of tile along the chalk lines. Match patterns and if necessary, adjust tiles before applying adhesive.

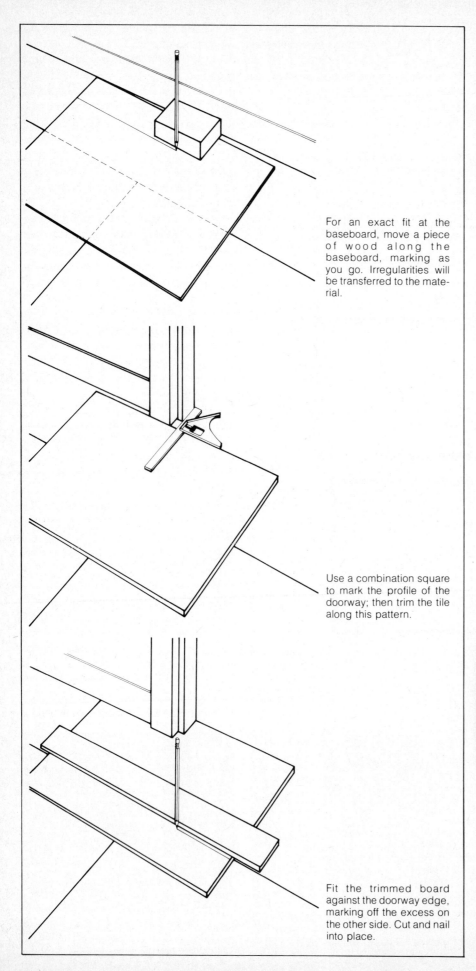

For an exact fit at the baseboard, move a piece of wood along the baseboard, marking as you go. Irregularities will be transferred to the material.

Use a combination square to mark the profile of the doorway; then trim the tile along this pattern.

Fit the trimmed board against the doorway edge, marking off the excess on the other side. Cut and nail into place.

sive even throughout the job. If lumps or debris appear in the adhesive, remove them as you go along.

Step 6: Laying Tile. Work in one quarter at a time. Place the first tile at the center of the room where the lines cross. The success of your layout will be based on the key center tiles. Work outward from each of the four center tiles, along the chalklines and then filling in one marked quarter of the room at a time.

Step 7: Cutting Corners and End Tiles. When you come to the last tile against the wall in each row, you may have to cut it. To get an exact fit, place a whole tile against the wall, overlapping the last whole tile (which we will call Tile A) you have set. Align all edges perfectly. Now place a second whole tile so that fits exactly on top of Tile A. The tile which butts against the wall will be sandwiched between Tile A and this last tile.

With a marking pencil, draw a line on the sandwiched tile along the edge of the top (last placed) tile. Remove all loose tiles. Cut the marked tile along the cut-off line. This tile should now fit perfectly. Use the same technique for corners, but do the corners as your final step.

Step 8: Cutting Tile to Fit. Any obstructions or curves, such as an island or peninsula, will probably require that you make a template, which is a cardboard pattern of the shape. This technique can prevent waste and will ensure an exact fit.

Using any cardboard, trace the exact outline of the shape of the irregularity or

For special cuts, make a cardboard template the same size as the tile. This works for any tile material. The template size must match perfectly, or the actual tile will not fit.

curve, with a pencil. Carefully cut the cardboard to the shape with sharp scissors or a utility knife. You may find that a razor blade in a holder works best. Transfer the shape — the template — to your tile. Cut the tile to the same shape.

Applying Pressure. Some tile manufacturers call for use of pressure to firmly set the tile. Professionals use high-pressure rollers; in many areas you will be able to rent one.

Variations — Other Tiles

Peel and Stick Tile. When you use a peel-and-stick tile or similar self-adhering tile, you will not need to use an additional adhesive. Set up the chalk line as previously described. Start at the center of the room where the two lines cross. Remove the protective covering and press the tile to the subfloor. Butt the edge of each new tile against the preceding one already set. Do not press down tiles until you are certain they are properly aligned. If you try to move a tile even a moment after you have pressed it down, it will usually break.

Carpet Tile. Carpet tiles are set in almost the same way as other tiles. For best results, cut your carpeting with a utility knife. If your carpet squares have arrows on the back, make sure they all point the same way, unless the instructions of the manufacturer state otherwise. Some carpet tiles are sold with their own adhesives on the backing. If yours do not have this adhesive, you should secure the perimeter tiles with double-faced carpet tape, which is sold in rolls of various widths and lengths. To use double-faced carpet tape, lay the tape on the floor where the edges of the carpet square will fall, and press the tile to the floor.

Hardwood Tiles. Hardwood block or parquet tiles are manufactured with straight edges that are butted together or with tongues-and-grooves that fit into each other. Lay out the wood rectangles as instructed, in exactly the same way as for other resilient tiles. If self-adhering, there will be no need for mastic. Make sure that tongues and grooves are fitted into each other as you go along. When it is necessary to cut parquet tiles, make the cuts with a crosscut saw. Start the cuts on the finish side, working through to the unfinished back.

Hardwood block flooring usually comes tongue-and-grooved, in various finishes. Once the blocks are set, clean off any excess adhesive and polish the wood.

To match the grain or create patterns, first set tiles without adhesive, laying them pyramid-style. Mark each as you take it up so you can reset it quickly after spreading the adhesive.

With a notched trowel, spread the adhesive over only a small area at a time. Lay a uniformly thick adhesive bed. Remove any lumps or debris as the adhesive is spread.

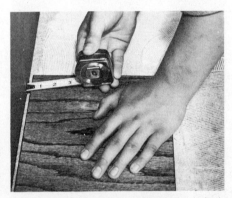

Space hardwood block tiles about ⅛ to ¼ inch from the wall. This permits expansion and contraction of the wood. The gap will be hidden by baseboard molding.

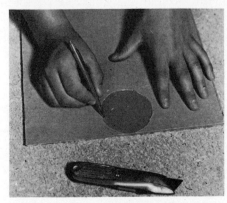

Cut the template to match the object around which you want the tile to fit, for instance a plumbing fixture. Then transfer this shape to the tile and cut along the outline.

Align the tongue in the groove. Lower the tile into the adhesive and press the tile in. Tiles may be adjusted slightly by sliding them in the adhesive.

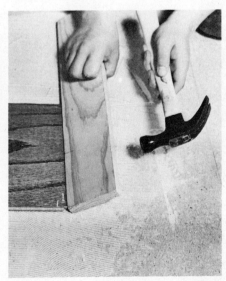

Tap stubborn tiles into position for a tongue-and-groove lock. Then press tiles into the adhesive. Remove any excess adhesive that oozes out between the tiles as you go along.

For resilient sheet flooring applied with adhesive, the key to a good fit is accurate measurements and markings. Draw up a room diagram noting positions of all room features.

In an area where flooring can lie flat, transfer diagram dimensions onto sheet. With sharp knife and straightedge, cut flooring. Cardboard under flooring protects knife blade.

At joints, sheet vinyl flooring can be adhered with double-faced tape. The tape gives a strong, neat joint that does not peel or bunch as the flooring adjusts to the subfloor.

Hardwood on Concrete. When installing wood squares directly over concrete, building experts recommend that you lay down a vapor barrier. First, cover the concrete with a special masonry primer. After it has dried, go over the floor with a thin coat of mastic adhesive. Then press 4-mil polyethelene film into the mastic. Allow the film to extend several extra inches, overlapping the baseboard area around the room. (The overlap will be trimmed later.) This film provides the vapor barrier.

Once the barrier is in place, construct a support for a subfloor. For this you will place 2x6s around the perimeter of the kitchen and 2x4s as the joists (sometimes called nailers or sleepers). Set the wood joists, flat side down, on top of the film,

Put flooring in place, rolling back half of sheet to spread the adhesive. Unroll sheet onto adhesive while adhesive is still wet. To finish room, repeat with remaining sheets.

Finish job with base molding to hide uneven cutting and give a neat edge. Nail molding to wall framing and subflooring, countersinking 10d finishing nails. Fill holes; finish wood.

using a cold-stick asphalt mastic adhesive. The joists should be on 12-inch centers. Then place 2x6s. Leave a space of a fraction of an inch space near the walls for expansion. The concrete floor is now ready for a plywood subfloor, over which you may then place wood in parquet blocks or planks.

CERAMIC FLOORS

If your floor is to incorporate a design, make sure you work out the design on graph paper to scale first, so you can easily transfer this to the floor. If the floor tile shades vary, lay them out for an eye-pleasing arrangement and then number the tile backs. Mark the numbers onto your design layout.

Surface Preparation

The first step is to prepare the surface and the room. Remove all doors that open out into the room by tapping out the hinge pins. In the case of older-style hinges, remove the screws from the back of the door. Check the door bottom to see if it will need to be cut off to allow for the height of the new floor. If so, place two tiles, one on top of another, against the inside door edge and mark a line across the bottom of the door. Cut this amount off the bottom edge of the door to enable it to open out into the room. Sand smooth, and refinish if necessary.

Remove the shoe molding, but leave the base molding unless you plan to tile the walls, in which case you will utilize a base tile instead. Insert a thin pry bar under the molding and gently pry out, starting about a foot from a corner, then gradually working along the floor until you have it completely removed.

Ceramic floor tile may be installed over most structurally sound and level surfaces that are free from any looseness or buckling. If plywood is to be applied to joists as the new undersurface, use nothing less than ½ inch Exterior grade. Cement floors must be made level and free of holes or protrusions. Painted floors should be roughened by sanding to ensure a good bond. Old tile or linoleum usually must be removed. The surface must be clean and completely dry. If special problems exist, consult your tile dealer. Actually, installing ceramic tile over a floor is one of the easiest of the ceramic tile jobs. As with any tile job, proper surface preparation is the key to a long-lasting result.

Over Wood Floor. Above all, don't lay ceramic tile over a springy floor. Nail down loose flooring, and if that is not sufficient, cover the existing floor with ⅜ inch Exterior grade plywood. For an older floor this is a good idea anyway, as it will help strengthen the old floor. A ceramic tile floor will add weight to a floor, so check it first to determine if it is structurally sound. If it is over a basement or crawl space, you may wish to add bridging (as shown) to further strengthen the floor.

For a plywood subfloor beneath ceramic tile, use a primer and seal the edges of the panel before nailing it in place. To nail, space 6d ringshank nails every six inches at floor joists. Leave ⅛ inch expansion joints between plywood outside edges and the wall. Fill the expansion joints with adhesive. For a floor that needs leveling, trowel on a plastic underlayment, working from a feathered edge up to ⁵/₁₆ inch thickness in one coat. Then cover with the Exterior grade plywood.

Over Concrete Floor. A concrete floor makes an excellent base for installing ceramic tile, but it must be level, free of holes or protrusions, and clean and dry. In the case of grease or other stains that may prevent the adhesive from adhering, use a chemical floor cleaner for concrete such as that found at auto supply stores. Chip away any excess of concrete, paint, and so on, using a wide flat masonry chisel, but make sure you wear safety glasses.

A concrete floor that is flaking, painted or has an extremely slick finish should first be sanded to roughen the surface and provide a good bond. This can be done using a rented floor sander and about No. 4 open-coat sandpaper. Make sure you wear a dust mask to cut down on breathing the dust produced. Then clean the floor again, first using a vacuum to remove all loose material and then washing thoroughly with a stiff bristle brush and clear water. All holes and cracks should be filled with an appropriate filler compound

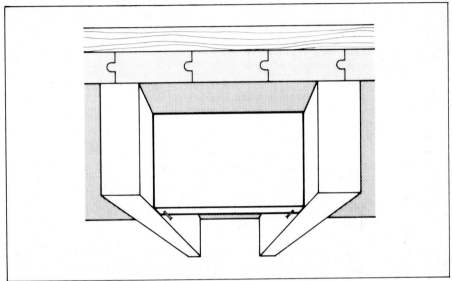

To add joist reinforcement, cut 2x6 or 2x8 needed for each span. Force new bridging between joists. Then toenail into joists at top and bottom of ends of new bridging.

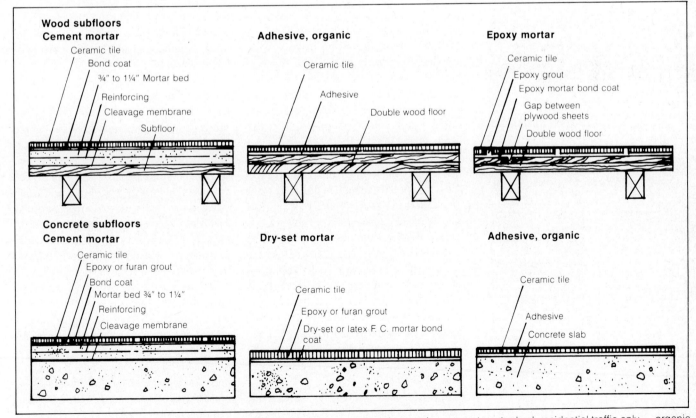

Top, left to right, tile adhesive on wood subfloors: structurally sound wood floor (any use) — cement mortar bed; residential traffic only — organic adhesive; residential or light commercial traffic — epoxy mortar. *Bottom, left to right,* tile adhesive on concrete subfloors: for floor subject to bending — cement mortar bed; for floor subject to chemical damage — dry-set mortar bed; for residential traffic — organic adhesive.

to level the floor. If using a mortar bed, fill the cracks and level the floor using an ordinary concrete patch compound. However, if the floor will be laid using thin-set mastic, use a mastic underlayment material as suggested by your tile dealer or the tile manufacturer. The main point is that the floor must be absolutely smooth and flat.

Over Resilient Tile Surface. Ceramic tile can be applied over existing resilient tile or seamless flooring if the tile material is of the rigid type, not cushioned. But the

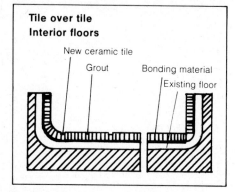

On a level floor of ceramic tile, terrazzo, stone, or slate you can lay new ceramic tile.

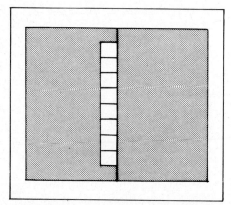

Lay a test row of loose tile so the spaces at each end of the row are of equal size. Neither should be smaller than the width of ½ tile.

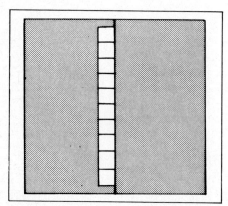

If space between wall and end tiles are less than ½ tile, you must cut a very small finishing tile — a difficult task. Instead, move tiles to end up with one, larger end space.

existing material must be securely bonded to the floor. There can be no loose tiles or areas, nor any holes, or chips. These, or other defects in the floor, should be patched with the appropriate material as suggested by your dealer. Epoxy adhesive usually is used.

Over Old Ceramic Tile. A new ceramic tile coat can be applied over old existing ceramic tile if the old tile surface is sound, solidly bonded to the floor and has no chipped areas. In addition, it should be thoroughly clean to allow the adhesive to adhere properly. Use a commercial ceramic tile cleaner to clean. If any tiles are loose, pry them up and re-adhere them in place before installation of the new tiles. Roughen the floor tile by using a rented floor sander, or use a heavy duty sanding disc in a portable electric drill.

If using a mastic adhesive, prime the floor area completely with the flat side of a trowel, using a waterproof ceramic floor tile adhesive as a skim coat. Pack all expansion joints as in plywood floors, and floor-wall joints, with adhesive. Then let dry thoroughly. Always tell the dealer the surface to which you will apply the tile, so he can recommend the correct primer, adhesive and grout.

Installing Ceramic Floor Tile

Establishing the Work Lines. Working lines for installing a tile floor are as for resilient tile. You should start by finding the approximate center of the floor. Snap a chalkline from wall to wall. Now snap another chalkline between the other two walls. Then lay out the tile (no adhesive yet) to find a layout that doesn't leave you with less than half a tile at the edge. Check with a carpenter's square to make sure that the lines cross each other at right angles of 90 degrees. Adjust the starting point, if necessary, to avoid ending up with less than half a tile at outer edges. In most instances ceramic tile setting is started at the center of the room, working toward the walls. This allows you to have the same amount of cut tiles around all sides of the floor. When working out the tile arrangement, make sure that none of the grout lines will fall over a seam in the underlayment.

Try to Avoid Cutting Tiles. Check the corner meetings of the four chalklines with a two foot square. Use the corner that is square, or nearly so, for a starting

point. Lay out a line of tiles in each direction to determine if full tiles can be used, or if some will have to be cut at the wall. If the last tile next to the wall will have to be cut shorter by just a bit, go back and make the grout lines just a fraction narrower. This trick often will eliminate the need for tile cutting.

If the opposite happens — that is, the last tile does not quite reach the wall by the width of several grout lines, then go back and slightly widen the planned grout lines. All this arranging is done "dry," with no adhesive.

Thresholds. Since the new floor will be higher than the existing floor, a transitional threshold will have to be installed in doorways to match up with existing floors. Strips of marble sometimes are used as such thresholds, or wooden thresholds can be added. Where there is carpeting in the adjacent room or hallway, one alternative is to shim up the carpeting at the joint and fit a metal trim strip to abut the tile surface. If the floor outside the room is not carpeted, you probably can use bullnose tiles for the transition; the rounded edge gives a neat, finished look.

In many instances floor tiles do not have spacer lugs, so you will have to use spacers that can be removed after the tiles are set in the adhesive and before grout is added. Thin wood strips may also be used, which will help ensure a straight, continuous joint.

Adhesives. While dry-set or thin-set mortar is suggested for some locations, a do-it-yourselfer will do better with one of the modern mastics or adhesives which bond tile to almost anything. This is especially true of epoxy-base adhesives. The epoxy is more expensive than other types of adhesives, but it will adhere when other types will not. Always carefully read the instructions on the container of mastic or adhesive you will use to apply ceramic tile. The instructions will tell you how to mix, what sizes the notches should be on the trowel used to apply the adhesive, and how long the adhesive will remain workable after it is applied. Also, while some modern adhesives are water-based and nonflammable, others have a flammable solvent base. This means you must keep away all fire and flames. You must not smoke when using the adhesive. Provide ample ventilation, to prevent the fumes becoming concentrated enough to cause a health hazard.

Tile adhesives all are applied in a similar fashion. A notched trowel, with notches along one side and one end and the other end and side smooth, is used to scoop the adhesive out of the container and onto the wall or floor. One of the smooth edges is used to spread a thin layer of the adhesive, then the notched edge is scraped across the adhesive to create ridges, with only a thin layer of adhesive left between the ridges. Check the instructions, as the notched trowel might need to be moved at an angle or in circles, according to the manufacturer's research. Trowel on the adhesive only in as big an area as you can cover with tile before the adhesive begins to set. If installing a thick-back tile (one with ridges), also spread the adhesive on the back of each tile. Spread only a little bit of adhesive along one edge of any wooden guides, if you are using them.

Setting the Tile. Set the tile in place using a slight twisting motion along one edge of the guides. Press firmly into place. Do not slide tiles against each other, or there will be excessive adhesive buildup in the corners.

Work along the chalklines or the wood guide strips from the middle toward the corners. From time to time get out the straightedge and square to see that all courses are true. Do not panic if they are not. If you are a bit out of line, gently tug the tiles until they are aligned. To make sure the tiles are flat and firmly embedded in the adhesive, slide a flat board across the surface, tapping lightly with a hammer. Cover the block with felt or thin carpet scraps to avoid scratching or marring the tile. The block should be large enough to cover several tiles at a time.

Fill in with needed cut tiles to complete each area. The tiles can be laid in with all joints lined up, or the joints staggered such as in brick fashion by offsetting the tiles one half tile, by starting every other row with a half tile.

Clean adhesive off the tiles as you go because it will be extremely hard to remove after it has set. Do not walk on the surface of the tiles just laid. If it is absolutely necessary to walk across, lay flat smooth boards over them to help distribute the weight.

Cutting Tiles to Fit. Tiles are best marked for cutting by scribing. The easiest means of doing this is to position the tile to be cut so that it aligns exactly

with, and completely covers, the last whole tile. Then place another tile against the wall so that it overlaps the previously positioned middle tile. Draw or scribe along the edge of the top tile onto the middle tile to mark for the cut.

The easiest way to cut straight lines on tile is with a tile cutter. This can be purchased or, in most cases, rented from the tile dealer. It's a good idea to practice on several scrap pieces before you start the actual tiling job.

Straight cuts on tile are also easily made without the cutter by using an ordinary glass cutter and a straightedge, preferably a steel ruler or steel bar. First, scribe a line onto the glazed side of the tile. The scribed line is then placed over a straight piece of wire approximately ⅛ inch in diameter. A wire coat hanger is an excellent choice. With the glazed side of the tile still up, press down gently on opposite sides of the line and the tile will snap.

Stay off the floor the time recommended by the adhesive manufacturer. Replace any molding, cut off the doors to fit, as described above, and re-install them.

Grout. A gray grout may be preferred on the floor. You can buy the grout pre-mixed, or you can mix it yourself.

Clean all debris from the joints; remove any spacers if necessary, and diagonally work the grout between the tiles with the flat side of a rubber trowel or squeegee. Make sure you follow the manufacturer's recommendations. When the joints are firm, wipe the tiles clean with a damp sponge. Polish with a soft cloth. Allow the grout to dry for another day or so before you wash the floor with clean mop and household detergent and water. Then polish with a soft cloth and add a grout sealer to the floor.

Using Mosaic Sheet Tiles

Mosaics are quite frequently used on floors. If ceramic mosaic tiles with perforated mounting are used, lay out sheets from the center point for the length and width of the room, dry laying without applying adhesive. Adjust slightly for the minimum number of cut tiles. Avoid excessively small cut tiles. Then begin by applying adhesive at the farthest wall and lay the sheets, working until you have filled in one of the room quarters. Fill in all cut tiles as they occur for each area.

Lay sheets in the other three quarters. Check each sheet to maintain straight joint lines. Allow the floor to set in place for 24 hours (or follow directions of adhesive manufacturer) before applying grout.

Refinishing Wood Floors

Removing an old finish and applying a new finish to strip wood flooring is a fairly easy job if the floor is not "cupped" or badly uneven between the strips — and if you can rent professional sanding equip-

Twist tiles into position. For tiles without lugs, adjust to ensure straight grout lines.

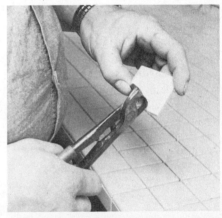

Use a tile nipper to cut odd shapes and curves, or to fit tile around obstructions.

A rented tile cutter eases the task of cutting tile — especially sheets of small tiles.

ment. Otherwise, the humps and dips of uneven flooring must be leveled with the smaller sanding machine in order for the machine to give the proper finish. In some cases, this can involve many hours of sanding to remove above-level wood.

Remove all furniture and rugs, and carefully remove the quarter-round molding nailed to the baseboard and the floor. Then vacuum the floor.

With a hammer and nail set, countersink any nail heads you find. During this inspection, renail any loose flooring, using 10d finishing nails. Countersink these nail heads. Vacuum the floor again.

Move the sanding equipment into the kitchen. Then seal off the doorways. Sanders create lots of fine dust, which can be tracked into other rooms. Turn off the heat or air conditioning to the room so the air circulation will not carry the fine dust into your heating/cooling system.

The First Cut. Use the coarse abrasive for the first sanding cut. Run the sander in the direction of the wood grain in the floor. Work carefully with the sander. It cuts fast and should be in motion at the start and finish of each cut. Do not let it sit and run on the floor. If you do, you will cup the wood, making additional sanding necessary. Practice.

Start at one end of the room with the sander and work toward the other end. Make each pass across the flooring as continuous a motion as possible. When you come to a wall, slowly push down on the handle of the sander, lifting the abrasive drum up off the floor.

The first cut should take the finish down to the raw wood flooring. Depending on the number of coats of finish on the floor, you may have to change the abrasive several times, since it can wear out fast or become clogged with sanding residue. Be sure to use an open-coat abrasive for this job. Do not use paint and varnish remover in conjunction with the sander.

Along the walls and in corners, use the hand-held disc sander to remove the finish. Start with coarse abrasive first. This is a delicate job because the disc sander must be moved evenly over the flooring to maintain the level of the floor and to match the sanding cut left by the larger drum sander.

On your first sanding attempt with the disc sander, we suggest you work in an area that won't be too noticeable.

The Second Cut. Use the medium-grade abrasive. Use both sanders, just as you did for the first cut. However, make this cut diagonally across the floor, removing all the old finish until the wood is semi-smooth. Do not work at right angles to the first sanding cut.

The Final Cut. Use the fine-grade abrasive for the third cut, running the sanders diagonally across the flooring. Make this third cut very lightly against the grain of the wood. The result should be a glass-smooth floor surface.

If you can't use the disc sander in corners or under obstructions such as radiators or shelving, you will have to use a hand sanding block, teamed with paint and varnish remover and a stiff-bladed scraper or putty knife. Ventilate the room when using the chemical finish remover.

When the sanding job has been completed, go over the floor once again with the vacuum cleaner, removing all sanding residue. Then, with a tack rag, go over the entire floor again.

To complete the job, replace the quarter-round molding and/or baseboard. If this trim should match the floor finish, you will have to remove the old finish by hand. Do not attempt to use a machine floor sander or disc sander on the trim.

Finishing Hardwood Floors. If the floor is oak (which it probably is) or a similar hardwood, you will have to go over the floor with a wood filler made especially for this purpose.

Generally, you should thin the filler slightly with turpentine or mineral spirits so the filler has the consistency of thick paint. Apply the filler to the floor with burlap cloth. Rub the filler onto the floor across the grain of the wood. Work in a small confined area.

When the filler begins to appear dull, wipe off the excess filler with clean burlap. Then complete the job by wiping the area again with a clean piece of burlap.

Let the wood filler dry for two days. Then lightly buff the floor with No. 2 steel wool, working with the grain of the wood.

Vacuum the floor to remove all steel wool and filler residue. It is a good idea to again go over the floor with a tack rag.

With a lamb's wool applicator, apply penetrating wood finish to the floor. Don't use too much finish. Spread it fairly thin with the applicator, but do not miss any areas. Try to keep a light between you and the finishing operation; this way you can see the wet finish and can catch any dull spots that have been missed.

Let the finish set for about 20 minutes. This gives it time to penetrate into the wood grain. Again, go over the surface with the applicator to remove any finish that has not penetrated into the wood. Cover the entire floor with the sealer, and then let the job set for about 24 hours.

In a corner that will not show, test the finish with a knife blade to make certain that the material has dried completely. If not, the finish will curl and stick to the surface of the knife blade. Wait another day. Then try the test again.

If the finish is dry, go over the entire floor with No. 2 steel wool. Don't bear down on this abrasive; just lightly buff the finish, removing any gloss from it. Vacuum the floor, removing all residue.

Apply the second coat of sealer with the lamb's wool applicator. Let the finish set for 20 minutes or so. Then remove any excess finish with the applicator. Wait three days, or until the finish is hard. Vacuum.

With a polisher, apply a semi-soft wax to the floor. Be sure the wax product is made especially for hardwood floors. Do not use a water-based wax. Wax the floor with the grain of the wood and let the wax dry. Then go over the floor with the polisher to complete the job.

Finishing Softwood Floors. Softwoods such as pine do not need a wood filler, although any holes and cracks should be filled with a matching wood plastic following the final sanding of the floor. Press the plastic in the holes with a putty knife; let the plastic set for 30 minutes; sand the patch smooth.

Apply the first coat of finish to the floor; with a lamb's wool applicator or brush made for oil-based finish. This coat of finish should be thinned slightly.

Let the finish dry for at least 48 hours. Check the finish with a knife blade to see if it has dried hard. If so, go over the floor with No. 2 steel wool just as you would for a hardwood floor.

Apply the second coat to the floor; let the finish dry; apply wax and buff and polish the wax. Do not use a water-based wax on the softwood floor.

Your finish may call for additional coats. If so, always lightly buff the finish between coats with No. 2 steel wool, and remove the residue with a vacuum cleaner and tack rag.

8
WALLS AND CEILINGS

WALLS

Unlike floor coverings, materials used on vertical surfaces do not have to be durable enough to withstand constant traffic. However, you should limit your choice of materials for your kitchen walls to one or two favorites. Avoid the mistake, which many homeowners make, of combining too many different types of materials so that the beauty of each material becomes lost among the clutter. Remember also that you will probably have little surplus wall space to be covered in your kitchen once you have provided the basics. Windows, wall cabinets, open shelves, wall ovens and your display objects will have used much of your available vertical space. For this reason, you will have to consider the remaining space carefully, considering both the practical aspects of the material you use as well as the decorative scheme you have chosen for your kitchen.

The most common coverings for kitchen walls are paint and wallpaper. In addition, simulated brick and stone are becoming popular. Fabric can be stapled or glued to walls instead of wallpaper, and moldings, ceramic tiles, certain metals — such as stainless steel or copper — cork or vinyl tiles are often chosen as accents. You might choose instead a rather unique finish, such as cutouts or wall murals.

Walls of Wood

Wood not only helps disguise many existing wall problems, but it is also very durable and works well with almost any style of decoration you choose.

Wood is available in a variety of different styles. You may use wood molding to create a chair-rail — a molding which is placed around the entire room in a continuous line, at the height of the tops of the chair backs. Wood flooring also is suitable for walls, or you can cover your walls with V-grooved or rough cut lumber, or any other type of plank that runs horizontally, vertically or diagonally. Just about any type of wood that can be purchased from a lumberyard will make a suitable wall covering. In addition to these less familiar wood materials, you can choose to cover your walls with traditional wood paneling, placing it over half the wall, the entire wall, or even extending it to cover the ceiling.

If you decide to panel your walls, you will find a variety of options. Paneling may be solid wood, veneered, or plasticized veneer. It can be wood-grain paneling with photographic reproductions of wood-grained patterns or a

Wood walls are attractive in themselves, but the same material, or contrasting, can be used for shelves, cabinets and counters.

grain-printed paper overlay. Paneling comes grooved or ungrooved, with or without a cross-scored pattern between the grooves to enhance the appearance of solid planks. Plywood covered with decorative printed designs is also available. Panels can be painted, stained or given a clear finish. The price of paneling varies according to quality, availability, and cost of manufacture. Moldings and trim are made to match most prefinished panels.

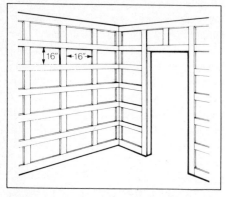

Apply horizontal and vertical furring strips to the wall to ensure a smooth surface and a longlasting paneling job. Seams should fall over the furring strips.

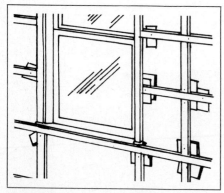

Use shingle shims behind furring to produce a smooth vertical surface.

For small hole repairs, fill in wallboard or plaster with spackling compound that has the consistency of thick mud. One pass of the putty knife usually is sufficient.

Paneling may be installed directly over the wall framing (studs) or to gypsumboard or plaster. Furring strips generally are not used when paneling is installed directly to the framing members. In wallboard and plaster applications, the paneling probably is attached to furring. It also can be cemented right to the wallcovering with building adhesive. The adhesive method is fairly new. If your house is older than 1970 it probably will not use it.

To repair extensive damage to paneling, you almost always have to replace a complete panel. This is an easy job if the paneling is installed over furring strips or nailed to the framing, but a difficult job if the paneling has been glued.

Plaster and Gypsumboard

Small Dents. If the damage is not deep enough to hold even a small patch, you will have to enlarge the problem area.

If the wall is of gypsum wallboard, use a razor knife to score the paper covering the gypsum core, making a square or rectangular cut. Just cut enough of the paper to surround the entire damaged area. Then, using the knife blade, peel the paper back to the scored lines. Again with the razor knife, remove a quarter inch or so of the gypsum core, making a little void in the core. This area need not be smooth and finely cut; it is better to leave it rough because the rough edges will hold the patch better.

After this point the procedure is the same for plaster and for wallboard repair.

Mix a small amount of spackling compound in the mixing container. Add spackling to the water and stir it with the putty knife until the mixture is about the consistency of putty. Balance the mixture on the putty knife and press the spackling into the hole.

Be sure the hole has been filled with spackling. You can probe into the patch with the tip of the putty knife to compact the mixture. When the hole is full, use the edge of the knife to smooth the fresh spackling. The putty knife serves as a trowel.

Leave the patch slightly higher than the surrounding surface of the patch. The spackling will shrink as it dries. Let the patch set for about two days.

Once the patch has dried, lightly sand it, working away the rough spackling and blending the patch in with the surround-

ing area. Check often; spackling sands quickly.

Spot prime the patch with paint. Let the paint dry. Sand the area lightly again, and then apply a second coat of paint. If the wall has not been painted for some time, you may have to repaint the entire wall to hide the patch, since the new paint will not blend in with the old paint.

Nail Hole Repair, Plaster or Gypsumboard. Mix a small amount of spackling compound with water. The spackling should be a stiff mixture, about the consistency of putty or stiff whipped cream.

Press the spackling into the hole, using the tip of a putty knife. Then, with the putty knife, level the spackling in the hole. Let the spackling dry an hour or so. Then sand the area with medium or fine grit abrasive.

Touch up the spot with paint. Try to feather out the paint into the surrounding area. Sometimes just a daub of paint on the spot works best. You can try both and decide which looks better before the paint dries.

Patches for Plaster. Clean the break with a razor knife, cutting back to the hard plaster. The patching area should be free of loose debris; don't enlarge the damage more than necessary. Clean the area to be patched with water and a brush. Mix the spackling compound (or plaster patching material for a large, deep hole from which the metal lath is missing) to a fairly stiff consistency.

If the metal lath is still in place, you will follow these steps: Rewet the area to be patched; this prevents the plaster from absorbing water from the spackling mixture. Trowel in the spackling with a scraper. Level the patch and smooth it. After the patch has dried for several days, sand it smooth so it blends with the surrounding surface. Spot prime and paint the entire wall or ceiling.

For larger patches, substitute a mason's trowel for a wall scraper to apply and level the patch. Another possibility is to use a section of gypsum wallboard instead of spackling. The wallboard can usually be butted against the plaster and then taped and smoothed to match.

If the metal lath (a heavy mesh available in hardware stores) is missing, follow these steps. After cleaning the patch, as above, mix the plaster patch material according to instructions. Cut the mesh so it is a little larger than the hole — about 1 inch larger all around. Tie 5 or 6 inches of string through the center of the lath. Holding onto the string, bend the lath just enough to fit it through the hole, then flatten out the mesh. Tie a pencil to the string, and twist so that the pencil spans the hole and keeps the metal lath in place.

If the hole is fairly small, apply plaster patching to within ¼ inch of the surface and let it dry. Once the patch is dry and holds the mesh in place, cut the string and remove it and the pencil. Then put on another coat; allow it to dry, and sand smooth. If the hole is large, you will apply three layers rather than two. Fill the patch so that it will form a bond between the metal lath and the wall; let it dry; remove the pencil and string.

Large Hole Repair, Gypsum Wallboard. Clean out the break with a razor knife. Do not try to enlarge the hole, just cut away the loose gypsum down to the firm inner core.

Mix up a large batch of spackling compound and make the mixture stiff. Then stuff the hole full of mineral wool insulation. The fibers of the insulation will catch on the gypsum board surface and hang in place.

Fill the hole with the spackling compound, being careful not to dislodge the insulation. You want to use the insulation as a backing material for the spackling. You may be able to tack the insulation to the back of the hole with small gobs of spackling.

When this initial job is finished, let the spackling dry a day or so. Then go back and fill the hole full of spackling. Level the spackling with the putty knife, but leave it a tad high for normal shrinkage.

When the spackling is dry, sand the area lightly so it is level with the surrounding surface. Then, touch up the patch with paint.

Even Larger Hole Repair, Gypsumboard. Can you patch the hole with a piece of gypsumboard, or is it so large that you should remove the gypsumboard panel and replace it with a new panel? The latter may be easier than the former.

Using a straightedge or square, outline the damaged area with a pencil. Include all the damage within the lines, but no more than this area. The patch should be adequate, but as small as possible.

Score along the outline with the razor knife, bearing down hard on the knife. If

you can, cut completely through the gypsumboard at this time. If you cannot cut completely through the material, repeat the scoring procedure with the knife until you remove this part of the wall. You now should have a nice square or rectangular hole where the damaged area once was.

Measure the hole and transfer these measurements to the scrap piece of gypsumboard, plus 2 inches on all four sides. The extra material will be used for gluing. When you are done, you will have the patch for the wall.

Since you need to be able to hold onto the patch while you fit it into the wall, punch two holes all the way through the patch with a nail. Aim for the center of the patch and space the holes so the ends of the wire come through the front of the patch.

Now coat the face of the patch with glue; use a lot of glue. Place the patch inside the hole, seating the patch in the glue. Pull the patch toward you with the wire so that the glue makes a good bond with the back of the wall.

When you are sure the patch is seated, wrap the wire around the 1x3 or dowel,

which should bridge the patch. Then twist the wire around the 1x3 or dowel and tighten the wire with pliers. This will anchor the patch on the wall so that the glue makes a good bond.

Remove the 1x3 or dowel from the wall when the glue dries, after at least a day, and test the patch. If it seems to be wobbly in the wall, very carefully "tack" the recessed edges of the patch with a stiff spackling compound. Let the spackling dry a day.

When the patch is securely in place, fill the recess between the patch and the surface of the wall with spackling compound. Use the wide wall scraper for this, troweling in the spackling mixture and smoothing it level. Use the surface of the surrounding wall to help guide the wall scraper so that the patch will be level with the wall. Or, cut another patch of gypsumboard the same size as the hole.

Check that the patch fits, then peel off the paper covering on the front side of the patch. Use the razor knife for this. Go right to the gypsum core on the surface of the patch that will face the room. You need not be too careful with the razor;

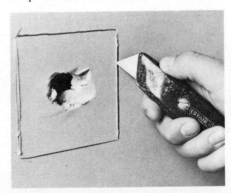

Mark a square or rectangle around the damaged area and score it with a razor knife. Cut and lift out the damaged piece; slightly bevel edges of the patch toward the back wall.

Run wire through the patch; spread glue on its face. Angle patch through the hole. Pull the wires toward you for several minutes until the glue sets enough to hold the patch.

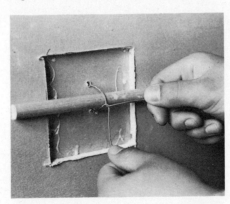

Before continuing with the patch, clamp it while the glue dries. Apply pressure by twisting the wires; use pliers. Pressure should be firm, but should not damage the patch.

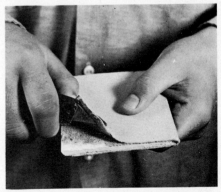

Cut a second patch. Remove the paper covering on one side of the core; it will come off more easily if wetted first. The patch fits over the one already in the wall.

the gypsum core should be a bit rough. Glue the patch in position. When the glue dries, fill the joints with spackling compound.

Once the spackling compound has dried — give it three days — sand the patch smooth, blending the patch into the surrounding wall surface.

Spot prime the patch with paint. Then paint the entire wall so the patch won't show.

Replacing a Gypsumboard Panel. When the hole is so large that you can't mend it with a spackling compound or a gypsumboard patch, you will have to

Glue second patch over first, paper to paper, with exposed core facing toward you. Wait another day while glue dries. Apply spackling to joints and over the patch.

Let the spackling dry for several days. Sand the patch smooth, feathering the edges and raised areas so they will taper into the surrounding, existing wallboard.

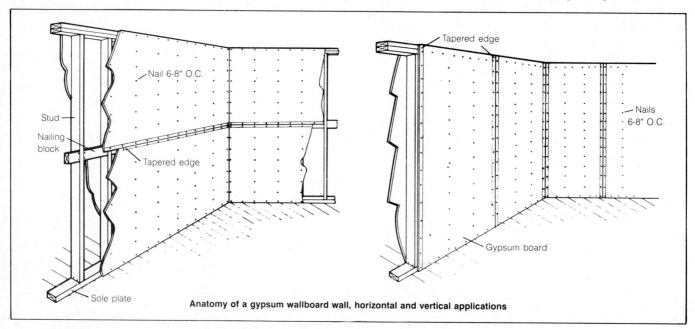

Anatomy of a gypsum wallboard wall, horizontal and vertical applications

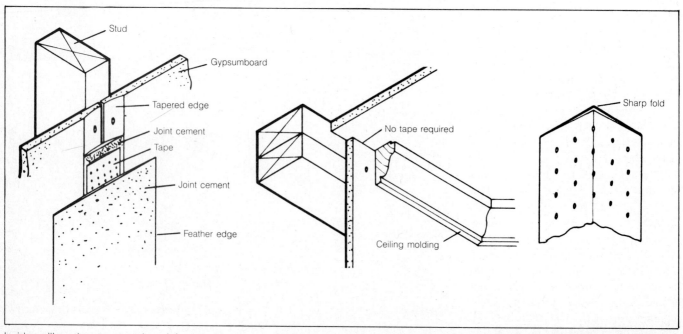

Inside wallboard corners can be reinforced with metal, or taped with joint tape. Have spackling or joint compound about the consistency of thick whipped cream so tape smooths easily. Outside gypsum wallboard corners should be reinforced with a metal strip for protection. Nail the strip to the corner; add joint compound; embed the tape into the compound. Smooth the tape with a scraper.

replace the panel. This is not especially difficult, but you need patience and must be careful not to damage the good surrounding panels.

Remove the base molding from the wall on which the damaged panel is located. Use a pry bar and hammer for this and take it easy when you pry; you want to save the trim and reinstall it after the repair has been made. When the molding has been removed, tap and pull out the nails and store the molding out of your way.

With a hammer, break out the damaged gypsumboard panel back to the studs to which the sides of the panel have been nailed. If you go very slowly, you can remove the entire damaged panel by removing chunks of the panel and pulling the nails as you go. Do it in small pieces rather than jerking off the whole panel at once.

When you come to the panel joints, you probably will have to cut the gypsumboard tape that spans the joints along the sides and at the ceiling line. Do this with the razor knife. Again, be careful not to rip into the adjoining panels or the ceiling.

With the panel removed, you should have a neat, clean hole in the wall with the studs exposed and the "good" gypsumboard panels overlapping the side studs by about half their width.

Insert the new panel over the framing members. You will need a helper to handle the new panel so that you can mark and fit into position. Then remove the new panel and make any necessary cuts for correct fit using the razor knife.

Nail the new panel to the framing members with gypsumboard nails. Space the nails about three inches apart. When the nailheads are flush with the panel, hit them one more time with the hammer. This creates a "dimple" in the surface of the panel and countersinks the nailheads below the surface of the panel. These dimples will be filled later with spackling compound.

When the panel is in place, check the edges to make sure that they do not project above the surface of the surrounding wall. If the edges do project, you may be able to trim them down slightly with the razor knife. It is likely, however, that the panel will fit perfectly.

Mix a stiff batch of spackling compound. With a putty knife or wall scraper, trowel on a thin layer of the spackling at the joints and along the ceiling line. Then embed the joint tape into the spackling compound. Run the wall scraper over the top of the tape, pressing it into the spackling. Give the tape a downward swipe with the scraper.

With the tape embedded, fill all dimples with spackling compound, leveling the compound in these depressions using the wall scraper or putty knife.

Let the spackling dry one day. Apply a layer of spackling over the tape; let dry another 24 hours. Add a third coat. Once dry, sand the spackling lightly and prime the new panel with paint. Once the paint has dried, give the panel a light sanding and dust off the residue. Add a second coat of paint.

Replace the baseboard, nailing it to the studs with finishing nails. Countersink the nail heads using the nail set, fill the holes with a wood putty or wood plastic, and touch up any spots with paint or stain.

Wallpaper

Wallpaper is a popular choice for the kitchen, although these days it need not actually be paper. You can find "wallpaper" that is made of vinyl woven fabric bonded to paper, or vinyl bonded to fabric. Vinyl is excellent in kitchens, provided it does not have too much of a sheen; the sheen will spotlight imperfections in the wall surfaces. These wallcoverings are easily washable, and some manufacturers make a special vinyl coating for their products that increases washability, and durability and prevents staining. Other types of coated fabrics and papers also are well suited to kitchen use.

When smoothing tape into wallboard seam, apply even pressure in a downward movement.

Wallpaper is the total decorating theme in this kitchen/dinette. The same paper covers the walls, the soffit area, the cabinet doors and drawers and the backs of the open shelves.

Some of the adhesives that have been developed recently eliminate problems that were formidable in the past. Glidden, for example, manufactures a special adhesive, designed for their vinyl wall-coverings, which will adhere to metal, glass, tile, or other vinyl.

Wallpaper is available in a large variety of colors and patterns. The most attractive patterns will not necessarily appear in your local store's wallpaper books. A number of places with especially good patterns do some of their business by mail. If you cannot find a pattern that pleases you, try visiting or writing to one of those in Appendix B. Most have outlets in cities other than the main office listed below.

Most of these companies have coordinated vinyl papers and fabrics, which may give you ideas for tablecloths and curtains, or other matching accessories.

Contemporary wallcoverings, grouped as wall "papers", range from actual paper material to plastics such as vinyl and mylar to fabrics such as burlap and percale (bed sheets). Because of the smoke, grease and other airborne dirt associated with a kitchen, it is most practical to use vinyl coated papers or other plastic wall coverings in kitchens. However, if you find a plain paper which you like very much, you will probably be able to seal and coat this type of paper with a clear urethane varnish and make the surface practical for kitchens.

Wallpaper will adhere only to clean, smooth, well-prepared surfaces. A thorough washing and rinsing will be required under any circumstances. Use a detergent that will cut through any grease buildup on the walls. No matter how clean your walls may look, there will be some grease. A product containing trisodium phosphate is usually recommended. After washing, rinse very well. Any detergent residue left on the wall will prevent the paste from sticking.

If you have cracks, dents and other breaks in the surface of your plaster or wallboard, repair carefully with spackling compound or patching plaster so that your wall surface is even and flat.

A wall painted in an enamel which has a shine (high or semi-gloss) will have to be sanded lightly with a medium grit sandpaper to break down the smooth, slippery finish. If this seems to be a difficult task, and if you do not have an electric sander available to you, a product is available that is applied like a paint and acts as a bonding agent. It breaks down the surface of paint just enough to create a slightly tacky texture.

Hairline cracks that have not changed over a long period of time may simply be covered by the paper; however, if you are in doubt about any crack, repair it. Wallboard joints which are uneven or have popped must also be repaired. This may mean retaping and covering the tape with spackle. As a rule, tape is applied then covered with spackling compound, which is allowed to dry 24 hours and then sanded. The spackling process is repeated three times. Plan your wallpapering project carefully to allow for each of these steps. Rushing or skipping wall preparation results in a less than satisfactory job.

An additional consideration is the general finish of your walls. If the plaster or wallboard is not smooth, either because of a naturally granular surface or because of general wearing, you will probably have to apply a lining paper to level the surface and to provide a good bonding layer for your wallcovering. The lining paper will be applied in the same manner as the final wallpaper, but it is of a lighter weight and is wider than regular wallpaper rolls.

Estimating Quantities. To determine the amount of paper you will need, you must work out three figures. The first is the square footage of the walls you will paper. Measure the height and width of each wall, and multiply. A wall eight feet high and ten feet long will require 80 square feet of paper to cover. You may subtract the square footage of windows and doors; however, you will need extra paper for matching the pattern above and below the windows and above the doors, so it is best not to subtract for an opening unless it takes up most of a wall.

The second measurement is the distance between repeats of the pattern. This will help you find the third number, which is the amount of paper that will be wasted when matching your pattern. If your wall is 8 feet high (96 inches) and your pattern repeats every 23 inches, the figures would be as follows: you will plan to use five pattern repeats (115 inches) for each strip put up — this includes 96 inches plus the 2 or 3 inches at each end to trim off at the top and bottom. You will have hung 100-102 inches, and will have wasted about

one foot each time in order to begin the next pattern match. This is for a straight random match. Drop-match patterns may have even more wastage. Work out a sample allocation when buying drop-match patterns, in order to plan accurately.

Equipment. Wallpaper must be measured, cut, pasted and applied. For this you will need a table at least 3x6 feet, a cutting board, a yard stick, scissors, razor knife, several brushes, rollers, buckets, sponges, sandpaper, drop cloths, and a stepladder. For your own safety, your step ladder should be a good, sound ladder that is tall enough to allow you to reach the ceiling of the room without ascending the top two steps.

You will also need a sealer to cover any newly patched areas of your walls, so that the moisture in the adhesive is not soaked up by the spackle or patching plaster. Unless you have already applied a bonding agent, give your walls a coat of size. This is especially important if your walls are porous.

Old Wallpaper. Loose, peeling wallpaper must be removed before application of new paper. However, if the old paper appears sound, you may be able to paper over the old.

To remove the old paper, wet down the paper with a sponge, let stand a few minutes and then pull or scrape off. There are wall paper removers available in paint and wallpaper stores which may speed the job. They are messy but quick. Place tarps over your floors to protect floors from water. If the paper adheres stubbornly in some places, you may have to rent a steamer to remove these sections.

This small assortment of tools is all you need to cut, paste and hang wallpaper correctly in any normal situation.

Consult your wallpaper supplier for rental and instructions.

Application of Lining Paper. A lining paper will give a smooth surface for wallpaper application, absorb excess moisture from paste, and protect expensive papers from any "bleed through" of old surface materials. Premixed vinyl adhesive is applied to the lining paper, which is cut ⅛ inch short of full length of the wall so the edges adhere to the walls. Pieces which butt against window frames and door jambs are cut ⅛ inch narrower as well as the ⅛ inch shorter. This allows a fraction of the wallpaper to contact the wall for absolute adherence. An emulsion bonding agent should be applied before the adhesive if the wall has a glossy finish.

Chalklines. For wallpaper to be attractive and effective, it must hang straight. To determine a straight vertical line, measure the width of a roll of wallpaper. At the ceiling level, measure this distance, less one inch, from your starting point — preferably an inside corner (the less visible, the better). Drive a small nail or brad into the wall at this point. Now hang and string with a weight (plumb bob) at the end from the nail. Rub chalk on the string. When the string and weight are perfectly still, hold the string against the bottom of the wall with one hand and pull the string away from the wall, toward you, with the other hand. Snap the string away from the wall, toward you, with the other hand. Snap the

string to create a chalkline. This will be your guide for applying your first length of paper. The last strip will extend around the inside corner to meet the chalkline.

Cutting and Pasting. Look at the edges of your wallpaper; you will find marks which indicate the pattern match. Using these marks as a guide, decide where in the pattern you want the strip to begin. Cut the paper about 4 to 6 inches longer than your wall to allow you to cut 2-3 inches off once the paper is in place. Match the pattern for the next strip and cut in the same way using a razor knife. Cut against a yardstick as a straightedge. Prepare three to four lengths in sequence, then paste.

Apply paste to the back of half the strip, pasting from the center out and from one end to the middle. Then fold the pasted end to the center and paste the other half of the strip. For good coverage and easy application, use a paint roller with a ⅜ inch nap. Fold the second end over, meeting the other end at the center, paste to paste. Prepare other strips in the same fashion, keeping them in the proper order.

Applying Paper to Wall. Carry the first piece to the wall and unfold the top half. Climb your ladder carefully and line up the edge of the paper with the chalkline previously made. Adjust the paper so that the design aligns the ceiling line, leaving 2 to 3 inches overage at the top. Smooth the paper from the center, working to the edges and up and down. Do not move the

paper around once you have positioned it correctly. Unfold the bottom section and smooth it in place. Use a brush, a sponge and *clean* hands to smooth the paper until it is flat. Work out any air bubbles from under the paper to ensure a smooth appearance and complete adherence to the wall. Repeat with next strip: match the paper; smooth the paper. After you have hung several strips, go back to the first strip and trim off excess at the top and bottom for an exact fit against ceiling line and the baseboard. Roll the seam flat with a roller. Keep returning to trim and roll each strip after the adhesive has set and the strip is securely held.

Windows and Doors. Working around frames of windows and doors is less difficult than it may appear. Measure from last full-length wallpaper edge to the frame edge. Cut the strip to desired length, then cut down the width to one inch more than distance just measured from last full-length seam to the frame. This allows a one inch overlap above the door, or above and below the window. Apply, matching the pattern, and cut excess from around the frame. Use short lengths above and below to fill, matching the pattern.

Special Problem Spots. Every room will have some places where smooth ap-

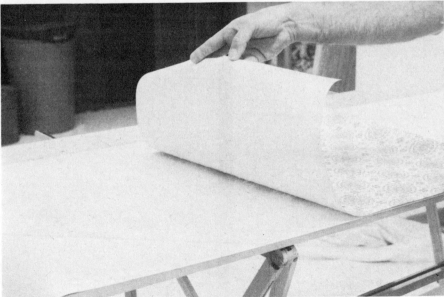

"Booking" the wallpaper makes it easier to carry pasted strips to the wall. Paste half of the strip and bring the pasted end to the center, so paste meets paste. Then paste the other half and place that end in the center, so it nearly touches the other end.

Cut paper larger than space from the previous seam to a door or window frame. Trim excess for a precise fit after hanging the paper.

plication of wallpaper is more difficult than in others. Switchplates and outlet covers can be removed easily and covered with paper themselves. This takes a little extra time, but is not unusually difficult. Measure the location of the outlet or switchplate and mark your paper. Then carefully cut an X over the area of the outlet or switchplate and trim out paper. The cut-out area should be smaller than the box so that the coverplates will overlap the paper. Cover the plates with paper, cutting to match the pattern as closely as possible. Turn edges under and press firmly. Let dry before reinstalling over openings.

Any object which is permanently mounted to the wall and cannot be removed will be a bigger problem. To handle this, measure the area and cut an X in the paper. Check measurements two or three times before cutting. Apply paper carefully, slipping the cut portion over the object and then trimming once paper is smooth.

A radiator can also cause a problem because the space behind it is limited. After paper has been applied to the wall above the radiator, slip a dowel into the fold and roll it down slowly. Do not pull the upper section out of line. Smooth the paper, using a padded yardstick.

Special Considerations. Wallpapers are made of many different materials and each requires different paste and handling. Ask questions when you order the paper. Make sure you know what material the "paper" is made of. Will it crease easily? Does it breathe? Is it subject to mildew? Can it be washed? Is it strippa-

ble? Can it be painted? It is much easier to ask these questions before you decide what to buy for a kitchen wall than after you have put up the paper and discovered that it is failing to adhere to the wall or is staining or fading.

Prepasted Wallpapers. Many papers today come prepasted. They require far fewer tools for application and come in a wide variety of materials and patterns. These papers come with specific instructions. They are relatively easy to handle and to apply; however, experience has shown that they sometimes need extra adhesive applied to the seams. The paper tends to pull away from the wall at that point. Discuss this with your wallpaper salesperson, and consider pasting at the seams.

Soffits and Corners. The soffit above your cabinets is really just wall, and should be marked with a chalkline and handled similar to wall areas when matching and trimming. However, you will have to deal with an outside corner somewhere and will have to turn it under the angle of the soffit just above the cabinets.

To turn an outside corner, apply paper to one surface and fold the excess around the corner. Smooth the paper lightly. Apply paper to the second surface, overlapping the excess. Align the two strips exactly, so the pattern at the overlap is a perfect match. With a razor knife cut through both layers of paper, at about one inch beyond the corner. Lift up top paper and remove excess from first, underneath piece. Put the second strip's new seam edge back in position. Smooth down the

freshly cut seam with a damp sponge, cleaning off paste at the same time. This procedure requires careful matching of the pattern so the seam will not show.

To paper a soffit edge, which is overlapped by the top of the cabinet door, simply bring the paper down and under the soffit edge, smoothing firmly and trimming to an exact fit.

Paint

Paint is a popular choice for covering kitchen walls. If you decide to paint, semi-gloss is a good choice. Flat paint is more difficult to wash and wears away after scrubbing. Most homeowners find that a high-gloss paint has too much reflective shine. Various kinds of textured paints are also on the market, making it possible for you to give your walls a plaster or stucco appearance. These are an excellent coverup for uneven walls, although they may attract and retain more of the airborne grease than will the smoother finishes.

How to Buy and Use Paintbrushes. A quality paintbrush costs more than a cheap one, but it will be easier to use and to clean and it will last for many years. A quality brush can have natural bristles or synthetic bristles. In either case, the brush, when gripped around the bristles, should feel full of bristles. Natural bristle brush has tiny "flags" at the tips of the bristle. You can see these flags by isolating a single bristle and holding it to the light. The flags let you load the brush with more paint. Synthetic bristles on quality brushes are "exploded" at the tip.

Make sure the ferrule of the brush (the

To strain oil-based paint, place screen wire across the top as a strainer. Always strain paint to be applied with a spray gun; otherwise, lumps can clog the nozzle.

"Boxing" paint helps blend paint from a partially used bucket with that in a new bucket of the same finish. This method also is suggested to mix paint to which you have added tint.

Never dip a brush more than ⅓ the length of the bristles. After dipping, gently slap sides of brush against walls of bucket. Do not wipe the bristles across the bucket rim.

shiny metal band around the bottom of the handle) is a rust-and-corrosion-resistant metal such as stainless steel, and that the ferrule is screwed or riveted to the handle, not nailed.

When buying a paintbrush there is only one inflexible rule: never buy a pure or natural bristle brush for use in water-based paints. If you use one in water-based paints, the bristles bunch and the brush operates like a long string mop. Use synthetic bristle brushes for water-based paints and natural bristle brushes for oil-based paints.

Before you use any paintbrush, spin the brush in the palms of your hands to flip out any loose bristles and remove any stray bristles by snapping them off against the metal ferrule.

How and When to Use Rollers. On large, flat surfaces you can spread paint very quickly with a roller. Compared to brush application of paint over a given area, a roller can cut work time in half. For most painting jobs, however, you should team a brush with a roller for best results — use a brush for trim and cutting in walls and ceilings; use a roller for the big surfaces.

Roller handle assemblies are very inexpensive. Size depends on the width of the roller cover needed. If painting ceilings or high side walls, buy an extension handle for the roller which will provide additional reach so you won't have to move the ladder often. This may eliminate use of a ladder altogether.

The best roller frame is the wire or birdcage design because the wires are easier to clean than a solid block frame.

Whatever the material of roller paint trays, usually aluminum or plastic, it is most important that a tray be constructed with ridges across the pan. This will give the roller traction as you load it with paint. If the tray does not have the ridge feature, you can cut a small piece of hardware cloth to fit the bottom of the tray and this wire will provide necessary traction.

If your painting job will stretch out over several days, buy two roller covers and alternate the covers on work days. In this way, the covers will be dry each time you start painting. Always buy roller covers that match the type of paint you plan to use. This information usually is stamped on the roller cover package.

Painting the Wall. Remove all draperies and window shades from the kitchen. Move furniture out of the room or to the center of the room and cover it with a dropcloth. With wide masking tape and newspaper, go around the baseboard of the room, covering the flooring. One edge of the tape should butt against the baseboard and the opposite edge of the tape should be pressed down against the newspaper. A dropcloth may be laid over the newspaper to complete floor protection. If you do not want to paint them, remove the electrical switch and outlet plates. Use a screwdriver to back out holding screws and a razor knife to pop plates off the wall. Many homeowners do paint switch plates and outlets, because paint hides these plastic or metal rectangles so they then blend in with the wall surface. If you decide to paint them, spot-prime the plates before painting the

wall — you may have to spot-prime with two or three coats.

Cut in the ceiling, trim and corners of the wall with a paintbrush, or mask the ceiling for a straight line, if you plan to use a roller on the large surfaces. Run the paint about 6 inches down the wall from the ceiling, up the wall at the base and onto the wall at the corners. Work across the wall from left to right, if you are right handed — the opposite way, if you are left handed. Do one section at a time, working down from ceiling to baseboard.

When you apply paint with a roller, run the roller in all directions against the wall because this multi-directional application helps distribute paint more evenly. Always apply the paint from the unpainted surface to the just-painted corner and other cut-in areas.

If you are using a wide wall brush to apply the paint, also work from the unpainted surface to the fresh paint. Work the paint evenly; then smooth it with the tip of the brush. At windows, run the roller or stroke the brush across the wall in the direction that light comes through the window — usually horizontally along the wall. If there are any ridges in the paint they will follow the same direction as the light and will not show.

Load paint rollers with paint just short of the dripping point. As you roll on the paint, watch out for roller tracks in the paint surface. Tracks occur at the points where a roller has been set down on the wall prior to rolling out the paint, or where a roller skidded on to the wall.

When using a brush, inspect the wall from time to time for brush marks. These

Punch holes around the rim of the original container so that paint lodged in the rim can drip back in. We recommend using a paint bucket instead of the original container.

Always paint from a dry surface into the wet area being painted. Use tips of the bristles to smooth out laps and brush marks. Wipe brush handle often, using a clean cloth.

A paint roller will cover large areas quickly and smoothly. Different roller covers are designed for different paints and types of surfaces. Use the right cover.

marks are caused by spreading the paint too thin or by starting or stopping the brush on a freshly painted surface.

To remove a loose bristle from freshly-painted surfaces, lightly tap the tip of the brush against the loose bristle, gently flicking off the loose bristle. The loose bristle will stick to the paint in the brush so you can then remove it with your fingers.

Paint the trim, windows and doors last. If the doors are flush panel, remove the knobs and paint the panel; a brush is the best painting tool. Do panel inserts first, then paint rails and stiles and finally the edges of the door. Using a brush, paint window mullions first; then paint window stops, casing and sills.

Brick

If you wish to use brick on your kitchen walls, you can choose between real brick and synthetic brick.

Real Brick. For kitchen use of real brick, which is either glazed or unglazed, glazed brick is the better although more expensive, choice. It is easily washable and impervious to water. These features make it especially suitable on the backsplash between the counter and the wall-hung units, as well as the facing near a stove or barbecue. Unglazed brick is a poor choice for the kitchen walls unless it has been sealed or painted.

Synthetic Brick. Synthetic brick serves as a reasonable alternative if real brick will be too expensive, too heavy or too difficult to install.

Nonceramic Brick. One brand of non-ceramic brick, Z-Brick, offers several advantages over real brick for kitchen installation: It is lighter, less expensive, and easier to install. Z-Bricks, which are nationally distributed, are offered in five colors. The mastic adhesive manufactured by the company comes in black, white, and natural, which makes it possible to key the mortar to the color of brick selected.

Since each Z-Brick unit has a thickness of $5/16$ inch, brick sufficient to cover a square foot weighs only two pounds; this is one reason it is easier to install. It is non-combustible, making it suitable for barbecues, stove surrounds, and kitchen walls or dividers. It is not a firebrick, and should not be used to line fireplace interior openings.

Installing Z-Brick. Before installation, try a few applications of Z-Brick on a scrap of wallboard or plywood before you install it on your actual surface, in order to get a feel for the material. Experiment with different widths or mortar joints, so that you can learn to control the effect. Try both a mitred and butted corner to see which you prefer. Score and snap off a few bricks until you feel comfortable doing it. Allow your sample bricklaying to dry thoroughly before proceeding. If you sample does not look exactly as you wish, make another trial run before installing the Z-Brick on your actual surface.

Using a ¼ inch square, notched trowel, spread a layer of Z-Ment adhesive mortar

$1/16$th inch thick. Use the adhesive over any clean and sound surface, such as wallboard or plywood. Press each individual unit of brick firmly into the adhesive, one at a time, squeezing the surplus adhesive into the mortar-line areas. You may make the mortar joints as narrow as ⅜ inch, or as wide as ¾ inch (rarely, as much as one inch). Smooth the adhesive with a narrow brush to seal all edges of the brick.

According to the makers of Z-Brick and Z-Ment, the working time for their adhesive mortar is about half an hour, allowing you to work on one small section at a time before it hardens. A strong, final set is achieved in two hours.

After the final set is achieved, seal the brick and the mortar. The makers of Z-Brick recommend two coats, 48 hours apart, of their product, Z-Sealer. It provides a clear, acrylic, indoor-outdoor seal that is flat and weatherproof, which does not affect the color of the brick.

Plastic Laminates

In most parts of the country, plastic laminate is the material preferred for kitchen countertops. Many new and innovative patterns simulating wood or brick or metal, are now on the market. If you have already used plastic laminate on the kitchen counters, it also is a good choice for the backsplash. However, you need not limit use of plastic laminates to matching countertops and backsplashes. For attractive and unusual kitchen design, use a textured plastic laminate on the back-

Z-Brick applied to the support pillar and the backsplash gives a rustic look to this kitchen. Z-Brick is fireproof, safe for kitchen use, and adds excellent protection to surfaces subject to heat.

A Z-bricked wall in the eating area and behind the stove help unify this kitchen's decor.

splash, or one that contrasts with that used on the countertop. You can surface anything from kitchen windowsills to entire walls with this material. Instructions for installation of plastic laminate countertops will be found in Chapter 10.

Ceramic Tile

Ceramic tile is available in a large choice of sizes, shapes, colors, patterns and finishes. It comes in large squares or tiny mosaics, solid colors with or without texture and with or without coordinated patterns, shiny or matte finishes, glazed or unglazed, machine or hand-made. Unusual alternatives also include: ceramic tiles on which to paint your own design before having them baked in a kiln; elements of either a small or large picture or mural, portions of which will be in every tile. You can find tiles imported from Holland, Italy, Spain, France, Mexico and several other countries, as well as American-made tiles.

Although installation of ceramic tile has in the past been a time-consuming chore, manufacturers are developing products to make this process easier. For example, American Olean has developed several application systems that are infinitely easier than setting tile in mortar. One is called Redi-Set, in which tiles are supplied in pregrouted glazed-tile sheets. Their Mosaic-Set, for small tiles, works in such a way that there is no paper to peel or residue to remove, making sections simple to align. They also have ceramic tile that can be dry-set or set with a latex

cement mortar over their own product, Wonder-Board.

For instructions on how to tile a countertop, see Chapter 10.

Stainless Steel and Other Metals

Stainless steel, copper, aluminum, and porcelain-enameled steel are all made in tile or sheet form. Although they are not as often seen in home kitchens as other materials, they are excellent for backsplashes, countertops, and surfaces around and behind stoves.

Vinyl Tiles

The same vinyl tile used for floors can also surface walls or backsplashes. However, keep vinyl away from the heat of cooking areas.

Corian

Corian, the trade-name of a synthetic marble, is a top-quality but costly material that lends itself to almost any kitchen surface. Where counters are of Corian, you can cover backsplashes with it to produce a unifying effect. Corian, however, can be used anywhere and you may find it very attractive near the stove or sink.

Fabric

Fabric can be used near eating areas, but not near stoves. It can be stretched over walls and stapled to a frame. Because the fabric stretches on a frame which is a fraction of an inch away from the wall, it hides wall flaws. You can eliminate most of the sewing and cutting by using Indian

throws, patterned sheets or fabric already manufactured in rolls. On a smaller scale, fabric can be stretched and stapled to replace or cover cabinet doors on base or wall cabinets, or it can be hung like curtains over either opening. Coordinated fabrics and papers are made by a number of firms.

Personalized Wall Design

Paper Displays. Imagination can be the prime ingredient of your kitchen walls. Renowned cook and author James Beard has papered his kitchen walls with the huge world maps available from the U.S. Government for modest sums. If you have posters, reproductions, sheet music, or other similar items, coat the paper with a suitable protective coating once you adhere the materials to the wall. When your paper decoration is to cover an entire wall, as Beard's does, an inexpensive lining paper hides surface irregularities and makes the final papering easier. (For details on application, see "Wallpaper", above.)

Cut-outs. You can use individual small cut-outs of paper or fabric to create a frieze or border-design complementary to your kitchen colors and theme. The designs can be copied and stenciled, or they can be revised and adapted to your purpose either as stencils or as freehand copies.

Kitchen Murals. If you have the available wall space, you might like to use a kitchen mural on your walls. You may purchase them ready-made, or you may have them custom-made. For instance, a good photographer in the family could prepare a photo-mural in color or black-and-white on one wall of the kitchen to give it individuality. You might want to try a photo-montage of the family and its ancestors from the previous several generations. You should protect photographs, like any other paper on the wall, with a cover of clear plastic or an appropriate liquid coating.

You may use other unique creations for murals. Mount children's drawings you like best to cover all or part of a wall; enlarge or reproduce them via photography or Xerox copying. One project might be to divide the wall into sections and to hang sheets of paper, giving each child an opportunity to create a picture for his or her own rectangle, using a washable paint. This enables you to control the col-

Ceramic tile behind a stove resists heat and grease and can be easily cleaned.

These original tin walls only needed fresh paint to complete restoration.

ors and organize the design. A delightful mural, though expensive, can be devised from tiles available from Country Floors or other tile distributors.

Wall Space for Miscellaneous

While planning which materials you are going to use on your walls, reserve some space for useful items. You will probably want to include a bulletin board or chalk board, on which family members can leave messages for one another, or on which they can jot down reminders. If you are planning to have a wall-hung kitchen telephone, decide in advance where it is to go. Buy an extra-long cord that will allow you to walk freely around the kitchen. A pass-through to the next room, called a "hatch" by some, is handy in certain layouts — but it, too, occupies wall space.

To make as full use of your walls as of any other surface in the kitchen, and to double their usefulness and appeal, buy a grid system in chrome, steel, natural wood, brightly colored plastic or plastic-coated metal with hooks or pegs, and hang your cookware from the grids.

Building an Arch

Constructing an arch to enclose a burner top or range or used simply as a decorative accent is a relatively simple process. First, decide on the overall size. Refer to the illustration below for basic guidelines. Since the size needed will vary depending on your space, we suggest drawing a 1-inch-to-the-foot front view of the entire unit to help determine height and other dimensions. It also is a good idea to superimpose a line at head height and another at eye level to make sure you will be com-

fortable working at an enclosure of this size.

For the framing procedures, see the drawing. The most difficult part of an arch is in the way depth is given to the arch itself. This is created by cutting a second piece of plywood in a mirror image of the front piece. They fasten together with screws into the spacing framing on each side. The void of the arch is covered by bending a material such as ⅛ inch Masonite to the curve of the arch. Fastening this piece with coated subflooring nails is satisfactory, but use screws wherever possible for the most stable construction. Tape plywood and Masonite joints with joint compound.

After joints have been filled and sanded, cover with the finish material — tile, stucco, brick or other. Be aware that if you elect to use one of the stucco-like

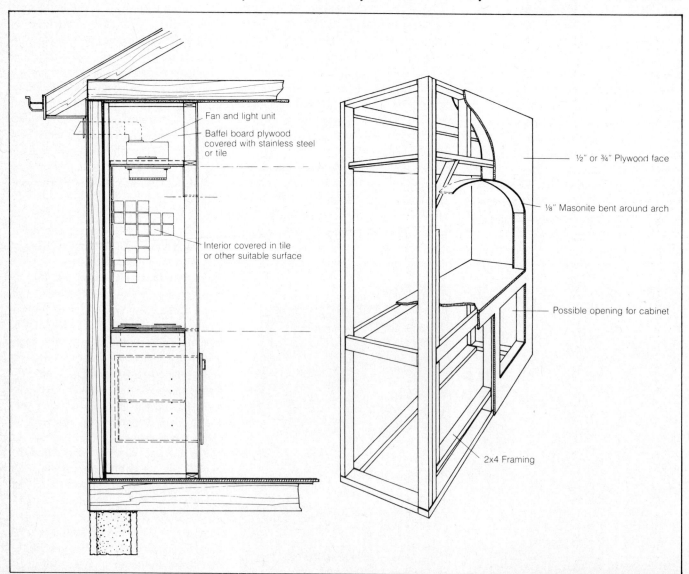

Arch framing may be built against the wall or free-standing. If an oven or cooktop is built in, be sure to observe fireproofing clearances for both the framing and surfacing, keeping combustible materials away from areas subject to heat.

materials, there is a possibility that cracks may develop at the joints of the facing due to expansion and contraction of the wood. At the very least, fill any voids with an elastic caulk and make sure the covering material has some latex or similar base to allow for some movement.

A Pass-through

A pass-through is basically an unglazed window in an interior wall and is a project within the scope of the do-it-yourselfer. Plan your pass-through so that you will get maximum use from the completed opening, with minimum difficulty in construction. If you discover that the wall in which you want your pass-through is a loadbearing wall, refer to the section following on removing a wall.

Unless you are planning to add a pass-through to provide additional natural light to an interior room, you will not need a very large opening to hand plates and trays from one room into another. After you have decided the approximate location for your pass-through, locate the studs by knocking on the wall, using a stud finder, or driving nails until you hit the stud. Studs are usually (in contemporary homes, at least) 16 inches o.c. You can have a pass-through nearly 30 inches wide, after all finishing, by cutting through and removing a section of only one stud. Center your pass-through at the location of a stud. Mark the height you want for the bottom of the opening and the top. Remove the plaster or wallboard following the same instructions given for enlarging a window (Chapter 9).

Allowing for the thickness of the sill plate and the header, cut the stud, which is centered in the opening. Mark the desired height of the opening on each of the side studs. Cut 2x4s to that length, less the thickness of the header, and nail these 2x4s to the side studs. Install a double header across the top of the opening by nailing into the tops of the newly added, side 2x4s from above and into the cut stud from below. Mark the desired height of bottom of the opening and cut 2x4s from above and into the cut stud from below. Mark the desired height of bottom of the opening and cut 2x4s to that length, less the thickness of the sill plate. Nail these short 2x4s into the already doubled side studs. Nail sill plate from above to the new 2x4s and the cut stud.

Apply wallboard or plaster, and finish with tape and spackling compound. Final finishing depends on your decorating wishes. The opening may be left plain, painted or wallpapered. You may wish to make the sill into a serving shelf by adding a piece of board, any size from 1x6 to 2x12, to the sill. This board should be carefully cut for exact fit and installed with countersunk wood screws.

If you wish a more elaborate decorative finish to the pass-through, add wood molding as a frame with mitered corners or rim it with ceramic tile.

Removing a Wall

The crucial issue is whether you can plan such a removal without interfering with necessary ceiling support. The first step is to find out which way the ceiling joists run. In a one-story house you can go up to

The built-in cooktop and ceramic tile backsplash are made more attractive by the installation of the decorative arch and the useful and attractive plate rail.

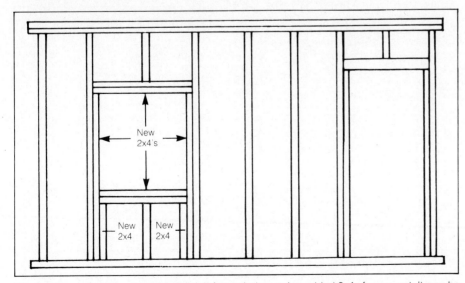

Framing for a pass-through resembles that for a window, using added 2x4s for support. It may be finished with casing, wallboard, a wooden sill, or with other decorative molding.

the attic to look at the ceiling joists, but in a two-story house there is no easy way to check the direction of the joists.

If your roof is supported by a truss, the interior partition is probably not load-bearing. However, trusses have only been in frequent use in residential construction for the last 10 years. If your home does not have a prefabricated truss, and the span is long, you should have a center beam to which the joists are connected. If the interior partition you are considering removing runs directly beneath the beam, it will be load-bearing. If the wall runs parallel to the beam but not directly beneath it, the wall usually will not be load-bearing. If the interior wall runs perpendicular to the joists, the partition probably was not intended to serve as a load-bearing wall. However, in both these latter cases the house has probably settled over the years, which may have caused the wall to become partially load-bearing.

As is probably evident by now, from your own inspection you can determine probabilities but not certainties. However, most localities require that a building inspector look at your existing home before issuing a permit for the proposed remodeling. Even if it is not required by code, call upon your local building inspector to determine whether or not the wall is load-bearing. The negative results of a wrong conclusion could be dangerous and expensive.

Before beginning wall removal, trip the circuit breaker or remove fuses, as necessary, of wiring that services the wall. It is not enough to just have all the switches in that wall turned off. Use a voltage tester (see Chapter 9) to check that none of the other circuits are leaking current into that circuit. If there is plumbing in the wall, cap pipes at some point before they enter the wall.

For access to the plate nailed to the subfloor, remove baseboards. It never hurts to use a support 4 or 5 feet behind the portion you are removing, even if the wall is nonload-bearing. Use a plate at the ceiling to distribute weight; wedge 2x4s for support, similar to that shown for enlarging a window (see Chapter 9). If you are absolutely positive the wall is not load-bearing you can cut through the wall and the studs with a Saws-all. Start at the top of the wall and work downward. If the wall is plaster, then whatever you cut out will be heavy. Take out a maximum of 28 inches by 2 feet. If cutting wallboard, you can cut out larger blocks. You can even remove the wallboard panels (as in Chapter 9) and carefully cut out the studding for later use. In this case, you will want to do as little damage to the materials as possible, so start at a corner at the ceiling.

ZIP CUT

TUFF BACK

SPRING BACK

GENERAL PURPOSE

GENERAL PURPOSE

SAWZALL DELUXE

PLASTER CUTTING

ALL-PURPOSE

SCROLL
TUNGSTEN CARBIDE

TUNGSTEN CARBIDE

SPECIAL
(KNIFE)

METAL SCROLL

TWIN EDGE

SUPER-TOUGH

WOOD SCROLL

METAL SCROLL

METAL CUTTING
(HIGH SPEED)

METAL CUTTING
(FLEXIBLE BACK)

PRUNING

A reciprocating saw accommodates different blades in order to cut a variety of materials.

A reciprocating saw (shown is the Milwaukee Saws-All) can cut through walls, floors, and other surfaces. It is easier to handle than other saws often used for this type of work.

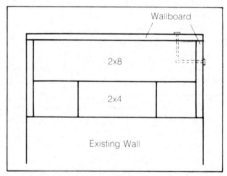

Wallboard

2x8

2x4

Existing Wall

A wallboard surface may be added to match the existing surface of the wall portion still in place. With this finish, the construction work will not be evident. Use gypsumboard nails.

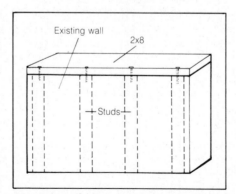

Existing wall   2x8

Studs

Shown is a sill used when part of a wall has been cut away. It is less strong, but easier to accomplish, than the other 2 methods given. A facing may be added to cover the cut wall edge.

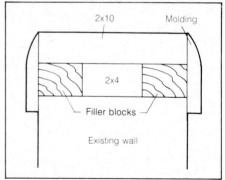

2x10   Molding

2x4

Filler blocks

Existing wall

For strong support and a nice finished edge, use a finished hardwood for the sill and add curved moldings to cover the adjoining edges of the wall and the lumber.

Score at the corner and ceiling. Then use a Saws-all and cold chisel. Do not strike the cold chisel with a claw hammer; use a ballpeen hammer — a brick chisel also will handle the job. Tear out wall material, using a pry bar (such as a Stanley wonder bar). If you do not have a Saws-all (which will cut through wiring) or do not want to damage the wiring, disconnect the wiring and reverse the fishing procedure (see Chapter 9) to pull the cable out of the way. When you reach the floor level (remember, you started at the ceiling) take out the 2x4 plate, using a pry bar. If saving lumber, take nails out first, then the drywall or plaster, and then cut out lumber.

Removing Part of a Wall. To remove the top half of a wall, leaving just a divider over which you can work and serve, first measure a horizontal chalkline and mark it just below the cut-off point. After cutting, as described above, cover the wall section with a wood inset attached to the studs (for example, a 1x10 or whatever lumber is needed to match the thickness of the wall). For extra strength, first cap the half-wall with a 2x4 and put the larger piece of lumber on top. This will require a filler block and casing in order to finish it off neatly. Another possibility is a 2x4 cap with a second piece of lumber attached to create a frame for wallboard, which you can tape and spackle. Wallboard in or patch the surrounding surfaces as necessary. Check with your local building inspector as to regulations; he may be required to inspect the work before you wallboard in and patch.

If removal of the wall, or the top half of it, has damaged the ceiling, you can put drywall over the entire ceiling. First attach furring strips to joists. Use nonrusting drywall screws. If there are no drywall screws available, use drywall nails (barbed nails). Apply wallboard on top, countersinking and spackling. If the ceiling is uneven, you will have to shim first.

CEILINGS

Ceilings may be painted, papered, covered with tile (acoustical or otherwise), or paneled with wood of any type. A kitchen ceiling can benefit from one or more skylight openings when it is feasible, and an entire ceiling or selected portions of one may be raised or dropped. Textured or printed fabrics can be used to advantage on some kitchen ceilings, and materials such as burlap can be used with or without a coat of paint. Ceiling beams can add a pleasing, rustic effect to the kitchen. Even straw matting in squares or rolls is worth considering for the ceiling. Let's examine some of the choices for your kitchen ceiling.

Paint

Paint has traditionally been the favorite choice among homeowners for ceilings. If your ceiling is in perfect condition — whether it is made out of plasterboard, plaster, or wood — use a glossy, white paint. This type of paint will reflect more light and your kitchen will appear brighter. If your ceiling is less than top condition, the best course is to fix these problem areas (see below). Colors other than white, as well as nonglossy paint, can be used successfully on kitchen ceilings, but as the darkness of the shade increases, more light is absorbed, making the kitchen appear dimmer. This effect occurs whether your lighting is natural or artificial. Textured paints in colors and reflective glossy paints rarely are attractive on a kitchen ceiling, although in a few rare instances, they may be adequate.

Some authorities suggest that you apply a lining paper (see Wallpaper discussion under "Walls") before painting a newly plastered ceiling. Whether or not you choose to follow that suggestion, however, you must be sure that you first prepare the surface according to the manufacturer's recommendations, no matter what surface you are painting or papering. When painting a ceiling, remember that rollers can be fitted with long handles that allow you to paint from the floor, without using a ladder. For best results, roll paint on in one direction first, then roll the second coat in the other direction.

Preparation — Patching Gypsumboard or Plaster Cracks.
The size of the cracks we are discussing here range from hairline to about ¼ inch wide. The repair technique for cracks in gypsumboard and for plaster walls is the same. If there are large cracks and lots of them consult a professional; there could be structural damage to the house.

Clean out the crack with a razor knife. Undercut the crack with the knife to form an inverted V. This configuration will help hold in the patch.

Mix a fairly stiff batch of spackling compound. Trowel the compound into the crack, smoothing it with the tip end of the wall scraper or putty knife. Leave the patch a little high; spackling shrinks as it dries. Let the patch set for two days. Then sand the area lightly and touch up the patch with paint. If the patch is large, you probably will have to repaint the entire wall, or room.

Sagging Gypsumboard Ceilings. Wear safety glasses. Be sure the stepladder is fully opened and locked before you climb the ladder. Do not climb the ladder above the third rung from the top.

Impact from foot traffic on the floor above could have caused the nails in the gypsum wallboard on the ceiling to loosen. Loose nails, in turn, can cause the ceiling to sag or appear uneven.

Locate the ceiling joists, which probably are spaced 16 inches on center. Renail the ceiling to the joists (or rafters), spacing the nails about 2 inches apart. To help hold the gypsum wallboard in place for renailing, build yourself a T brace from scrap 2x4, nailing the cross of the T on. Wedge this brace between the floor and the ceiling. You can kick it into position to apply needed pressure.

Water Sags. First find and stop the leak. Let the ceiling dry. This may take weeks, even months sometimes, but the wait will save you money.

Once the ceiling has dried out, try renailing the gypsum wallboard back in position, as described above. If this works, you will have to spackle the nail holes and repaint the entire ceiling. But first coat the water spots with 4-lb.-cut shellac. Shellac will prevent any water spots from later bleeding through the paint job.

If renailing does not work, and the sag is not too large, you can try the same panel replacement technique previously described for walls. However, we would

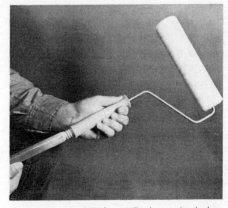

An extension handle for a roller is required when painting the ceiling.

recommend that you replace the entire wallboard ceiling instead. It should not cost much more for the whole ceiling than for a large-area replacement, and will look much better. The panels can be nailed directly to ceiling joists once the old material has been removed. Slightly dimple the location of each nailhead using a hammerhead — being cautious lest you damage the surface of the paper. Finish the joints and nailheads as previously described.

Painting the Ceiling. Remove all draperies and window shades from the kitchen. Move as much of the furniture to the center of the room as is possible. You may have to move it to one end of the room, or remove if from the room, in some cases. Cover surfaces with drop cloths, securing the edges of the dropcloths to flooring using masking tape. Paint brushes will drip paint and rollers will emit a fine spray that settles in a room like dust, so be sure you cover everything that won't be painted.

If you are painting only the ceiling, or painting the ceiling a different color than the walls, use a brush to paint the ceiling area where it meets side walls and light fixtures. (This is called "cutting in".) You can do this easily if you have a steady hand and a keen eye for straight lines. If not, mask around the ceiling/wall junctions or lights using a 2-inch wide tape. As insurance against paint stains, you may want to cover the top of any fixtures with newspaper. Fasten the newspaper in place with small strips of masking tape.

Apply paint across the narrow width of the room, working from the unpainted central areas to the just-painted corners. Work completely across the ceiling painting a strip about 3 feet wide. Start another strip when this is completed. In brief, do not apply paint at random across the ceiling. Start and complete one section before you begin another.

At windows, apply the final brush or roller strokes in the same direction that sunlight enters the room. When painted in this fashion, brush and roller marks won't show when sunlight strikes the surface. Use a brush to paint ceiling ducts and registers with the same paint used for the ceiling surface.

Wallpaper

As mentioned in the section on "Walls", wallpaper today is often made of materials other than paper. It comes in many different colors, patterns, and textures.

Patterns. If you are considering a pattern, keep in mind the following rule: while a small print on the ceiling can add a certain coziness to the room, the darker the print's background color or the larger and darker the print itself — or the more surface it covers — the smaller and dimmer the kitchen will appear. This is usually a disadvantage.

Textures. Textured papers, like textured paints, can help to hide minor imperfections on the ceiling. However, it is considered more difficult for novices to hang this type of paper than other types. Since any type of wallpaper is more difficult to hang on a ceiling than on a wall, no amateur should attempt to apply it to a ceiling without an assistant. Some papers require a lining paper first.

Preparation. Wash and rinse the ceiling. Remove the ceiling fixture if there is one, and turn off power to the wiring. Sand the paint if it is slick or shiny. Patch obvious cracks and dents, then seal.

Cutting and Pasting. When papering a ceiling, you will be working over your head and dealing with relatively long strips. Cut strips to fit across the narrow measurement of your room. Match your pattern as you would for walls, using the pattern matching marks on the paper edge. Cut three or four pieces at a time. Paste and accordian fold without placing any weight against the paper; this avoids creases at the folds.

Application. Unless your kitchen is extremely narrow, you will probably need an assistant to help hold and feed the pasted paper to you. You will also need to create a scaffold (see illustration). If you attempt to apply the paper from one ladder, you will either over-reach the safe limits of the ladder or you will have to climb down, move the ladder, and climb back up every few feet. All this risks your own safety and puts stress on the paper — which becomes softer and weaker as the paste soaks into the strip.

Smooth each strip, roll seams, and wait until adhesive has set enough to hold up the paper. Then trim off excess at the ceiling/wall line, and replace any ceiling fixtures.

Ceiling Tile. Ceiling tile may or may not be acoustical. If you prefer acoustical tile, which deadens sound within the kitchen, make certain that it is what you are buying rather than a look-alike. You may glue or staple tile to the existing ceiling, which will cover most minor defects in the ceiling. It may be necessary to suspend the ceiling (see "Dropped Ceilings"), Some ceiling tiles are prefinished, although you can paint most of them. You can cover the ceiling completely with tile, or you may leave openings for lights if you have chosen to suspend the ceiling.

Dropped Ceilings

When a kitchen is too high in proportion to its other dimensions, a lower, sus-

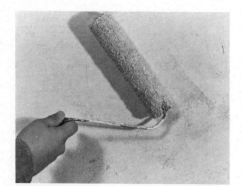

Roller "tracks," exaggerated here for illustration purposes, result from starting and stopping roller movement in fresh paint. Apply paint from dry into freshly painted surface.

Hanging wallpaper across a ceiling requires careful handling of the pasted and, therefore, soft paper. It also requires careful balance on a ladder. You should have a helper.

pended ceiling can improve appearances and possibly reduce heating costs. It can enable installation of recessed fixtures where they would not have been feasible. Dropped ceilings can be made from any of the materials suitable for kitchen ceilings. They can also be made from heat-proof translucent plastic panels that will diffuse a light system built in above them. This treatment is not satisfactory if you plan to utilize high, extra cabinets they install for storage of seldom-used equipment. One major disadvantage is that a low room may become overheated during the hottest weather. In addition, a high ceiling is ideal for placement of a fan.

Another option is to lower the ceiling selectively. For example, a dining area might be more intimate when tucked under a low ceiling, in contrast to a work area with soaring height (the reverse might even be more appropriate for your situation, each case varies). If you do raise or lower a ceiling selectively, the change in levels can be reinforced visually by a change in color or materials, but guard against a cold showroom effect.

Raised Ceilings

A possibility especially attractive to people whose elderly house has an infirm old plaster ceiling is to remove the ceiling altogether. (This is a very messy job.) You will never know what is underneath it unless you look. You may be lucky and find old beams or rough-finished wood joists that would be highly attractive once cleaned and stained or painted. If your kitchen is under a sloping roof line, you may be able to achieve a cathedral ceiling effect by uncovering it.

There are several perils to keep in mind when removing a ceiling, however. Sound will carry from the lower to the upper floor (and vice versa) more easily,

which may become a nuisance if there are occupied rooms overhead. If the kitchen is in a one-story house or one-story extension, on the other hand, insulation should be installed whether or not there is a ceiling. Furthermore, just as a dropped ceiling can conceal plumbing and electrical lines, so the removal of a ceiling can expose these necessities.

Creative Ceiling Materials

If you decide to opt for an unusual ceiling surface, you have several alternatives available to you.

Wood Ceilings. You can attach wood ceilings directly to the ceiling joists or lower them to whatever degree is required. Tongue-and-grooved boards are said to be the simplest for the nonprofessional to handle, but planed pine boards are less expensive. If you use boards with fractional spaces left between each strip

to cover sagging ceilings, you can first cover the original ceiling underneath with a matte black or dark grey paint, which will make these spaces virtually invisible.

You can finish your wood ceiling with a clear finish, stain or paint. If you paint it, try to use good quality, knot-free wood, which makes the painting easier. You may want to consider extending the wood ceiling down along one or more walls, for design benefits.

Fabric. In addition to fabric wallpapers on ceilings, you might consider woven materials such as burlap, monk's cloth, and linen. You may leave these materials in their natural color or paint them. Some of these are materials sold as wallpaper by-the-roll, with a paper backing and in a range of colors.

Straw matting, usually imported from China, sold in "tiles" as well as rolls, can reinforce a countrified decorative scheme

Ceiling fans are easy to install and need minimal maintenance. This fan hangs from a sturdy hook screwed into a ceiling joist. Electrical connections are hidden beneath the canopy.

A ceiling lowered with wood strips also provides a surface to which track task lighting can be attached in areas where soffits are not available for local lighting installation.

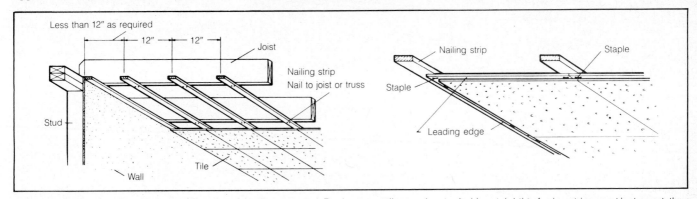

Shown at left is how a ceiling tile looks with some of the tiles removed. Replacement tiles can be stapled (as at right) to furring strips or, at last resort, they can be glued using building adhesive.

when applied to the ceiling. It can camouflage irregularities and mute sound, as do acoustical tile and cork.

Ceiling Beams. If you are extending the kitchen or adding a new kitchen, consider leaving the beams exposed. (This may cause insulation problems in a one-story home). If your old ceiling needs extra support, think about adding exposed beams. These beams attach to vertical members (wall studs) or other supports. New beams for any ceiling can be made from new or old wood. Genuine old beams are sometimes available from old buildings being torn down or from wrecking yards. Simulated ceiling beams offer advantages because they need less support and are easier to install. Boxed beams may also be built and then painted.

Placement of Ceiling Beams. Lay out the positions of the beams. We will use 4x6s in our example, but the same criteria would apply for larger or smaller beams.

Work out a scale drawing of the ceiling, taking into account any fixed soffits, pipe chases or light fixtures. Some people prefer half beams on each end of the room; others would rather use all full beams. If you will use supporting side beams, deduct the amount of space they will take from the total. Then divide up the remainder of the space for the number of beams you desire, depending upon spacing. Average spacing is often 36 inches, but as close as 30 inches or as far apart as 48 inches is also common.

Fastening the Beams to the Ceiling. For hollow, lightweight wood or hollow styrofoam beams, fasten a 1x2 strip (or whatever size fills the width of the recess in the beams) to the ceiling, using coated nails or screws. When the strips run in the opposite direction to the ceiling joists this is a simple operation, since you can nail directly into the joists. If the strips are to run the same direction as the joists, you will have to use Molly bolts or wall anchors for fastening the beams so they do not fall under a joist.

Cut the beam to length. Lay a bead of panel adhesive along each side, far enough in so it will not squeeze out onto the ceiling when placing the beams. You can nail through the sides of the beams into the nailing strips to help hold them in place until the adhesive sets up.

If you want to avoid using the wood strips on the lightweight plastic beams, it is possible to install them using only panel adhesive. To do this, you must use upright support rods, wedged between the beam and the floor, to hold the beams in place until the adhesive sets up.

For heavier wood beams it is advisable to use a more substantial fastening procedure, as shown.

The ceiling in this kitchen has been decorated with exposed beams. The area above the cooktop and ceramic backsplash is further defined by 2x4 stud lengths fitted at right angles.

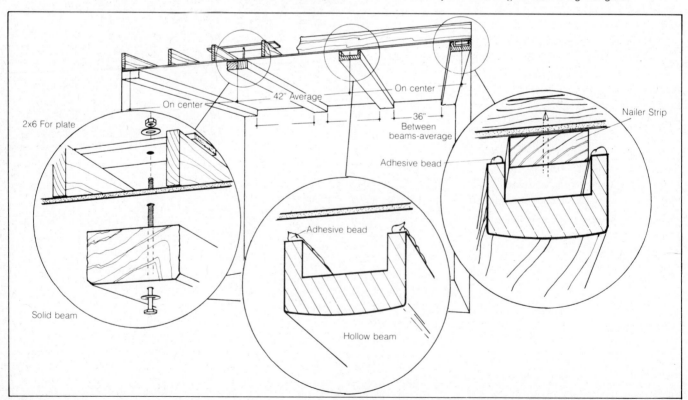

Fastening methods used for installation of ceiling beams will depend upon the weight and material of the beams, and the positions of the ceiling joists relative to the locations of the beams.

Skylights

Ready-made, mass-produced skylights are sold in dozens of shapes and sizes including flat, domed, or bubble shapes. They may be made of safety glass, window glass, or acrylic; they may be single, double, or triple-glazed; the glass may be treated to reduce heat or glare from the sun. Some skylight windows are stationary, others are able to be opened and closed. Manufacturers who aim for the nonprofessional market usually include instructions with their units. Skylights are sold by a variety of outlets, including small and large mail-order firms, home centers, major chains and catalogue stores, and hardware stores. Distributor or manufacturer instructions will no doubt vary somewhat.

Homemade Version. One solution to the high cost of skylights was developed by Alex Wade, author of *30 Energy-Efficient Houses You Can Build*. He installed a plexiglass sheet similar to a large shingle. Plexiglass (acrylic plastic) has advantages as a skylight material: it has less chance of breakage and does not transmit as much heat as does glass. To prevent skylight leaks, he suggests sliding the skylight top beneath the roof shingles which are at the skylight opening's top edge. The plexiglass then overlaps the opening by about 4 inches all around the bottom and sides. Use a clear silicone to seal the plastic, anchoring it using roundhead screws and rubber washers. An additional plexiglass layer installed on the inside of the house is a good idea to prevent heat loss and condensation at night. It would be very wise to seal the inside sheet of plexiglass where it meets the ceiling opening, using a narrow strip of rubber seal. This will prevent leaks from condensation.

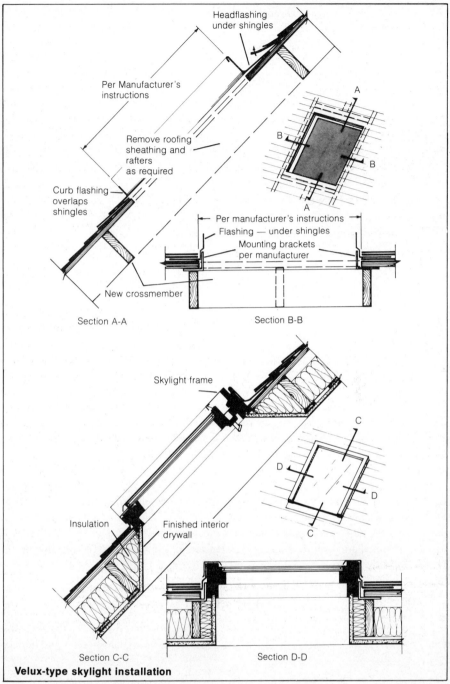

Velux-type skylight installation

Shown are principles for skylight installation; details vary according to product purchased.

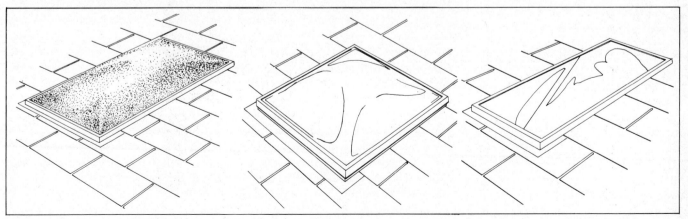

Skylights come in many sizes, shapes and styles and contain either translucent or transparent material. You have many choices available.

9
WIRING AND LIGHTING

When setting up a kitchen plan, keep in mind that many of your electrical requirements will be governed by local building codes. These are based upon the National Electrical Code. States and cities can add to the NEC, but cannot discount any of its requirements. The codes lay out general and specific requirements for all construction and remodeling projects. For instance, they dictate that at least two circuits must feed into a kitchen and that these must be at least 20-amp circuits. Codes will also state that a garbage disposal, microwave oven or dishwasher must have a circuit of its own, and new outlets must accept three-pronged plugs. All of the requirements are written for safety reasons; improper wiring can result in shock, fire, or damaged appliances.

The next most important note is that electricity operates according to specific, precise scientific rules. If you do not want your lights to dim every time your refrigerator cycles on, you must assess the energy needs of your kitchen and meet them adequately. You must become aware of basic electrical terminology before you will understand why the television picture in the living room might get smaller when you turn on the dishwasher.

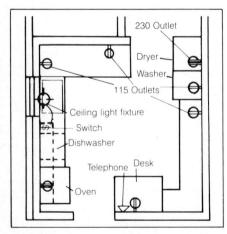

Many homeowners do not recognize their kitchen's electrical needs until they find themselves searching for an outlet. Shown are likely locations for outlet and switch placement.

Even if you do become knowledgeable about electrical systems and how they work, you still should hire a professional electrical contractor to do any extensive wiring projects. Indeed, local building code may require you to do so, or else will require that you pass an examination. At the least, a building inspector or an electrician will have to inspect the completed work. The dangers from one miswired fixture are too great to take the more complex work on yourself unless you have considerable wiring knowledge and experience.

ELECTRICITY FOR YOUR KITCHEN
Electricity is distributed by the electric company, which supplies electricity to a transformer that steps down the voltage to a 3-wire home system. The supply wires feed into a main service entrance box in your home. Then the service box distributes the energy supply as required by means of circuits. Each independent circuit serves a specific group of outlets and lights.

Basic Terminology
Any discussion of the circuits in your home or the appliances, lights and outlets fed by those circuits will incorporate some or all of the following terms. The more familiar they are to you, the safer you will be.

Volts. Voltage, in nontechnical terms, can be loosely compared to the pressure in a water pipe. Pressure makes the water flow when you turn on a faucet. If you turn on a switch, voltage causes electric current to flow through a wire. The main electric service entering most homes consists of three wires: two live, or "hot," wires and a neutral wire. There is 220 to 240 volts between the two live wires, and 110 to 120 volts between each of the live wires and the neutral wire. The voltage in most of the outlets in your home is maintained at between 110 and 120 volts, with

the exception of special outlets for an electric stove or clothes dryer. These outlets only accept special plugs and are wired to deliver 220 to 240 volts. The voltage level remains consistent at every outlet unless a problem exists in the home's circuitry. When your lights dim or brighten, an unusual circumstance, such as a storm, has suddenly decreased or increased the voltage.

Although the main service to most homes is 120/240 volts, not all homes utilize the 220/240 volt availability. If you are uncertain about the level of your service, call your electric company. The larger service is highly recommended, given the electrical demands of most households.

Amps. Amperes measure the number of electrons — the amount of current — that passes through a point in a circuit. Circuits themselves are described in terms of the number of amps — 15, 20, 30, or more — that they can safely handle. Some appliances, although not all, are described in terms of the number of amps of current they consume. Homes with 120/240 service typically have up to 200 amps of power available to them.

Watts. Wattage can be discussed in two ways. First, wattage is a measurement of the amount of power available in the circuit. If you multiply the volts times the amps in a circuit, you will find out how many watts are being used (V x A = W). Thus, a 15-amp circuit of 115 volts can supply 1725 watts of power.

The second way to discuss wattage is in terms of the rated watts of a given appliance. A 100-watt light bulb will consume 100 watts of energy, converting it to heat and light. A freezer consumes between 300 and 588 watts of energy. Calculations based upon the wattage rating of an appliance result in the Energy Efficiency Rating discussed in Chapter 4.

Resistance. Just as the rate of water flow in a pipe depends upon the amount of pressure behind the water — which forces it to flow — it also is governed by the amount of resistance offered to the flow. Electrical resistance of a wire depends upon its thickness and length. Thick wires offer less resistance, and thin wires more. The longer any wire, the greater its resistance. The resistance of the wiring itself is only a small fraction of total resistance compared to the resistance of lights and appliances. The resistance of a light or an appliance determines how much current will flow. Since the voltage (pressure) is constant, turning on more lights will lower the resistance and more current will flow. In other words, the decreased resistance results in an increase in current. Of course, increased resistance results in less current.

Circuits

If you work on the wiring in your kitchen, you will be dealing in most cases with 115-volt circuits. These are designed to meet the needs of light fixtures and most appliances, such as toasters, clocks or blenders. Because the demands upon a given 115-volt circuit are not high, it serves several fixtures, which often are located in several rooms. The area a circuit can serve is governed by the size of the wire, fuse or circuit breaker and potential connected load. Typically, it ranges between 375 and 500 square feet per circuit.

Cable Types. There are three basic types of cable for circuits. Inside the cable are three wires that are color-coded. Black (or sometimes red) stands for live wires, white for neutral, and green (or

sometimes bare) for ground. The kind of cable in your home may be determined by local code. For any of the projects included in this chapter, find out the code requirements for your particular area.

BX. This cable is enclosed in a flexible metal casing. The black hot and white neutral wires are paper-wrapped; there will also be a green ground wire or a bare ground wire. BX flexes to turn easily around corners. It is good for use in dry indoor locations, especially in areas where wires need protection from nails for later carpentry or decorating projects.

Plastic-coated Cable. This cable is enclosed in a plastic sheath. All three wires inside are paper-wrapped. It is very flexible. The size of the wire is stamped along the outside of the cable, as are designations for use areas. "T" cable adapts well to a variety of temperatures. "TW" is used in damp settings. "NM" cable is for use indoors in dry settings.

Conduit. In homes with very thin walls, cable is usually enclosed in galvanized steel pipe called thin-walled conduit. In some areas, conduit is required when more than 3 feet of BX cable is exposed in a basement. When using conduit, run insulated single-conductor wires — black, white and green — through the pipes. Do not try to run plastic or BX cable through a conduit. A conduit can hold a number of cables. It comes in a variety of diameters and in 10-foot lengths. Couplings and joint pieces make it adaptable to most settings.

Wire Types: Solid or Stranded. The wire in the cables of circuits is solid.

However, wire in light fixtures is made up of several strands twisted about each other. The distinction is important when splicing two wires together.

Safety System

Before starting any project, you must turn off the circuit with which you will be working. To do this you will go to the service box, where the main service lines of the household divide into circuits. There you will find either fuses or circuit breakers. Remove the fuse, or switch off the circuit breaker. Never change any switch, fixture or outlet without first breaking the circuit that feeds it.

A circuit breaker has toggle switches to activate or deactivate circuits.

A fuse service entry contains plug and cartridge fuses that are replaced when they blow out.

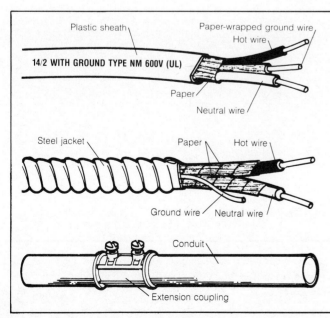

14/2 WITH GROUND TYPE NM 600V (UL)

Plastic sheath
Paper-wrapped ground wire
Hot wire
Paper
Neutral wire

Steel jacket
Paper
Hot wire
Ground wire
Neutral wire

Conduit
Extension coupling

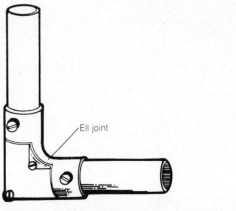

Ell joint

On the plastic-sheathed cable, markings indicate whether or not the cable has a ground wire, wire size, no. of conductors, and the type of cable. The steel-encased cable is recommended for areas where wires need more protection — such as within a wall where nails may penetrate. Conduit found within a home is usually thin-walled. Lengths are joined with connectors.

Although fuses and circuit breakers function differently, both serve the same purpose — to limit current flowing through a given circuit. A fuse is a screw-in device constructed with a ribbon of metal that has a low melting point. If the current exceeds the ampere rating of the fuse, the metal ribbon melts and opens the circuit. For example, a 15 amp fuse will blow out when the current exceeds 15 amps. To restore service to circuit you must replace the fuse. A circuit breaker performs the same function when its amp rating is exceeded. But it doesn't have to be replaced because its element functions to trip a switch. When the element cools off, the switch can be turned on again.

The amp rating of a fuse or circuit breaker is directly related to the size of the wire in the circuit cable. Together they determine the maximum amount of current allowed to flow in each circuit. The

circuits for living and sleeping areas typically are wired with No. 14 copper wire to provide a maximum of 15 amperes. The circuits for the kitchen (and possibly a garage or workshop) are wired with a slightly larger copper wire (No. 12) to provide a maximum of 20 amperes for each circuit. The smallest wire — for the doorbell or the thermostat — is No. 18 copper, which can carry about 6 amperes.

LARGER WIRE AMPERAGE RATINGS (75°C)

Size (Copper)	Rating
*No. 10 wire	30 amp max
No. 8 wire	45 amp max
No. 6 wire	65 amp max
No. 4 wire	85 amp max

*This is based on the 1978 National Electric Code for insulated copper wire.

If a circuit blows its fuse or circuit breaker trips, the device is responding to a current load that the wire cannot safely tolerate. Although the fuse or circuit breaker opening can be caused by an electrical storm, it typically is due to an overload on the circuit or to a short circuit.

Aluminum Wiring. In some homes the wires in the circuit cable are aluminum rather than copper. If that is true in your case, you should not attempt to do wiring projects yourself. Aluminum wire is difficult to work with. It presents special problems that should be dealt with by a licensed electrician.

Overloads

Appliances pull the power they need to function correctly. As more devices are switched on, the combined resistance in a circuit decreases and the flow of the current increases. When the black and white

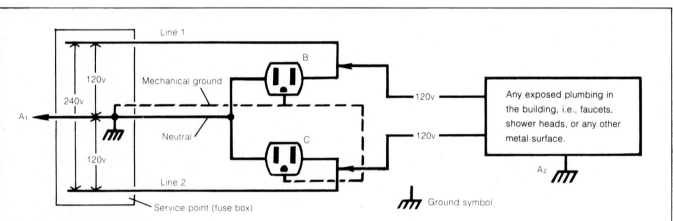

GROUNDING BASICS
Point A connects to a metal rod driven into the earth at the service entrance to the building or to a water pipe in older buildings. The earth, or water pipes which are also underground before they enter the building, will conduct electrical current. Points A and A₂ are common. A human being connected between "B" or "C" to any exposed plumbing will close a circuit and can receive an electrical shock. A human being can be connected to points B or C in several ways. For example:

1 If an appliance with exposed metal also has a 2-wire plug that is defective. Point B or C is making contact with the exposed metal surface; if a person touches the exposed metal he is subject to a shock.

2 The same as above, but with a 3-wire plug using a 3-to-2-wire adapter when the ground wire has been left unconnected.

3 Many cable model radios may have one side of the 2-wire plug connected to the metal chassis. Never place an item like this within reach of any plumbing (if you want to stay alive). Here is a scenario: While standing in the shower, you reach out to change the station on the radio. In the case given, when one side of the 2-wire plug is connected to the metal chassis, you can receive an electrical shock and be unable to release your grasp on the radio. This type of shock would probably be fatal.

What is an electrical shock? Shocks are caused by current flowing through the human body. A fraction of one ampere (a measure of the amount of current) can kill you. If you are not kicked free by the initial shock, your muscles may contract and

cause your hand to freeze around the appliance or conductor which you are touching — someone else would have to free you by using an insulated object (such as a wooden chair or a newspaper) to push you away or by turning off the current. These are the reasons why the integrity of the mechanical ground must be carried through to any device that has exposed metal. The third wire mechanical ground is internally hard-wired to the exposed metal of the appliance. In this way, if points B or C come in contact with the exposed surface, a fuse will blow, or sparks will fly. It must be emphasized that by lifting the mechanical ground with three-prong to two prong adapters, the shock protection of the mechanical ground is also suspended.

Adapter safety. When discussing adapters, many owners' manuals, books, and references, indicate that you can use a two-prong adapter if you connect its third wire or metal tab to the center screw which holds the faceplate to the wall outlet box. The center screw that holds the faceplate on an outlet receptacle is NOT ALWAYS grounded. Yet these publications advise connecting the pig-tail ground lead from the adapter to this screw to ground it. Since the nut for this screw in 2-wire outlets is embedded in the plastic of the receptacle and is not connected to anything, proper connection will require you to remove the faceplate and to check for a ground wire. Then secure the adapter's ground wire under the screw that secures the outlet to the metal box. If the metal box is properly grounded, the adapter's ground will then serve its purpose.

will also tighten around the terminal. The other end is then connected under the screw at the back of box in a similar manner.

Middle-of-the-run Junction. This hookup is more complicated than the first. In addition to the materials listed above, you will need a wire nut and electrician's tape.

Cut two pieces of new wire, each four inches long. From one end of each, strip ½ inch of insulation. From the other end of each, strip 1 inch of insulation. Turn loops in the ½-inch ends. You now have Jumper #1 and Jumper #2.

Attach the looped end of Jumper #1 to the green screw of the outlet. Now loosen the screw at the back of the junction box

and detach the two ground wires there. Fasten the looped end of Jumper #2 to the screw. Only Jumper #2 should be connected to the junction box itself. You now must splice together four ground wires — Jumper #1, Jumper #2 and the ground wires from the two cables that enter the junction box.

Splicing procedure depends on the type of wires involved. As noted earlier, most house wiring is solid, but wiring for light fixtures is stranded. If the wires are solid, keep wire ends pointing in the same direction, and twist them around each other with a pliers. If the wires are stranded, individually twist the end of each wire together very tightly. Then hold the ends together, facing the same direction, and

twist all the wires together. If there are both solid and stranded wires, strip off about one-half inch of insulation from the end of the stranded wire in addition to the one inch already removed (you will now have 1½ inches of stripped wire). Twist it so it is packed as solidly as possible; then wind it around the solid wire in a spiral pattern.

Once the wires have been joined, cover them with what is called a wire nut. This is a plastic cap lined with threaded metal. It screws on over the splice. Cover the entire splice and nut with electrician's tape so the nut cannot jar loose. Do not just twist the ends together and cover with electrician's tape. This will not meet today's codes.

Two-wire-cable Junction. In a two-wire cable there is no independent ground wire. Instead, metal wrapping on the cable acts as a built-in ground. To add the ground for your outlet, cut a 6-inch piece of new wire and strip a half-inch of insulation from each end. Create a loop in one end, and fasten it to the green screw on the outlet. Then, using a machine screw, fasten the other end to the back of the junction box.

Whichever hookup you have utilized, you now are ready to attach the hot black wires to the brass screws and the white neutral wires to the silver screws of the new outlet. Fasten the outlet to the junction box and re-attach the face plate.

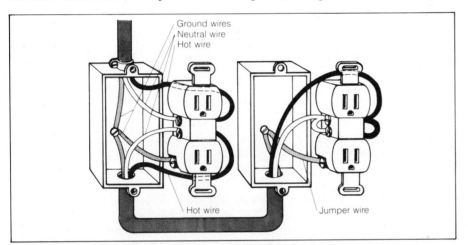

In an outlet, ground wires fasten to the outlet and the junction box for a continuous ground. At right is "end of the line" outlet; at left is "middle of the run."

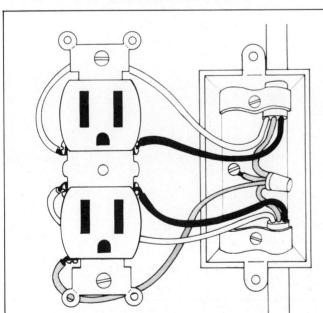

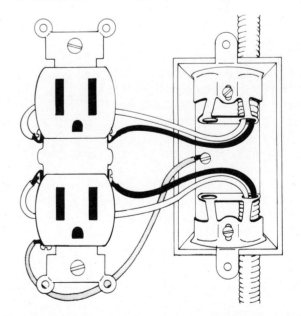

For 120-volt middle-of-run receptacle (at left) using plastic cable, bring in 2 cables. Wire cap connects jumpers to ground wires. Black wires attach to brass terminals; white wires to silver terminals.

For middle-of-run 120-volt receptacle using armored cable (at right), black wires connect to brass terminals, white wires to silver terminals. Jumper wire goes from box back, then to green terminal.

Special Outlets

All of us are familiar with the standard two- or four-outlet receptacles. However, specialized outlets can prove most useful in a kitchen.

Special Location Outlets. If your kitchen dining table is well away from the wall, plan for a floor-outlet receptacle. These have special covers that protect the outlet when it is not in use and prevent dust and other foreign material from entering the openings. Also available are wall outlets whose built-in supports hold up a clock and conceal the entire cord.

Outlets with Use Indicators. Most electrical heating and cooking appliances cycle on and off, rather than running constantly. Some, such as deep-fat fryers, have a small light that turns on when the appliance is using power, and turns off when it is not. For cycling appliances that do not have this convenience you can install an outlet with its own light to fulfill this function.

Metallic Multi-outlet Raceways. If you believe that the number of circuits in your kitchen at the present time is adequate, but you still would like more outlets, you can either extend an existing circuit by adding more cable through the walls of the kitchen or you can utilize a metallic multi-outlet raceway. A raceway also extends an existing circuit, but the added cable runs through a metal sheath fastened along the outside of the wall. It can contain receptacles, switches and even light fixtures. You can install it directly above the baseboard, above or below wall cabinets or shelves, or above a low backsplash. Raceways are grounded. However, do not run one through a wall or near ovens or surface burners. If you have baseboard heat in the kitchen, add a wood spacer strip over the baseboard and attach the raceway above the strip.

A raceway's power source is an already-existing outlet. As a result, the strip does not carry more current than is available in the circuit to which it is attached. It does not add extra current. If you are uncertain about the load to which you are subjecting the circuit, see the earlier chart of appliance wattage demands.

Extension Cords. Although it may seem simpler to buy extension cords rather than install a multi-circuit raceway, extension cords can be a hazard in the kitchen or any other room in the house. Few homeowners check to see that their extension cords have the appropriate wiring capacity and insulation necessary for the circuit and the appliances they connect. If you do use an extension cord, it should always be of the same type or have a larger capacity than the original cord attached to the mechanism. Never use an extension cord as a permanent attachment. Even if all cautions are rigorously followed, two hazards remain: (1) someone could trip over the cord and seriously injure himself; (2) the cord in time becomes frayed and thus dangerous.

Extending an Existing Circuit

If you do not want to install a multi-circuit metal raceway but still feel you need more outlets, the alternative is to extend an existing circuit. You also will have to do this if you wish to take advantage of special outlets. Remember that you still are not increasing the amount of available current in a circuit, so you will have to be careful that the circuit will not become overloaded as a result of your work. Check local building codes before you begin. Codes may dictate the kind of

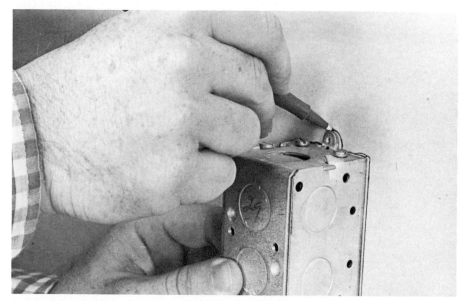

A new junction box fastens to a framing member — stud, joist or rafter. Locate that beam; then trace the junction box outline over the spot where the outlet or switch will be.

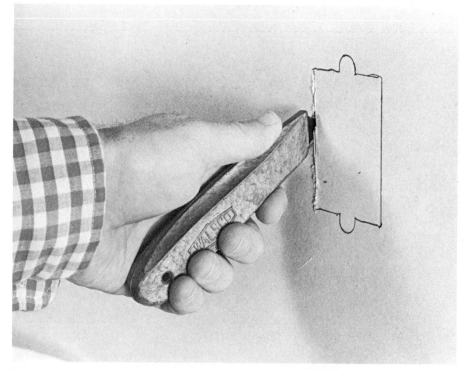

Cut the junction box opening in wallboard with a razor knife. A lath and plaster wall calls for a razor knife and a single blade hacksaw. An accurate cut eases later alignment.

cable you can use in a kitchen area. Some communities' codes will not allow circuits to be extended, stating instead that the only way to increase the number of outlets is to add new circuits. (If the latter is true, you should have a professional solve your problem.)

There are three basic steps to extending a circuit. First, decide where you want the new junction box and find the existing box nearest to that spot. Then you "fish" the new cable from the existing outlet or fixture to the new location. Finally, you splice one end of the new cable to the old cable and the other end to the outlet in the new junction box. Never splice old and new cable together in any location other than an existing junction box or fixture.

Step One: Creating The New Outlet. Your new outlet can go in any location you desire, with one stipulation. It must be located next to a rafter, stud or joist to which you can attach the junction box. The following discussion refers to studs, but the procedure is the same for finding joists and rafters too. The hunt for the stud requires a ⅛ inch drill bit, an 8-inch piece of coat hanger bent at a right angle in the center, and spackling compound.

Mark the spot where you want the new outlet, and drill through the wall. If you hit a stud, make another hole about 6 inches to the left or right of the original one and use the second hole as your outlet location. If the bit passes through the wall, insert the coat hanger up to the bend. Then twirl the coat hanger wire around in a complete circle. If you hit no obstacles, you have found an appropriate location. If you still hit something — either the stud or possibly plumbing pipe — make another hole about two inches farther away; test again. Assuming that you now have your outlet position, patch all holes except the last with spackling compound. The final hole will sit in about the center of your junction box.

Once you have found the stud, select the size junction box you want, given the number of outlets you desire. Trace the outline of the box onto the wall where the new outlet will go. If your wall is gypsum wallboard, cut around the outline with a razor knife. For lath and plaster, use a single-blade hacksaw. Careful work now will make later alignment easier.

Step Two: Which Existing Junction Box Should You Use? Your primary consideration here is to select the junction box closest to your new outlet. The second consideration is ease of installation — some junction boxes will be easier to work with than others. Your third consideration will be finding the route that involves the least amount of damage to the ceilings and walls. The best routes are those that run parallel to the joists of an unfinished basement or attic. However, one cannot always take advantage of such paths.

Outlets. The easiest place to attach your new cable is to an end-of-line outlet, as long as it is not controlled by a switch. (If it is, once the switch to the outlet is off, no power will go to your new outlet either.) As explained earlier, an end-of-line outlet will have only one cable entering the box.

If the outlet is at the middle of the line, two cables will enter the junction box. Since you will be adding to the number of wires and splices in the box, you may have to add another box onto the existing box. This is called ganging the box. Junction boxes are easy to expand (gang). Take two boxes. On the first one, locate the screw at the top. Loosen it so you can remove the right side panel. On the second box, loosen the screw at the bottom and remove the left side panel. Each screw has a flange right beneath it. This device will hold a corresponding notch on the partner box. Fit the two boxes together and tighten the screws. The outlet can now hold twice as much wiring as before.

Switches. You can extend the circuit from a middle-of-a-run switch. This switch will have a cable both at the bottom and the top of its junction box. If the box is small, it may have to be ganged just like an outlet.

Ceiling Fixtures. You can attach the cable to a ceiling fixture only if it has middle-of-run wiring. The number of cables running to it, however, will not necessarily tell you whether it is end-of-the-run or middle-of-the run. If the fixture connects to more than one switch, your outlet will receive power only when a particular switch to the fixture is on.

Coming from the fixture itself will be a black and a white wire. If these both attach to the same cable, the fixture is at the end of the run. If the black wire attaches to one cable into the fixture's junction box, and the white wire attaches to another cable, the fixture is at the middle of the run. Note: some ceiling boxes will have recoded wires. A wire will be white, but near its terminal or splice there will be black paint or electrician's tape. This wire is now a hot wire, having been recoded black.

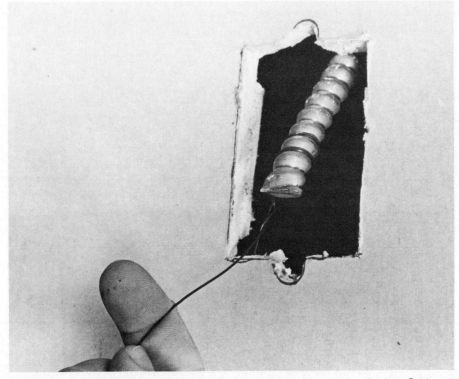

Use fishtape to pull BX or plastic-sheathed cable to the opening for a new junction box. Cable can originate at a nearby switch, outlet or ceiling fixture (codes permitting).

Main Junction Boxes. Below the floor of your home (probably in more than one location) in the vicinity of your kitchen will be a main junction box. Cable from one or more circuits will route through this box. You can attach new cable into this box, but be sure it connects to the correct circuit.

Step Three: Fishing the Cable.

Equipment List. Although some fishing routes are more complicated than others, the basic list of equipment is as follows: the required amount of cable; two electricians's fishhook tapes; screwdriver; drill, $^1/_{16}$ inch bit, $^3/_4$ inch spade bit; hammer and punch; electrician's tape; metal snippers (if cable is plastic); cable staples. To estimate the amount of cable you need, figure the distance the new cable must travel. Add 8 inches at both ends for connections to the boxes. Then add 20%, since cable will never lay perfectly flat.

Fishing Procedure, Hooking up through the Basement, Cable Parallel to Joists. This procedure begins with the cable already in the basement and a fishtape on both floors. The objective is to reach down into the basement and draw one end of the new cable up to the old outlet and the other end of the new cable up to the new outlet. Directly below the existing box, in the molding of the baseboard, bore a $^1/_{16}$ inch position hole. (You may also drill through the floor, if you prefer.) Go down into the basement, find the position hole, and mark a direct line from it to

the 2x4 bottom plate of the wall. This intersection should be directly below the existing box. Drill through the 2x4 plate, using a $^3/_4$ inch spade bit. You now have a channel between the basement and the inside of the upstairs wall.

Remove the faceplate and the existing receptacle. Using a nailset or a punch and a hammer, push out one of the U-shaped insets (a knockout hole) at the rear of the bottom of the receptacle. This must be broken off completely. To do this, make a loop of coathanger wire. Use this to wiggle the inset back and forth until it breaks off. Insert a fishtape through the opening from the upstairs. Have a helper in the basement push a second fishtape up from the basement, through the platehole. Hook the two together. Draw the upstairs fishtape down to the basement.

After unhooking the two tapes, remove 3 inches of your cable's sheathing and wire insulation. Loop the wires around the fishtape hook that you pulled down from the upstairs. Tape firmly with electrician's tape.

Pull the upstairs fishtape back up, with a helper feeding the cable until it emerges from the box. Unhook the tape from the cable end; then remove 8 inches of cable-end sheathing. Using an internal clamp, attach the cable's sheathing end to the box. The clamp has an adapter for metal-sheathed cable. For plastic-sheathed cable you will have to use metal cutters to remove the metal strip containing the two loops that extend down from

the solid section of the clamp. The clamp tightens onto the unstripped section of cable, not onto the wires. Screw the clamp down tightly.

Extend the cable across the basement ceiling. Use cable staples to attach it to the joist, stapling every 4 feet — or at the intervals specified by local codes. Do not pierce or damage the sheathing of the cable when you apply the staples. Now repeat the fishing procedure to draw up the other end of the cable.

Hooking Up through the Basement, Cable at Right Angles to the Joists. If the cable is to run at right angles to the joists, the installation process depends upon the type of cable you use.

Plastic-sheathed cable runs through holes drilled in the center of the joists with a $^3/_4$ inch spade bit. Drill the holes first; then run the cable through. Fish one end to the old outlet, the other to the new.

BX cable cannot be exposed for more than three feet in an open basement. For greater distances, you must use conduit. Here is an overview of the final hookup. BX cable will run from the existing out-

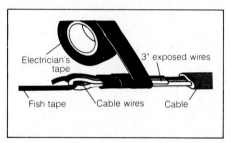

Pull tape through hole in bottom plate; unhook. Remove 3 inches of sheathing from cable end. Strip insulation from wires; loop wires through hook. Firmly tape wires and hook.

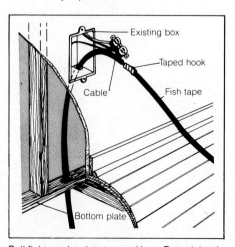

Pull fishtape back to tapped box. Detach hook; strip another 8 inches from cable end. With internal clamp fasten sheathed cable edge to box. Fasten cable every 4 feet along joists, using cable staples. Fish cable to new box; attach. Mount new box.

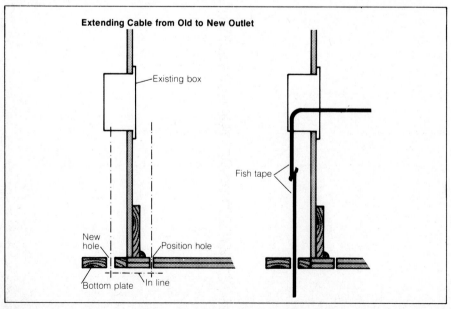

Extending Cable from Old to New Outlet

Bore $^1/_{15}$ inch position hole into floor below existing box. Following a line over to bottom plate, drill through bottom plate with $^3/_4$ inch spade bit. Repeat to bore hole in plate below new location. Pull receptacle out of existing box. Push fishtape in; hook to second tape.

let, down through the plate and across the basement ceiling for a distance of no more than three feet. (It is best if you make the ceiling section of BX as short as possible; preferably, it should end before the first intervening joist.) Then it will attach to a junction box fastened to the basement ceiling. Conduit will run from the junction box to a second junction box near the location of the new outlet. (This conduit can hang below the joists or run through them.) From the second junction box, BX cable will complete the run to the location of the new outlet. Like the first BX section, this BX cannot extend more than three feet across the basement ceiling.

Measure the space between the existing outlet and the first basement junction box, then the space between the new outlet and the second junction box. Add 12 inches to each figure. The totals will tell you how much BX you need. Then measure the distance that the conduit will travel; add 12 inches to that figure. The total will equal the amount of single conductor wire (black, white, and green) you will need. You will also need 2 junction boxes, wire caps, electrician's tape, and the conduit itself.

Install the junction boxes and the conduit first and fish the single conductor wires through. If the BX will pass through any joists, drill the opening(s) with the ¾" spade bit. Then fish the BX from the basement to the upstairs on both sides. Connect the basement ends to the junction boxes; splice the black wires together with wire caps. Do the same with the white wires and the green wires. Then fasten the BX cables to the old and new junction boxes.

Hooking up through a Wall to Another

Outlet. If you cannot work beneath the floor but must go through the wall, at each stud location you cut a rectangle in the wallboard that is at least 1 inch high, and extends 1 inch beyond either side of the stud. (Remember that studs are equally spaced, usually 16 inches apart.) Drill a hole through the center of each stud with the ¾ inch spade bit. Insert one fishtape through the U-shaped knockout in the existing box. Insert the second fishtape through the closest stud opening to catch the first fishtape and pull the end through. Fasten the cable to the free end of the first fishtape and draw the cable through the box and the stud. Pull the cable through the other studs to the new location.

Hooking up through the Wall to a New Ceiling Fixture. It is possible to extend your circuit from an existing outlet to a new ceiling fixture. But remember that unless the outlet is already controlled by a switch, the fixture will always be on. If the outlet is not switch controlled, you must add a new switch, then continue the new line to the new ceiling fixture.

If you decide to extend such a circuit, there are a few basics to keep in mind. The ceiling fixture must be placed between the joists, not on them. The cable in the ceiling must run parallel to the joists, not at a right angle to them. The cable will run straight down through the wall, then over to the existing outlet. Thus, part of your preparation will involve cutting through the wall, as described above, and cutting other access openings. The fishing process itself divides into three steps: up the wall to the ceiling; across the ceiling, moving from the new fixture to the wall; near the baseboard, from the wall over to the existing outlet.

To prepare the ceiling and the wall, first cut the hole for the new fixture. Following the joists, locate the place on the ceiling where the cable will turn to come down the wall. At this corner on the ceiling, draw a rectangle 2 inches long and 1 inch wide; on the wall, draw a rectangle 4 inches long and 1 inch wide. Cut away the ceiling and wall rectangles. The supporting boards behind form the top plate, and you have just cut "plate holes." If the wallboard is less than ½ inch thick, you will need to chisel a groove to hold the cable to the plates. Use a keyhole saw to make two cuts that are ¾ inch apart. Then chisel out the wood between the cuts.

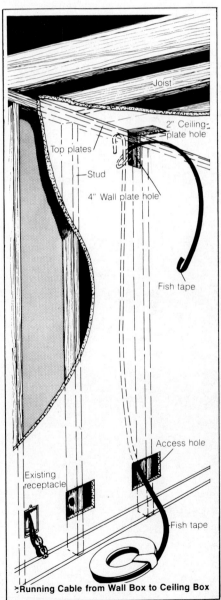

Running Cable from Wall Box to Ceiling Box

Cut ceiling opening. At top of wall, midway between joists, cut ceiling plate and access holes to bring cable in line with existing box. Push fishtape up to plate hole. Hook and fishtape; pull through. Disconnect; tape hook to cable. Draw behind wall to access hole.

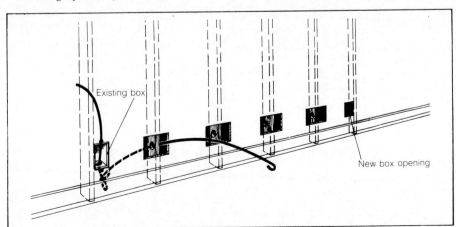

For route behind wall, first expose studs. In wallboard, cut 1-inch-high rectangle 1 inch beyond each side of stud. In plaster, cut with chisel and saw out underlying lath. Drill holes in stud centers. Remove knockout in existing box; use fishtapes to pull cable through.

Now cut a wall access hole near the baseboard. This should be straight down from the ceiling plate hole and straight across from the new outlet. Push the first

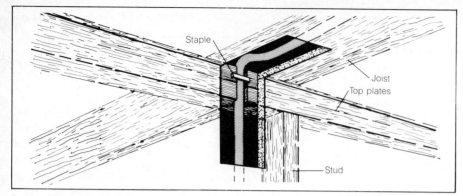

For a wall less than ½ inch thick, cut a channel in the top plates. Use keyhole saw for 2 parallel vertical cuts ½ inch deep, ¾ inch apart. Chisel wood out between cuts. Staple cable below top plate edges. For thicker wall, staple cable to top plates. Then patch.

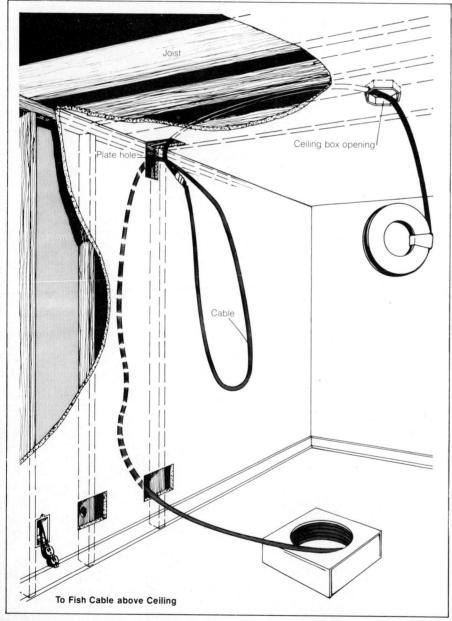

To Fish Cable above Ceiling

Push fishtape into ceiling box opening. Guide between joists to just beyond ceiling plate hole. Use short, 2nd fishtape to pull first through hole. Disconnect tapes; attach stripped cable wires to first fishtape. Feed cable into ceiling plate hole; draw to new box opening.

fishtape through the access hole up to the top plates. Insert the second fishtape through the wall plate hole and catch the first fishtape. Draw it through; fasten the cable to it, and then draw one end of the cable back down to the access hole. Detach the cable.

Move to the fixture hole. Insert the first fishtape and push it across the ceiling toward the ceiling plate hole. Insert the second fishtape through the ceiling plate hole. Catch the first fishtape and draw it through the ceiling plate hole. Attach the end of the cable which you have just fished up the wall to this first fishtape and draw the cable across to the ceiling fixture hole.

Finally, at the lower wall access hole, fish the cable from the access hole to the old outlet. Staple the cable to the top plates, or seat it into the chiseled space and then staple it.

If you must install a switch as well as a fixture, first cut the opening in the wall for the switch, and run the cable to it, using the fishtape procedure given above. Then you run another cable from the new ceiling fixture to the switch.

Step Four: New Cable to Existing Circuit. Almost every type of new cable installation will require at least one wire splice to fasten the old cable to the new. If you are uncertain about the acceptable method of splicing electrical wire, see the section on adding a new ground wire under "Outlets with Openings for Grounded Appliances" (earlier in this chapter). Any other method is not only unacceptable according to code, but creates a dangerous fire or shock hazard.

End-of-run Outlet. This is the easiest hookup to complete. Attach the black wire of the new cable to the unused brass screw. The white wire goes to the unused silver-colored screw. With a wire cap, splice the green ground wires together.

Middle-of-run Outlet. This hookup requires two new jumper wires — one black and one white — cut four inches long and three wire nuts. Select a matching pair of black and white wires on the outlet. Detach these from their terminals. Splice together three wires: the black wire you just loosened, the black wire from your new cable and one end of a black jumper wire. Attach the free end of the black jumper wire to the brass terminal on the outlet. Now splice the two neutral cable wires and a white jumper. Fasten the

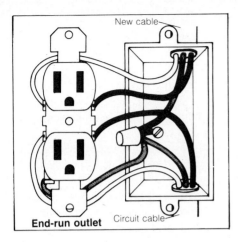

End-run outlet

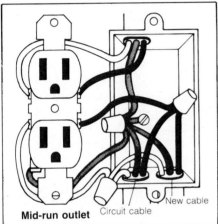

Mid-run outlet

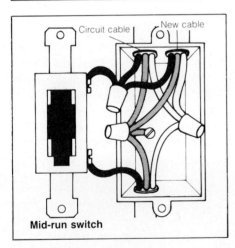

Mid-run switch

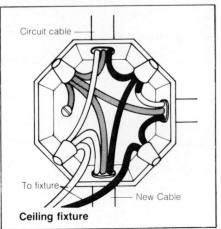

Ceiling fixture

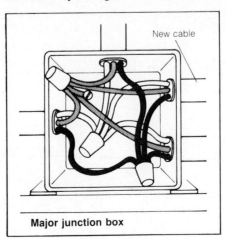

Major junction box

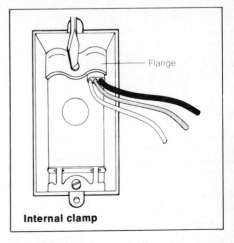

Internal clamp

white jumper to the silver-colored screw. Finally splice the new ground wires together. The hookup is complete.

Middle-of-the-run Switch. There are two sets of existing cable here. One set comes from the service box; the other runs to the fixture or outlet that the switch controls. Before you can hook up the new cable you must find out which set comes from the service box. (Otherwise, your new outlet will have power only when the switch is on.)

To determine which cable comes from the service box, use the voltage tester. First, disconnect the wires to the switch. Then, and only then, have an assistant turn on the circuit at the service box. Put one probe of the voltage tester against the metal junction box. With the other probe, touch one of the exposed black wires. If it is the live source (the one coming from the service box), the bulb of the voltage tester will light. If the bulb does not light, test the other black wires. The one that lights the bulb is the one you want. Then turn off the circuit again before you continue.

Now you must have two 4-inch-long jumper wires — one black and one green. Splice together the black wire that lit the bulb, the new cable's black wire and the black jumper. Fasten the black jumper to the brass terminal on the switch. Fasten the black wire that didn't light the bulb to the other terminal of switch. Splice together the green wires with one end of the green jumper, and secure the other end of green jumper under the screw at the back of the box. Finally, splice the three white wires.

Middle-of-run Ceiling Fixture. Again you must find which of the black wires in the existing cables is live and is not controlled by the light switch. This black

wire comes from the service box. Turn off the circuit at the service box. In the fixture will be at least two splices that connect black wires. The black wire coming from the service box will not be in the splice holding the black wire coming from the light fixture. Look for the former. Dismantle this splice and separate the wires so the bare ends do not touch anything. Turn on the circuit at the fuse box and use the voltage tester. The black wire that turns on the test light is the one to connect to the black wire of the new cable. Turn off the circuit. Splice together the black wire from the new cable and all black wires contained in the original splice. With the circuit still off, take apart the white wire splice and add the white wire from the new cable. Last, splice all green wires and one end of a 1½-2" green jumper. Fasten the other end of the green jumper under the box screw.

Major Junction Box. Several circuits may pass through this junction box. Have a helper turn off the circuits one by one, as you use the voltage tester to determine which cable controls the circuit you wish to tap.

Then splice together the wires — black to black, white to white, and ground to ground.

Step Five: Installing the New Outlet. There are two steps to this process: (1) fasten the cable to the junction box; (2) fasten the box to the stud in the wall.

Installing an Internal Clamp. The method used for internal clamps was discussed earlier. Basically, you bring the cable through one of the U-shaped knockouts in the junction box. Then screw down the internal clamp in the box over the sheathing of the cable.

Installing a 2-Piece Clamp. Two-part clamps attach the cable to the box through one of the round knockout holes. The larger section of the clamp is applied to the cable. The cable then passes into the box, where the second section of clamp, a nutlike fastener, tightens and holds the cable in place. Strip off about 6 inches of the outer sheathing from the cable. Slip the larger piece of the connector over the wires and the sheath. The threaded end of the connector faces the same direction as the stripped wires. The sheathing should not extend beyond the threading. Firmly tighten the screws on each side of the round knockout opening, along with the threading. Slip the nut over the wires and tighten it over the threading, using a screwdriver.

The cut metal edge of BX cable can cut or chafe through the insulation on the wires that extend from it. Therefore, if you are using BX cable you must install a standard plastic insulator that slips over the wires and sits between them and the sharp end of the metal sheathing. Do this *before* clamping the BX or installing a BX connector over the sheathing.

Step Six: Attaching the Junction Box. Once the wiring has been completed, attach the junction box to the stud with either nails or screws. (Screws may require the use of an offset screwdriver.) Some boxes also require the insertion of a bracket before the outlet can be installed. Now attach the new outlet.

Step Seven: Checking the Circuit. To check your work, you need what is called a continuity tester. This device consists of a pencil-like probe containing a small bat-

tery and bulb, and an attached cord ending with an alligator clip. With the circuit off, attach the clip to the terminal with the black wire. Touch the white wire terminal with the probe, and finally the metal box. At no time should the bulb light up. If it does, there is a short circuit in the new cable. Go back and check for bare wires that are touching, loose connections, or frayed insulation. If you cannot find anything, call an electrician.

If the bulb does not light, then test with the power on, this time using the voltage tester. Insert the probes in the respective slots of a given outlet. The light should light. If it does not, turn off the circuit and check the hookups.

If the circuit tests out perfectly, turn off the power and repair any holes in the walls or ceilings.

Installing a Range Hood

Some people replace an old hood with a new one because they desire one more modern. Others install a new hood whose design and style matches their new kitchen cabinets. Once you have learned to extend a circuit, you can complete this renovation with much less expense than if you had used a professional.

Install the hood high enough that its front edge does not impair the cook's view of the rear burners. If the depth of the hood is under 18 inches, place it no less than 56 inches above the floor. If the hood's depth is 18 inches or over, place it no less than 60 inches above the floor. You can install a ductless hood. However, if

you select a ducted one, plan as short and straight a path for the exhaust ducting as possible in order to get the best performance from the hood and to ease installation of the ductwork. In addition, ductwork should always vent outside your home. NEVER vent into an attic or unused house space; grease build-up would create both fire and health hazards.

When you select a new hood you will see that all have a "CFM" rating. The abbreviation means "cubic feet per minute," and the number preceding the abbreviation indicates the amount of air that the fan in the hood can move. Most kitchen experts feel that a rating of at least 200 CFM is required for minimum ventilation. Average sized hoods can have ratings of up to 400 or even 600 CFM. Anything rated above 400 will require larger ducting than ones with a lower rating. A barbecue fan, which often is rated as high as 1000 CFM, requires a round duct that is 10 inches in diameter. The size hood you purchase will not depend on the size of your kitchen alone. Also important are the length of the cooking tasks in a particular kitchen and the length of the ducting — a long duct will require a larger fan in order to function properly.

Replacing an Existing Hood.

Removing an Old Hood. To remove an old hood and add a new one, you will need a helper. Before removing the existing hood, turn off power to the circuit that serves it. Then disconnect the electricity that powers the exhaust fan and hood light. You probably will have to unscrew a

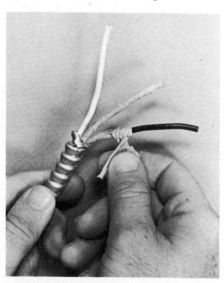

To remove BX metal casing, bend cable sharply — casing will crack. To complete removal without cutting the wires, use snips or knife. Then unwrap each wire's paper insulation.

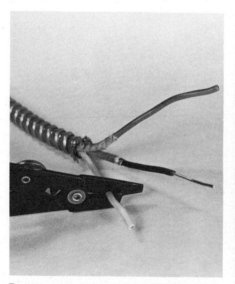

To remove plastic insulation from wires, use a wire stripper, not a knife. A notch in the stripper cuts through the insulation only. Rotate the stripper and pull off insulation.

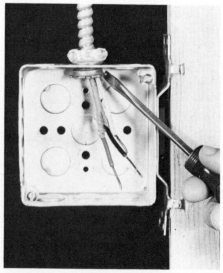

Insert a plastic protector between wires and cut metal casing. Then fasten cable to a junction box with a two-part cable connector. Tighten connector collar with a screwdriver.

metal pan covering that hides the junction box housing the electrical connections.

Use a screwdriver to loosen the terminal screws so you can remove the wires. Separate and tape the ends of the wires with electrical tape. Use plenty of tape; the wires should be completely wrapped.

Installation steps of range hoods will vary from manufacturer to manufacturer. Specific procedures are given in each manufacturer's package. However, options regarding duct planning and placement can be generalized and are presented here.

Selecting the Replacement. If you already have a ducted hood in your kitchen, you will save a great deal of time and frustration if the duct opening in the new hood is the same as (or similar to) the duct opening already in existence. If this is not possible, you may be able to use two pieces of elbow ducting to angle the channel over to the old vent. Then patch the old opening. If this procedure is not feasible, you must abandon the old duct and install an entirely new run. In fact, sometimes new ducting is the best course, especially if the old duct is too grease-laden to use safely.

If you do install a new duct, you can deal with the old duct in two ways. You can remove the old ductwork and patch the holes that remain. However, in the case of a house made with brick or aluminum siding, such repairs could prove to be prohibitive. The alternative is to screw down the damper in the exterior wall and caulk it closed securely. Then fill the duct with insulation and repair only the cabinet or wall opening.

Planning the Ductwork. Ductwork is the series of rectangular or round pipes that leads from the hood's vent to the outside of your home. It comes in several sizes and shapes to accommodate a variety of installations. Either wall or roof caps finish off the outside exit. Be sure to purchase metal rather than plastic ducting to prevent fire hazards.

Although most ducting is made of standard sheet metal, also available is flexible metal duct. Since it comes in only round duct, you will have to use a rectangular-to-round converter to use it with the hood. Flexible duct is quite easily dented or crushed, more so than conventional ducting. On the other hand, it is light and it goes around corners without requiring elbows and such.

The pathway you choose will depend upon your home's construction and the hood's location. If the stove sits against an exterior wall, the shortest path is straight out through the back of the hood. (However, once this installation is complete, be sure that the damper in the hood's duct and the one in the wall cap do not interfere with each other. If they do, either the hood exhaust will be impeded, or air will blow in from the outside. If this situation does exist, you can remove the hood damper.) Another satisfactory method is to install a short vertical pipe from the top of the hood, then angle through the wall. In most homes this duct path travels up through the cabinet or soffit above the hood, rather than through the insulation between the kitchen wall and the exterior shell.

If the hood is on an interior wall, your options depend upon home construction. Avoid extremely lengthy and twisted paths. Go straight up through the wall space to the roof, if you can. If this path is obstructed by a second story, you will have to pass the ducting through the soffit to an outside wall.

Installing the Ducting. As you work with ducting, keep one thing in mind. Although its primary purpose is to provide a passage for exhaust fumes and residue, unfortunately it sometimes also provides a passage for the flames of a grease fire. To be certain that any fire is enclosed in the metal ducting, as you connect sections of ducting together, tape the joints very securely with duct tape.

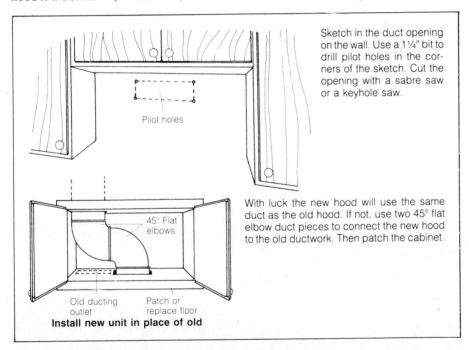

Sketch in the duct opening on the wall. Use a 1¼" bit to drill pilot holes in the corners of the sketch. Cut the opening with a sabre saw or a keyhole saw.

Pilot holes

45° Flat elbows

With luck the new hood will use the same duct as the old hood. If not, use two 45° flat elbow duct pieces to connect the new hood to the old ductwork. Then patch the cabinet.

Old ducting outlet

Patch or replace floor

Install new unit in place of old

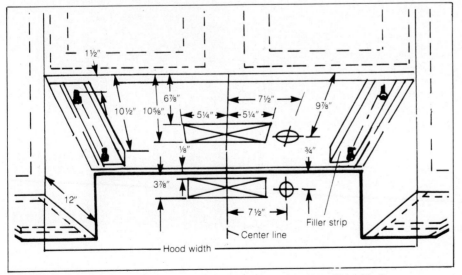

Different manufacturers' dimensions may vary, but the basic layout will be similar.

First cut the opening in the exterior of the house with a sabre saw or a keyhole saw. If you own a saw that has a blade that projects from the front, such as the Milwaukee Saws-All, your job will be much easier. This opening should be slightly larger than the ducting. (If local codes require, install casing strips around a wall opening in a wood house.) Then insert the ductwork.

The difficulties of this task will depend upon the complexity of the duct's path. A straight path will present few problems. Taping one section to the next, one at a time, lower the duct from above. If your path has a center angle, insert the section from the outside, and push the vertical section to meet it. If they meet inside a cabinet or above an unfinished attic, the junction will pose few problems. The same is true of a path through the soffit channel, provided that the soffit has not been finished off. In paths where the junction is enclosed, however, you will have to cut a small access hole at the junction point in order to tape the junction as securely as all other joints.

If the duct comes through an exterior wall, trim the duct even with the siding and attach a wall cap to the duct according to instructions. Then fasten the wall cap to the wall and caulk the opening well. If the duct comes through the roof, it should extend at least ¾ inch above the high side of the roof. Using plastic roof cement, completely seal the opening between the duct and the roof. Be generous so you prevent later water seepage. Then install the roof cap. Insert the high-side edge under the shingles and apply plastic roof cement all around the cap.

Final Hookup. The power must be off to make this connection. Fasten the cable to the hood with the connecter locknut. Now use wire nuts to splice the black cable wire to the black hood wire. Do the same with all white wires. Finally, using the green ground screw, attach the cable ground wire to the grounding bracket built into the hood. Comply with all local codes. Regulations may vary. Then replace the wiring box cover and screw. Be careful not to pinch any of the wires.

LIGHTING

Your kitchen's wiring system must be adequate not only for appliances but also for the lighting system. Assess the natural light available and then supplement with artificial light as needed. Daylight may come from traditional movable windows or stationary glass panels, from skylights or any combination of these. Artificial light may come from fluorescent or incandescent bulbs, or both. Wall switches and controls comprise a large part of the lighting plan. Consider also the colors and size of the room, as well as the needs of plants grown in the kitchen.

Natural Light

Natural light is a great energy conserver and contributes to your sense of well–being while in the kitchen. If the natural

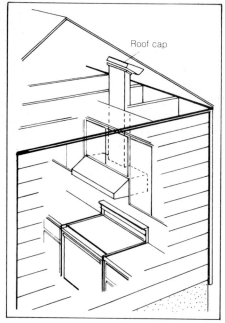

A straight duct offers least resistance to the exhaust of a hood fan. Extend the path up through the attic, then the roof. Seal finishing roof cap carefully with roofing cement.

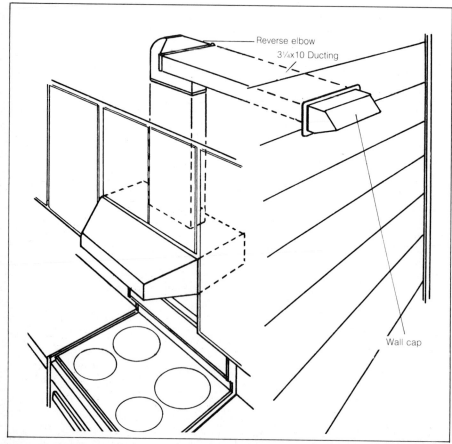

Use a reverse elbow piece to turn the duct that must go through a soffit. Then extend regular 3¼x10 pieces out through the exterior wall. Finish off the duct path with a wall cap.

The addition of a bay with over-sized windows brings in a great deal of additional light. Since the bay faces south, the windows also provide a passive heat source during the day.

light in your kitchen is inadequate, you can devise creative solutions when you remodel. The addition of a window is not particularly expensive, and many of the sizes and shapes do not require a special order.

Adding a Larger Window

If your kitchen needs more natural sunlight, you can either install a window where one has never been before, or you can replace a small one with a larger one. If you want one to provide light for a kitchen work surface, the lower sill should be from 3 to 6 inches above the work area. If the window is lower than 3 inches, it will become spattered during meal preparation; if higher, it will not illuminate the countertop.

You can place the window wherever you please. Although new windows do not have to be as wide as the old ones, they usually look better if their top edges line up with other windows in the room. Windows on the opposite walls have less need for alignment, and a large expanse of fixed glass often needs to have no obvious spatial relationship to other kitchen windows. Such might be the case when glass extends up through the normal soffit

level, a possibility that is extremely attractive when ceiling height and house construction permit.

There are the six basic steps to enlarging a window. After you select the window that you want, remove the trim, wallboard and the old window, and shore up the ceiling. You then cut the opening in the outside wall and build the "rough opening" in the studding. Finally you insert the new window and finish off the inner and outer walls. The amount of lumber required to create the rough opening will depend upon local codes on construction framing. Your local building supplier will help you determine the size and amount of lumber needed.

Materials and Tools List. You will need: new window; protective goggles; pry bar and hammer; razor knife; portable circular saw (use with caution) and carbide-tipped or flooring blade; handsaw; lumber for shoring ceiling; lumber for building "rough opening" — headers, studs, cripples, sill; shingle wedges for shoring and leveling; carpenter's level and square; finishing nails; insulation of desired thickness; staple gun; polyethylene film (at least 4 mil thick).

Window Sizes and Planning. Windows

lie between studs, which in most modern homes are on 16-inch centers. Even if you order a special window, installing it will be simpler if you design it in multiples of 16 inches. However, if you desire another size, or if your home has stud widths that are not compatible with the 16-inch norm — or if the window positioning cannot align with the present studs — you will have to add new studs before you build the rough opening — the framing for the new window. Discuss your specific situation with your building supplier. Although a ready-made window will come with an instruction sheet giving the required dimensions of the rough opening, in special cases your supplier is the best source for this information.

Step One: Removing the Existing Window. Once you have selected the window you want, draw in a sketch of its location on the inside wall so you know how many wallboard panels you must remove. Using the pry bar and hammer, remove the trim from around the old window and discard it. Then carefully remove the wall base molding and store it. Be sure you wear protective goggles when you remove the gypsumboard, and proceed with care and patience so that you

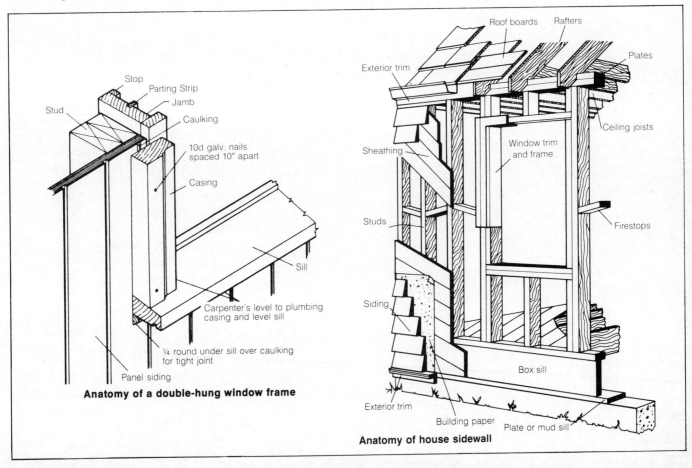

Anatomy of a double-hung window frame

Anatomy of house sidewall

will not damage a panel that the window opening will not affect. Turn off the electrical service so that you will not accidentally hit a cable and damage it — or hurt yourself. With the hammer, break out a wall section working out to the studs, but avoiding damage to the studs. Work methodically, removing chunks and pulling nails. Do not try to remove the whole panel at once. Use the razor knife to cut the gypsumboard tape at the side joints and the ceiling line. (For a more detailed discussion of wall anatomy and panel removal, see Chapter 8.)

Once the trim and panel are out, remove the old window. Cut away a section of the stool (inside still) and pull it out. You then can pull out the two remaining sections of stool since they fit into tongue-and-groove moldings in the side frames. The casing nails along the side of the window frame will look like oversize finishing nails. Pry these out. Then pry out the top (head) jamb and lift out the old window. What will remain is the old rough opening for the window.

Step Two: Cutting out the Exterior Frame. Refer to the specifications for the rough opening of the new window. Mark out the height at which you want the new sill to lie. From that line mark the position of the window's four corners. Drive nails through the sheathing and the outside wall siding. Go outside; mark the locations of the four nails. Check to be sure that the opening will be plumb and level. Then draw an outline between the nail points.

Cut along the lines using the saw and either a carbide-tipped or a flooring blade.

These two blades will withstand cutting through nails, which is inevitable here. Use the blade to notch the 2x4s; these you can cut through with the handsaw, but not until you have shored up the ceiling on the inside of the house.

Step Three: Building the Shoring. The exterior wall of your house is a load-bearing wall; that is, it supports the roof or second floor of the building. Although shoring up the ceiling is not necessary unless the window opening is to be more than 3 feet across, it is a good idea to have it before you remove any studs, especially in a two-story home.

The shoring system is a rough box, whose legs run from floor to ceiling. Use 2x8s or 2x10s cut 6 or 8 feet long. Place one on top of the other; fasten them together. Lay them parallel to the wall, about 3 feet from it. These two boards form a prop for the vertical supports. Measure the distance from the top of the second piece to the ceiling. Cut two supports to equal the distance measured minus about 1¾ to 2 inches.

Now you need to cut a length of 2x10 or 2x12 that at least equals that of the horizontal props on the floor. This will be sandwiched between the supports and the ceiling in order to protect the ceiling from gouges caused by the supports and to evenly distribute the ceiling weight between them. Lay the face of the ceiling support against the tops of the vertical supports. Move each support to about a foot in from each end of the protector and nail together. You will now need a helper. Place the open end of the vertical supports against the floor prop. Then tilt the shor-

ing structure up the ceiling itself. The vertical legs should rest on the top of the floor prop.

Now take two shingle wedges. Working at the bottom of one of the supports, drive a wedge on either side, between the top board of the floor prop and the support. Do the same for the other support. Later, as you work on the rough opening, periodically check these wedges to be sure that hammering on the wall has not loosened them. Once the framing is complete, you can remove the shoring and have more room to work.

Step Four: Creating the Rough Opening. Local codes often govern construction details for the rough opening. The process itself, however, is fairly standard. Add additional studs if one of the following conditions exists: (1) you are adding a window where there is no stud support; (2) a stud would add extra support the ceiling needs because the window is fairly wide. In either case, be sure that you allow sufficient space for construction of the rough opening. Check the width of the rough opening you have planned. It must allow for the width of the window, plus 3 inches (1½ inches for each side of the window). Now make a double header. Cut two headers to the above measure. Sandwich spacer strips between (½ inch plywood is a good choice) so that the thickness of the two is the same as a stud (3½ inches). Use three 16d nails spaced every 16 inches; nail at top, middle and bottom of the header (9 nails in all). Figure the height of the rough opening and nail the header across. Measure from the floor to the double header. Cut two short (or trimmer) studs to this measure and nail them in below the double header, to fill in at both sides of the window. Place a single header at the window's sill height. Support this with studs cut to fit. Then add cripples below the sill for support. If the double header above the window does not meet the ceiling, add cripples between the top of the double header and the ceiling. Once the framing has been completed, remove the shoring for the ceiling.

Step Five: Inserting the New Window. Many ready-made windows are designed to slip into the rough opening from the outside. Some of these come complete with exterior trim. Others require the addition of brick molding. If a self-trimmed one does not match the style of your other

Molding or casing for trimming a new or enlarged window (or for a pass-through, see Chapter 8) can be cut in a miter box for a neat, finished look and edges that meet exactly.

Ceiling

Wall

Wall

Rough box

Shoring   Shingle wedges

windows, you may decide to retrim the new one to match.

Slip the window in place and nail lightly with finishing nails. Check the inside for level and plumb. Being careful not to bow the sides of the window frame, insert shingle wedges between the window and the rough opening to correct level and plumb. To be sure the frame stays true, use a level that is at least two feet long. Slide it up and down the frame. Then check for square. Be very sure that the window is level, plumb and square to assure proper opening and closing later. Then nail with casing nails.

Step Six: Insulation. Once the window is in place, stuff insulation into the crack between the framing and the window. This can be remnants of that which you cut away when you removed the paneling. Then staple in either roll or batt insulation of the thickness best for your climate. To create a moisture barrier, staple sheets of polyethylene at least 4 mil thick over the entire wall. (Sheets thinner than 4 mil will not be impermeable to moisture.) Be sure that the sheets always end at studs and that you overlap the ends before you staple them down.

Once the insulation is in place you will be able to finish the wall. See Chapter 8 for instructions.

Replacement, the Same Size Window. The elements outside and the dampness and heat inside take their toll on the wood frame of a kitchen window. This is especially evident in older homes. In such a case you may decide to replace the window, even though you see no need to enlarge it. The steps for this process are the same as for installing a larger window, with two important exceptions.

Do not purchase your window before you have removed the wall surface. Otherwise, you will base your measurements upon that part of the frame visible to you with the wallboard and trim still in place. These measurements will be only approximations. You need exact figures if the new window is to fit the existing rough opening.

Completely remove wallboard as above. Then, *before* you remove the existing window, measure the rough opening from inside edge to inside edge of the 2x4 framing. Do not include the dimensions of the 2x4s in your figures. Then check with the local lumberyard or home center to see if the size you need is in stock. (The stock size will be ¾″ less than both the horizontal and vertical measurements of the rough opening.) It may not be — especially if the house is old — since stock sizes change over the years. If the size is not a ready-made one, your building supplier may suggest ways to alter the rough opening with extra studding. If this cannot be done, you must decide whether you want to install a larger size window, or to order one built to your particular specifications.

Artificial Light

Artificial light must meet two needs: it illuminates the room as a whole (general lighting), and it focusses on specific jobs or tasks — the most important areas for local lighting are at the sink, the food preparation center, and the range or cooktop. When the kitchen includes a dining table, local lighting should be included there. Both general and specific lighting can contribute to or detract from the mood and convenience of the kitchen.

Several factors will affect the amount of general or local light in your kitchen. One is placement of a given light fixture. Height affects the amount of space that a given light can illuminate. The higher the source of light, the wider the area it can light. A fixture installed behind a baffle — a valance or other construction used to obscure the light source — will have its light directed to a given area.

Size also affects the brightness of a given fixture. The light intensity of a single ceiling fixture of high wattage is greater than several smaller wattage bulbs, even if their wattage when added together equals that of the large one. In other words, one 150-watt bulb gives off more illumination than three 50-watt bulbs working together. As important as wattage is the lumen rating of a given bulb. Although two 150-watt bulbs use the same amount of power, they do not necessarily give off identical amounts of light intensity, which is measured in lumens. For the greatest amount of illumination, select bulbs whose ratings, given on the package, are highest.

The paint on your ceiling affects both the quantity and the quality of the light reflected down into the room from a ceiling fixture. The accompanying chart compares the reflectivity of given paint colors. Those with higher numbers reflect more; those with lower numbers reflect less. The texture of the ceiling's surface will also affect reflection capabilities. Glossy surfaces reflect the most light, but its quality is quite harsh. As a result, most people prefer the softer light quality of matte surfaces, which also reflect well.

LIGHT ABSORPTION BY COLOR

Color	Percentage
Black	1-5
Browns	5-20
Reds	5-20
Medium gray	15-30
Dark blues	5-10
Medium blues	15-20
Oranges	15-30
Medium greens	15-30
Light greens	40-50
Cream color	55-90
White	70-95

Shown are the percentages of light reflected back from various colors. The most absorbent, hottest colors are listed first, followed by the cooler colors.

If you can remove sash from frame without damage, replace it with prefabricated unit.

Repair window frame if needed. Fit new sash into frame; install as directed. When secure, caulk around sash unit and frame.

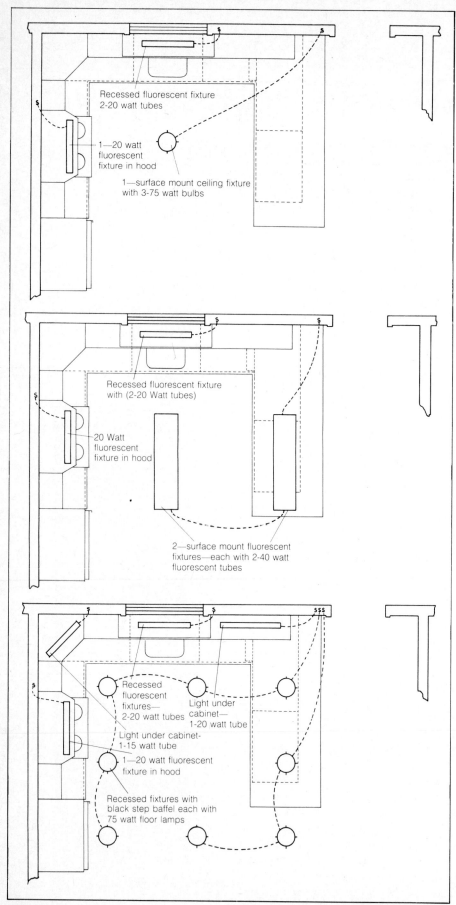

Recessed fluorescent fixture
2-20 watt tubes

1—20 watt
fluorescent
fixture in hood

1—surface mount ceiling fixture
with 3-75 watt bulbs

Recessed fluorescent fixture
with (2-20 Watt tubes)

20 Watt
fluorescent
fixture in hood

2—surface mount fluorescent
fixtures—each with 2-40 watt
fluorescent tubes

Recessed
fluorescent
fixtures—
2-20 watt tubes

Light under
cabinet—
1-20 watt tube

Light under cabinet-
1-15 watt tube

1—20 watt fluorescent
fixture in hood

Recessed fixtures with
black step baffel each with
75 watt floor lamps

Top to bottom: basic lighting layout of overhead light plus lights above sink and range; more elaborate lighting layout with fluorescent fixtures; installation with recessed incandescent fixtures for general lighting, fluorescent strips above range and sink and under cabinets.

Fluorescent vs. Incandescent. The type of light you utilize — fluorescent or incandescent — also will affect lighting quality. You need not choose only one type — many remodelers use fluorescent lights above or below wall-hung cabinets and as a ceiling fixture, but place incandescent lights as spots for specific tasks. Each type has advantages.

Fluorescent bulbs are discharge bulbs. The movement of electrical energy through a vapor or gas in the tube generates light that is even, glare-free and diffuse. A fluorescent's life span is about four to five years, during which time it uses about two-thirds less electricity than does an incandescent. The bulb does not become hot — which is an aid if lighting an area in which you have plants, as well as during hot summer months. However, its size and shape limits design possibilities. In addition, the direction of the light from a fluorescent is difficult to control.

For years one of the criticisms of fluorescents was that their colors were too cold and added a greenish-purple cast to other colors in the room. This is still true with cool white fluorescent bulbs. However, the light quality of the cool white deluxe bulb is somewhat more acceptable. Manufacturers have come out with a warm white deluxe whose color is close to that of a white incandescent bulb. This development, paired with the research on fluorescents which is now in progress, may well make this energy-saving light source a desirable option in home remodeling. If you decide to rely on fluorescents for your major light source, the American Institute of Kitchen Designers recommends that you plan for 60 to 80 watts of illumination for every 50 square feet of floor surface.

Even though incandescent bulbs are the usual source of lighting in the home, they can present problems. They create heat as well as light, although a new variety of cool beam bulbs create only two-thirds the heat of standard incandescents. They do not last as long as fluorescents, and they are more expensive to operate. On the other hand, because of their widespread use they come in more shapes and types than do fluorescents. Their light, which is warm and pleasant, is easy to direct toward a given location — one reason why incandescents are used for local lighting. If incandescents are to be your primary source of light, the American Institute of Kitchen Designers recommends you plan for 175 to 200 watts for each 50 square feet of floor area.

General Lighting

Most commonly, a central ceiling fixture supplies the general lighting in a kitchen. The fixtures may be recessed, flush with the ceiling, or suspended from a base on the ceiling. You may also select a hanging fixture designed in styles ranging from an elaborate chandelier to a simple industrial lamp. (Unless their height is adjustable, however, hanging lights provide only local lighting.)

There are several ways to increase the available light in your kitchen. One is to install a new ceiling fixture, such as a circular fluorescent fixture (a circline fluorescent). If you want to diffuse the light throughout the room, you may distribute several recessed multiple ceiling fixtures evenly throughout the room. (If you do choose this design, remember that you will have to work around the joists above the ceiling surface.) This plan does have drawbacks. Multiple sources tend to be expensive to install and operate because they require extra fixtures and supplies, and they do consume more energy than a single fixture. In addition,

because they are recessed, they do not direct any light upward. As a result, the light from the fixture is not supplemented by the bonus of reflected ceiling light.

An innovative way to handle recessed ceiling lights is to create an egg–crate louvre ceiling system. This system uses a grid of criss-crossed strips of wood, metal or plastic. The bulbs are hidden in the grid openings. You can construct this grid wide enough to create squares between the beams of a beamed ceiling, or small

enough to create single-light-size cubes.

Another way to increase general light is to transform the entire ceiling into a luminous light panel by hanging translucent panels below a grid of fluorescent lights. The panels, usually made of acrylic, allow light to pass through but are not transparent. The installation is a fairly simple one. You can buy luminous ceiling kits, or you can construct your own. If you decide on such a plan, provide 40 watts for each 12 square feet of floor area.

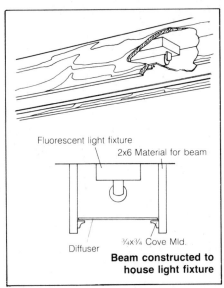

Fluorescent light fixture
2x6 Material for beam
Diffuser
¾x¾ Cove Mld.

Beam constructed to house light fixture

A fluorescent tube hidden in a beam behind diffuser uses cove moldings to hold panel.

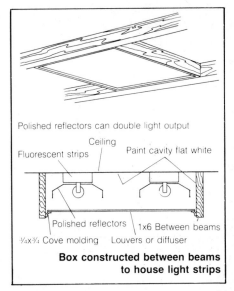

Polished reflectors can double light output
Ceiling
Fluorescent strips
Paint cavity flat white
Polished reflectors
¾x¾ Cove molding
1x6 Between beams
Louvers or diffuser

Box constructed between beams to house light strips

Polished reflectors double light output in a grid of 1x6s with louvers or diffusers.

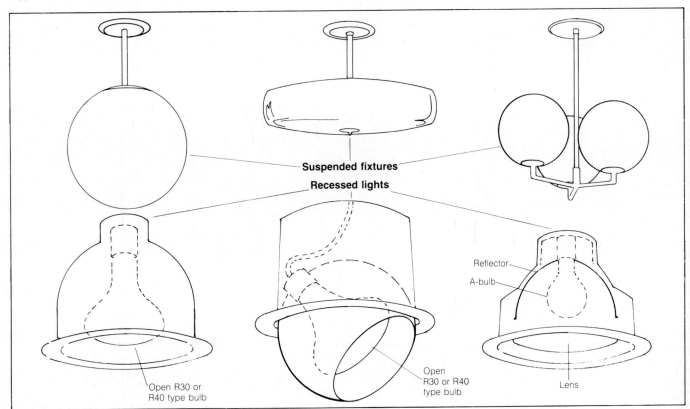

Suspended fixtures
Recessed lights
Reflector
A-bulb
Open R30 or R40 type bulb
Open R30 or R40 type bulb
Lens

Incandescent bulbs may be used in suspended or recessed ceiling fixtures. Observe local code requirements when recessing lights.

Luminous Ceiling. The best size fluorescent for use in a luminous ceiling is a 4-foot length of 40-watt rapid-start lamp. (Rapid starters also come in other lengths.) In order to determine the number of lamps you need, sketch out the dimensions of the ceiling. Plan for the lamps to lie in parallel lines that are between 18 and 24 inches apart. (The narrower space gives a more even light, but it is also more expensive.) On both ends, allow about 8 inches between the end of the line of lights and the walls. Now figure the length of the lines in feet, and divide by four. If necessary, supplement the 4-foot lamps with shorter ones to obtain the coverage you need.

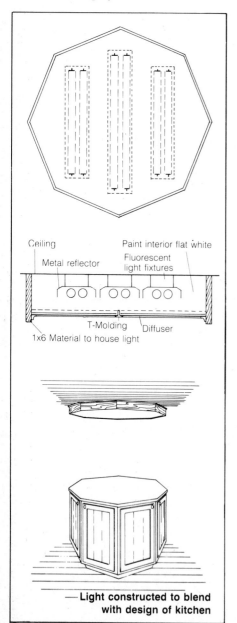

Ceiling
Metal reflector
Paint interior flat white
Fluorescent light fixtures
T-Molding
Diffuser
1x6 Material to house light

— **Light constructed to blend with design of kitchen**

Unusual shapes can be created using 1x6s and diffusers, resulting in a well-coordinated and integrated kitchen decor.

The Fluorescent Fixture. There are three parts to a fluorescent fixture. The body, called the channel, houses the wiring of the system and the ballast, which creates a momentary increase of voltage needed to light the fluorescent lamp. At both ends of the channel there are electrical knockouts. Along the bottom you will find several screwholes. At each end of the channel, protruding at right angles to it, is a metal strip, called a lamp holder. The two hold the fluorescent lamp. The second section is a protective lid for the channel. Openings are provided, through which the lamp holders fit. Once on, the lid fastens to the channel, over the wiring and ballast, with one or two screws at each end. Finally, there is the fluorescent lamp itself, which snaps into the receptacle at each end of the fixture. During most of the installation of the luminous ceiling (or of any fluorescent fixture) you will work only with the channel.

Power Source. A luminous ceiling relies upon a central, switch-controlled junction box in the ceiling. If you do not have one, you must install one. Remember to shut off the circuit that feeds the fixture before you begin work. If a box is already in place you need only remove the old fixture. Fasten a box extender to the junction box in the ceiling. (The extender will look just like the box in the ceiling, except it will have no back.) The extender will house the cable for the lines of lights. The lines themselves will be connected to each other with jumpers and then to the junction box. For a good, reflective surface, paint the ceiling with two coats of flat white ceiling paint.

Step One: Installing the Channels. To fasten the channels to the ceiling, you will need a screwdriver, screw anchors (to ensure the stability of the installation), and channel connectors to hold adjoining channels together. Then starting at either end, hold the channel against any of the lines on the ceiling. Draw in the positions of the screw holes. Continue on; remember that the channels in an individual line will butt right against each other. Install the screw anchors.

Before you secure the channels in place, remove the knockout holes at the ends of the individual channels that will butt against each other. Fasten the channels to the ceiling, butting the ends together as you go. Use a ½ inch conduit connector, which comes in two parts, a screw and a lock nut, to secure the butted ends of the two channels. Run the screw through the knockout holes of two adjoining channels; fasten with the lock nut.

Step Two: Connecting the Wiring. To connect the channels to each other you will need single conductor wires (black, white, and green) equal to at least one and one-quarter times the total planned length of your lines. You also will need wire nuts, electrician's tape, a wire cutter, a wire stripper, and two-part cable connectors to secure the cable to the junction box.

Finally you will need cable. Be sure you purchase the same kind of cable already in the circuit you are tapping. To determine the amount of cable you need, multiply the number of lines of lights you have by the distance between each line, (or 24″). Then select one end of an outer-

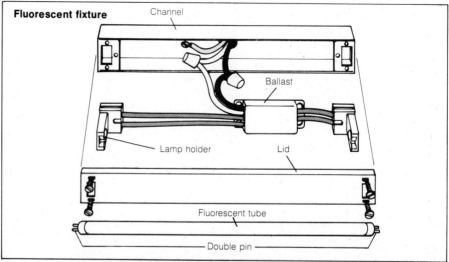

Fluorescent fixture
Channel
Ballast
Lamp holder
Lid
Fluorescent tube
Double pin

A fluorescent fixture consists of 3 parts: the body (also called a channel); the ballast; and, the fluorescent tube (also called a lamp).

most line of lights. Measure the path that a cable will have to take from that corner in order to connect with the ceiling junction box. Add this to the above total; divide by 12 to convert from inches to feet. To allow for connections and for the fact that the cable will never lie completely flat and straight, plan on using one and one-half of the total feet.

To wire the adjoining fixtures in a line of lights together, you will need to use jumper wires. Begin with the first fixture in an outermost row. Measure the distance between its black wire and the black wire in the next fixture. Cut a jumper equal to this length and splice the black wire of

channel one and the jumper wire together with a wire nut. (For splicing instructions see "Installing a Grounded Outlet," earlier in this chapter.) Do the same with the white wire and a white jumper. Take the two jumper wires and pass them through the channel connector between channel one and channel two.

Cut jumpers to connect the black and the white wires of the second channel to the third. Then splice together the black jumper from channel one, the black jumper from channel two and the black wire of channel two. Do the same with the white wires. Then pass the channel two jumpers through the channel connector to

channel three. Continue this process until the entire line of lights is connected. Do the same for all the lines.

When you have wired all the lines, you are ready to connect the lines to each other and then to the junction box. Move to the end of an outermost line. Remove the knockout at the end of the last channel. Then remove the knockout at the end of the last channel in the next line. (The two knockouts will be directly across from each other.) Cut 30 to 32 inches of cable. Strip 2 inches of sheathing from both ends of the cable, exposing the black, white, and green wires inside. Then strip about an inch of insulation from those wires.

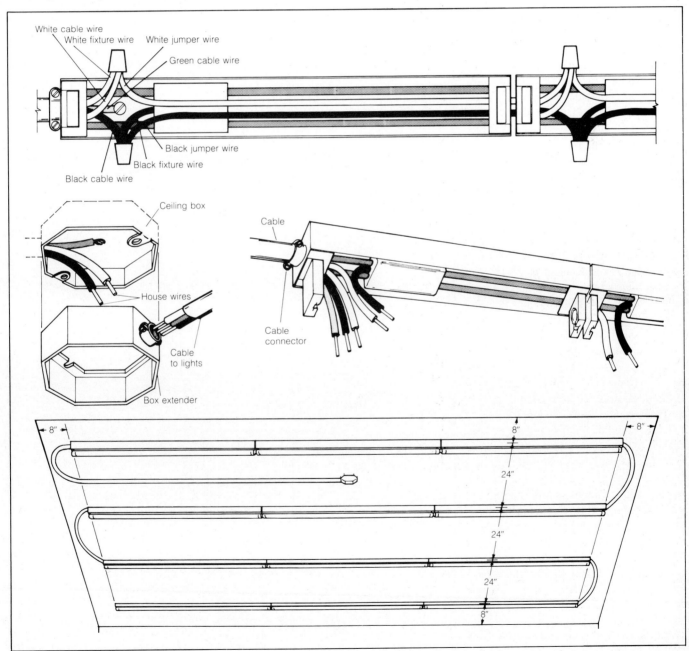

Rather than connect each individual row of lights to the central junction box, connect the rows to each other with jumper cable. The finished pattern should resemble a long zigzag. Once the lights are connected, run jumper cable from the final row to the central junction box.

Using a 2-part cable connector, fasten one end of the cable through the knockout in the outermost line. Splice black to black, and white to white. With a metal screw, fasten the green ground wire to the channel. Now move to the next line and fasten the other end of the cable to the knockout you prepared earlier. The first and second row are now connected to each other at one end.

Move to the opposite end of the second line. It must be connected to the third line, in the same manner as above. Once completed, connect the third and fourth. Continue until all the lines are connected. The result will look like a continuous zig-zag pattern.

When the lines are all connected, you are ready to connect the final line of lights to the junction box. Strip 2 inches of casing from one end of the remaining cable. Now run the cable from the channel to the junction box, attaching it to the ceiling as you go, using cable staples. (Be careful so that you do not pierce the cable sheathing.) Strip about 8 inches of sheathing from the cable end and then an inch of insulation from the wires. Connect the cable through the opening in the extender box, using a two-part cable connector. Splice the black fixture wire and the black circuit wire. Do the same with the white wires. Fasten the two green ground wires to the base of the junction box.

Attach the protective lids to the channels. Insert the fluorescent lamps into the lamp sockets, turn on the circuit, and test to make sure that everything works properly. Then turn off the circuit.

Step Three: Installing the Panels. The panels will be suspended in a metal grid. It should be installed from 10 to 12 inches away from the lights, and the distance between it and the floor should be no less than 7½ feet. The grid includes these components: an L-shaped metal framing, which fastens to the wall; main L-shaped runners, which hang from the ceiling by means of eye screws and hanger wires; and T-bars, which span the main runners.

Decide on the height of the luminous ceiling and draw a corresponding line on the walls all the way around the room. Using a carpenter's level, check that the line is completely level. Then nail the edge framing along the line.

The manufacturer's instructions will tell you how far from the edge framing the first main runner should be (usually 2 to 4

feet). Measure out, and draw a line along the ceiling, parallel to the wall. Measure every so often to be sure that the line is straight. Install the eye screws every two feet along the ceiling line. If your ceiling is of wallboard, you should first install screw anchors and then insert the eye screws. If the ceiling is plaster, you will have to drill holes first, using a bit size slightly smaller than the eye screws. You can then install the eye screws directly into the ceiling.

Now cut the hanger wires; their lengths should be twice the distance from the ceiling to the runner. Pass a fourth of the hanger wire through the screw eye; fold the end back against the wire itself; twist the end around the wire. Now lift the runner into position — have a helper for this. Pass the free end of the hanger wire through the opening provided in the main runner. Check the runner's height to be sure that it is the same as the distance between the ceiling and the edge frame. Hook the wire so it will support the runner. (Your helper probably will have to hold the runner for a while, until you have hooked several wires.) Go on to the next screw eye and repeat.

Once you have completed the hangers for a runner, check to be sure the runner is level. Make any necessary adjustments.

Then bend the hooks closed and twist the ends firmly around the wires. Place all the runners in the same manner. The distance between them will be determined by the size of the plastic panels you are using.

Once the main runners are in, install the T-bars. These will fit into special slots built into the main runner. The size of the plastic panel determines the distance between the T-bars. Once the T-bars are in place, you need only to slide the panels in to cover the ceiling.

Indirect Light. A luminous ceiling is designed to create even lighting for an entire room. It needs no supplement. A central ceiling fixture, on the other hand, sometimes needs to be supplemented in areas some distance from it. In this situation, use installations that contribute to general illumination by means of indirect

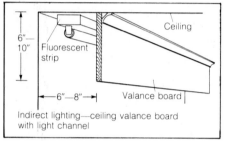

Indirect lighting—ceiling valance board with light channel

One method of indirect lighting utilizes a ceiling valance board, with a light channel for the fluorescent lamp.

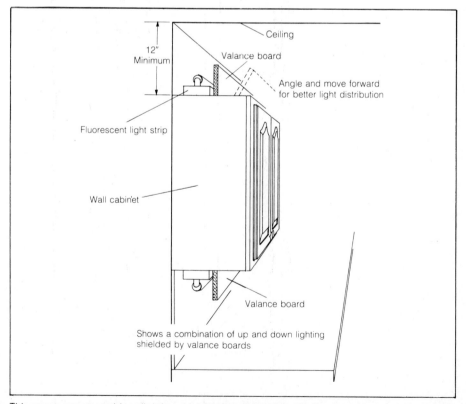

This arrangement combines lighting shielded by valance boards above and below cabinets. The boards can be angled forward for better light distribution.

light — that is, light that is diffused into the room by bouncing off a reflective surface. Most indirect light installations depend upon fluorescent tubes for their light source, although some have long, tubular incandescent bulbs called linear filament lamps. Whatever type of tubular light (or T-bulb) is used, the bulb is installed behind a baffle. This is the opaque shield that hides the bulb itself, and aims the light in the desired direction.

There are two basic types of baffles: the valance and the cove. The valance is a single board which is attached to a wall, cabinet or ceiling. When it concentrates the light downward, it accents such items as furniture, fireplaces or windows. When it directs the light upward, however, the light bounces off the ceiling and creates a soft, general light. In some settings, a valance directs light both up and down.

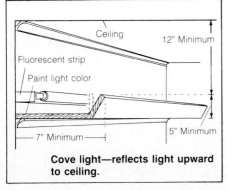

Cove light—reflects light upward to ceiling.

This cove light reflects light upward to the ceiling, from which it is reflected in an even, glare-free manner.

A cove baffle is especially constructed to create indirect general light. The base of the cove is parallel to the ceiling and perpendicular to the wall. It is attached at a level no more than 12 inches below the ceiling. The light fastens to the cove base. A second board, no less than 5 inches in width, attaches to the outer edge of the cove base, at a 45° angle. The light is directed both up and out, away from the wall and into the room.

Task Lighting

Make sure that your plan provides for more than only general lighting. For specific tasks that demand good light, diffused light is never as satisfactory as direct, localized illumination focused on the job. While it is possible to design a good kitchen without general light fixtures and with task lighting only, the reverse is seldom rewarding, even in tiny facilities.

Sink Area. For an average-size sink, a double 30-40 watt fluorescent fixture or two 75-watt incandescents (either recessed into the ceiling or cupboard, or concealed behind a valance) will supply the needed light in the sink area. Fluorescents and incandescents also can be hung vertically on both sides of the sink. If the sink extends beyond three or four feet, the lighting requirement will increase proportionally.

Another option is to use a reflector bulb, which has a coating designed to throw light in a desired direction. Reflec-

tor bulbs are made with wide (flood) or narrow (spot) beams in many sizes and types. They are excellent for task lighting. Because all their light is thrown exactly where it is wanted, bulbs of lower wattage can achieve the same intensity as nonreflectors of higher wattage.

Range Area. Most range hoods conceal a light source; some of the better-designed ones have space for either a fluorescent fixture or two incandescent bulbs. Older hoods contain outlets for only a single incandescent. Lights built into ranges themselves, on the other hand, provide very little illumination. Most homes need additional direct light over the range area.

A small opening for a recessed incandescent bulb can be cut into the floor of a cabinet built over a range or countertop burners. However, this sacrifices some cabinet space—an undesirable option if your storage space is limited. An alternative is a fluorescent fixture or a single incandescent hung under the cabinet. Some people prefer a strip containing several incandescent bulbs under the wall cabinet. The strips of fluorescent or incandescents cannot be left uncovered, however, because cooking directly below the lights will coat them with grease. Unfortunately, after prolonged exposure to cooking heat, moisture and grease, the plastics that usually cover such strips and act as diffusers of the fixture's light will discolor and distort the light. If you want a fixture in this location, you would benefit from replacing the plastic with a glass pane—either transparent or translucent.

An attractive and functional option is track lighting. A track light has two parts. The first is a grooved metal strip that fastens to a ceiling (in most cases). It connects to a power source, either directly through a ceiling junction box, or indirectly through a cord adapter that plugs into an outlet. (If you choose one that attaches to a junction box, you will probably have to extend an existing circuit, since ceiling boxes often are not close enough to the track's location to provide a power source.)

Electrical current passes through the strip. The second part of the system consists of lights or fixtures that plug directly into the track. Light from the track should hit the wall or work surface at a 35° or 40° angle for the best illumination. The loca-

Soffit lighting

Shown is a more elaborate method of incorporating fluorescent lighting for a work area; placement in a soffit creates a built-in look.

tion of the track on the ceiling is governed by the necessary angle of the light.

Tracks come in two types. Open channel tracks allow the fixtures or lights to plug in at any point you desire. Closed channel systems have specifically designated locations for fixtures and appliances. Although open tracks lend desirable flexibility, closed tracks are better for a kitchen setting because they do not become clogged with grease, as do the open ones.

Because you are able to aim the lights in a track system, and since the track itself can be as long as you wish, it is one way to light several problem areas at the same time. Also available are several adapters that give the system even more flexibility. Track lighting is sold in kits and is fairly easy to install.

You also might want to investigate clip-on opaque fixtures, which are adapta-

tions of those used in factories. These "portable" fixtures can attach to pot racks or other supports in the burner area. You can even clip them to the outside of a hood to cast a pool of light directly upon the burners or cooktop.

Work Areas. Countertop space below an overhanging cabinet is one kitchen area that is especially prone to shadow. Light this area with strips of fluorescent or incandescent bulbs concealed under the cabinet, installed either with or without a valance. If you do use a valance the light will illuminate a narrower area than if you don't—an undesirable situation on a deep countertop. If the light source is incandescent, remember that this type creates heat as well as light—which can be bothersome in the enclosed area under a cabinet.

If there is no cabinet over the countertop you have more options from which to

choose. Track lighting, of course, is one; recessed spotlights in the ceiling is another. Remember that reflector lights also create heat as well as light. This can be an advantage during the winter, but it also shortens the longevity of the bulb.

If you do not desire spotlights, you may hang any of a number of pendant lamps from the ceiling. An opaque shade will direct the bulb's light down onto the work surface.

Plant Lighting. If you wish to grow herbs and houseplants in your kitchen, you have another reason for installing special lights at the base of an upper cabinet. Plants usually do best when the conditions under which they live are similar to those of their natural habitat. As a result, several manufacturers produce fluorescents to meet the broad color spectrum that most houseplants require. Even an ordinary incandescent light backed by a reflector can produce sufficient light for many plants, especially some special blue-coated incandescents. However, many plants suffer from the heat of an incandescent, especially if set close to the light.

Many people who grow plants in their kitchens hook timer devices to their lighting systems. The timer is set so that the plants receive 10 to 16 hours of light, just as they would if they were outdoors. Plants' light requirements are one reason why it often is unwise to try to grow plants in the window above the sink. Since many people use the overhead light there in the evenings, the plants do not thrive as well as they would in another spot.

Very recently, manufacturers brought out special mercury vapor lamps, which are very good for plant growth and which also can contribute to local lighting. The color spectrum of some are unpleasant; however, others, such as Wonderlite, do not present this problem.

Herbs and other plants can be grown in well-lit windows. Hang them from the ceiling or set them on sills. A device called Clinger Clips enables you to clip plants to the insides of windows. You may even decide to use special brackets that attach small glass or plastic shelves to the inner window frame.

Task lighting is valuable not only in food preparation areas, but also in above a work center such as this desk built into an old closet recess.

10
CABINETS, COUNTERS, RECESSED SHELVES

CABINETS

In addition to the cost of using manufactured cabinets, there is the necessity of compromise. Ready-made cabinets may not fit your kitchen space precisely, and you may have to sacrifice part of your plan and accept something a little less than you wanted. Custom cabinets can be made for you, but that may increase your costs so significantly that you have to forego other features you planned.

One answer, provided you have the time and the skill, is to build your own cabinets to your own specifications. A basic kitchen cabinet is not beyond the skill of a patient and intelligent person with some carpentry experience. If you can continue to live with your old kitchen until you have completed the new cabinets, you will have an essentially unlimited time period in which to build them.

Plywood is available in a number of veneer finishes, which means you have a wide choice of cabinet finishes. Plywood is also relatively easy to work with; it is strong and can be cut to any size necessary within the usual overall dimensions of 4 by 8 foot panels. It is not cheap, but in comparison to the cost and the time required for dowel jointing and gluing boards together to size, it is economical of both time and money.

Before starting your particular project, you will have to measure your space and draw plans. Give plenty of thought to your design and take sufficient time to work out your plans. Time spent at the drawing board — drafting your plans — is never wasted. Do not hurry through this step. You will essentially be building your cabinets on paper. Check and recheck your measurements — the spaces for your cabinets, the sizes of your appliances, the clearances for the doors, as well as placement of the doors.

Do floor plans, elevations, and plans for each cabinet. Figure how much material you will need and find out the cost. Do you have enough room in your workshop

to both store and construct the cabinets? Can you move the completed cabinets from your workshop into the kitchen easily? A basement workshop is sometimes located so that large objects cannot be maneuvered out and up the stairs without damage.

Presented here are directions for building one set of wall-hanging and base kitchen cabinets. These units are only 30

inches wide as designed; however, the basic carpentry skills needed for any cabinet will be the same as those called for in this project. You should have a good idea of how to go about designing and building cabinets if working from these instructions.

These cabinets follow standard specifications. The upper (hanger) cabinet was designed to hang below a soffit. The base

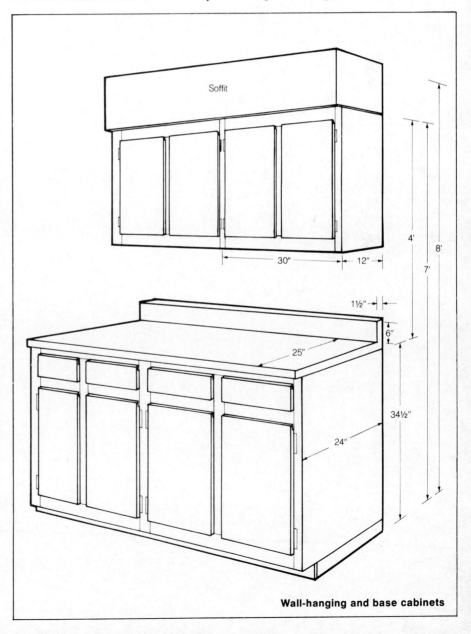

Wall-hanging and base cabinets

unit was designed to be even with the usual height of a range once the countertop has been added.

Wall-Mounted Unit

Following the accompanying illustration, cut the sides for the hanging cabinet from ¾ inch plywood. Cut ¾ inch dadoes in the top and bottom, 2 inches from the edges. Cut ⅛ inch dadoes ¾ inch in from the back of each side. Cut one bottom and one top to the size indicated; nail and glue these between the sides. Nail and glue the back in place. Attach the back mounting members at the positions indicated in the illustration. Cut and assemble the front rails and stiles using glue and dowels. Secure this frame assembly to the cabinet with glue and nails.

Doors. A simple overlay door is suitable for this project. Cut door panel 1¼ inches wider and 1¼ inches higher than your opening. Rout a ⅜ inch cove recess all the way around the edges of the back side of the panel to create a finger pull and allow room for concealed hinges. You may prefer instead to attach door pulls. Use magnetic or friction catches to hold doors closed.

A lip door is not very different from an overlay door except that the recess cut into the back along the edges fits into the opening. You will have to add door pulls. To create a lip door, cut your door from ¾ inch plywood. The door will overlap the frame by ¼ inch all the way around the frame. For a 10x16 inch opening, cut your door 10½x16½ inches. On the back of the door, cut a ⅜ rabbet all the way around the edges. This will allow a ¼ inch overlap and ⅛ inch for clearance. Round off the exterior edges with a plane or a router and finish smooth with sandpaper. Attach with appropriate hinges.

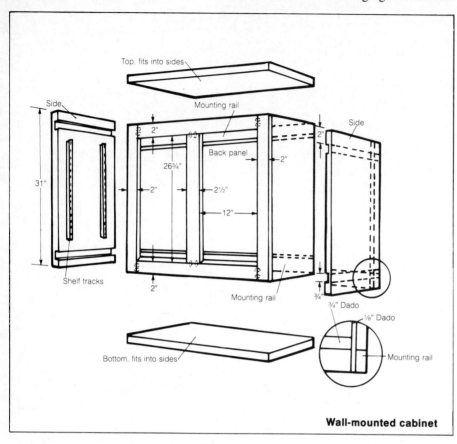

Wall-mounted cabinet

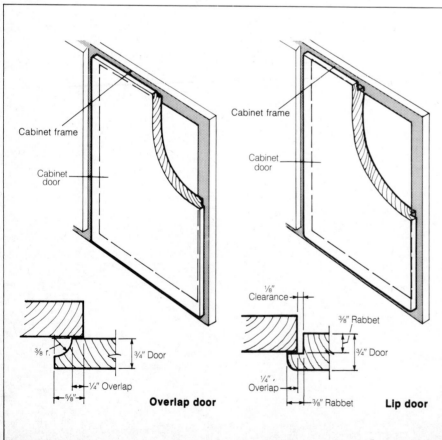

Overlap door

Lip door

To install a ⅜ inch concealed hinge use a router to create a backside cove or recess.

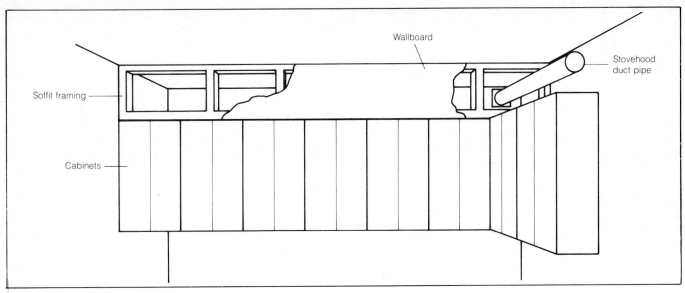

Although the primary purpose of a soffit is decorative, the space can be used to hide ductwork and electrical conduit.

Miter cut the first piece of molding and place it at the top of the cabinet at the ceiling.

Use previously cut molding as a guide for the angle cut on the second piece of molding.

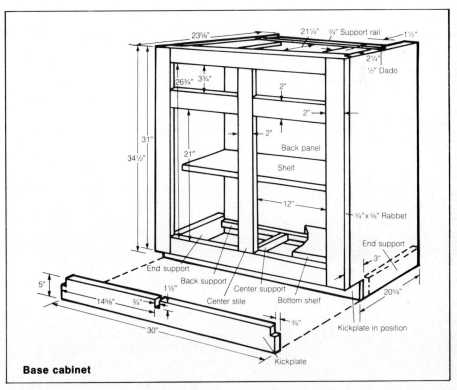

Base cabinet

Construction of Base Cabinet

Construction of a base cabinet is a little more complicated than the steps involved for the hanging cabinet. However, it actually requires only a bit more time; nor is it as difficult to install as the wall unit.

Cut the sides out of ¾ inch plywood. The sides will be 32⅝x34½ inch rectangles before cutting out the 3½x3 inch notch on each side for the kickplate.

Cut dadoes into the sides to hold the top back support rails and the bottom shelf. Cut rabbets in the sides; these will hold the front frame at the front edges. Cut the front stiles and rails and assemble as the

front frame, using dowels and glue. Then install front frame in rabbets. Attach to the base cabinet, with countersunk screws going through sides into the edge of frame. Cut the kickplate as shown in the drawing, using a ¾x5 inch wide piece of stock. Glue and nail this piece onto the side panels.

The back is cut from ⅛ inch plywood and glued securely to the dadoes made ½ inch from the back edges of the sides. Now nail through the back and sides to secure the middle and lower shelves. The last construction step is to attach a 6 inch reinforcing piece at the top edge, across

the back as shown.

Install drawer guides before adding the countertop. The countertop is usually ¾ inch Exterior plywood to which tile or plastic laminate has been adhered, as discussed later in this chapter. Other countertop materials include butcher block or synthetic marble.

Drawer Hardware. Measure the openings for the drawers, and the depths of their interiors. Plan to use side-mounted hardware. This requires the installation of a hardware support in the center of the cabinet, running from the center front stile to the back partition. Cut a piece of 1x3 stock so it is ¾ inch shorter than the space between the stile and the back. Attach a piece of 1x3 that is 4 inches long to the first piece of 1x3; this will form a "T". At the other end of the "T" attach a ¾x¾ inch block approxi- mately 4 inches long. Attach the block with screws, perpendicular to one side of the length of 1x3, but flush with its end.

After your drawers have been com- pleted, you will attach the side-mounted hardware to the drawers, to the sides of the cabinet, and to the "T" piece. Attach the "T" piece to the stile with screws driven through ¾ inch block. Brace the "T" against the back of the cabinet, prop- ping it up with 1x3 (or equivalent) stock. Firmly attach the "T" to the back only after you have tried the drawers and are certain that the hardware rolls smoothly.

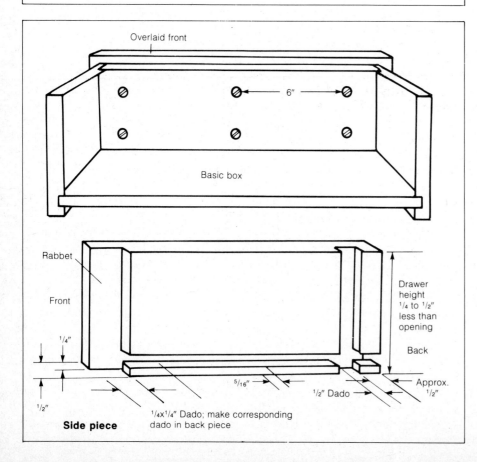

Side mounted hardware

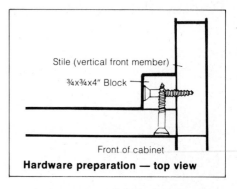

Hardware preparation — top view

Drawers. The simplest drawer to make is an overlay drawer. This is basi- cally a box with an extra layer added to the front. The front will overlap the frame by approximately the same amount as the door overlap.

Cut the drawer sides to the depth re- quired by the space, but to a height be- tween ¼ and ½ inch less than the height of the opening. Cut the front and back pieces the same height as the sides, but 1½ inches shorter than the width of the open- ing. This will allow for the side-mounted hardware.

The bottom should be cut from ¼ inch plywood and installed in dadoes cut into the front, back and sides. Carefully mea- sure the positions for the dadoes before

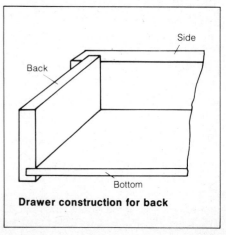

Drawer construction for back

cutting. Rout rabbets at the front edges of the sides for the front facing, and then dadoes to hold the back piece. Dry fit the front, sides and back, measuring the interior and dadoes to find the exact size of the bottom. Cut the bottom and dry fit into place. If everything fits properly and the drawer is square, glue and nail together with 3d finishing nails. If there is any problem, sand and smooth the edges and dadoes until the fit is good. Then pull the drawer into square, and complete the assembly. The overlay face now attaches, using No. 8 flathead wood screws. Locate screw positions around the perimeter of the box front. Drill pilot holes and drive screws through the box front, from the inside of the drawer, into the front overlay.

Attach drawer hardware and pulls. Install hardware in the cabinets and try the drawer in place. If the drawer rolls smoothly, tighten the back "T" into position. Remove the pulls before finishing the surface of the drawers.

Position your cabinets in your kitchen, apply any finishing necessary and install.

PLASTIC LAMINATE COUNTERTOPS

Home centers offer partly finished kitchen countertops that already have plastic laminate tops in place. They come in various lengths, which can be modified for the user. The major advantage in using this product is that attaching plastic laminate to its core can be tricky, as a run-through of the process in the following pages suggests. These prefabricated tops eliminate this step. In addition, the factory-laminated top can be cut to size. If your countertop must turn a corner, your dealer can miter it for you. We recommend buying a factory-made top, although it may somewhat limit your choice of pattern or color.

Producing your own laminated countertop also may offer you a more accurate fit than would a ready-made one. Another drawback is that there are very few avail-

able with full backsplashes; most of the ready-made tops have either no backsplash or reach 4 inches above the counter. In order for the splash to continue up to the wall cabinets, you would have to glue an additional piece of laminate on the wall. Another point on which to check is whether the dealer will make the cut-outs for the sink or appliances. If so, measure carefully and let the dealer do it. It can save you time, and avoids possible material damage.

Making Your Own

Core Material. Countertop core material may be ¾ inch plywood, particleboard or chipboard. Old plastic laminate without tears or bubbles can be covered with new plastic laminate. Remove bubbles in old surfaces by breaking them and filling in gaps; any missing or broken portions should be filled in or repaired. A good material to fill in the gaps would be a regular plastic automobile body repair material. Let it harden; sand smooth. All trim and edging must be removed, too. Unless you can repair old plastic laminate to smoothness, do not use it as a base for a new surface, as the old scars and irregularities will show through. Instead, cover the old surface with one of the recommended core materials before resurfacing. This will create a thicker, higher surface, which usually is not a disadvantage. Whatever material is used for the core, however, check that it is absolutely clean and dry before applying the adhe-

The simplest drawer can be made using hand tools, with a bottom made of ⅜ inch or ½ inch plywood. The bottom extends ⅜ inch beyond the sides of the drawer to form a lip. Ease the edges; apply paraffin for smooth operation.

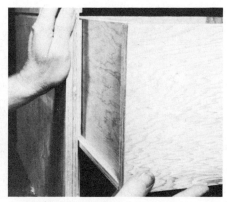

The extended bottom of the drawer fits into slots formed by gluing pieces of ⅜ inch plywood to the inner surface of each side of the cabinet. A gap just wide enough to take the lip is left between these pieces.

This drawer (shown upside down) can be built using a saw and hammer. Butt joints are glued and nailed. The bottom is of ⅜ inch or ½ inch plywood for rigidity. Drawer front extends down to cover front edge of bottom.

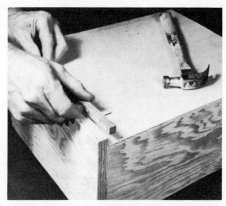

An additional strip of wood, glued and nailed to the front panel, reinforces the bottom of this second type of drawer made with hand tools. The reinforcing permits use of economical ¼ inch plywood for drawer bottom.

Plastic laminate can be purchased in exotic and unusual patterns and textures.

sive and laminate. This means that any debris from sanding and cutting must be wiped or brushed away.

Adhesives. There are two main types of adhesives for plastic laminates. The water-based ones are preferable for home use. The petroleum-based solvents are toxic and flammable; the water-based adhesives are not. Petroleum-based adhesives require extreme caution — no smoking, of course. In addition, when using the petroleum-based product, turn off all pilot lights and work in a very well-ventilated room. Even better, work outdoors if the weather is not much above or below 70 degrees. Weather much cooler or warmer adversely affects all laminates and their adhesives. Our suggestion is to play it safe and use a water-based product, even though it may provide a slightly weaker bond.

Plastic Laminates. As discussed earlier, plastic laminates are manufactured in an infinite number of designs, colors, and qualities. Their sizes range from 2x4 to 5x10 foot sheets. The $1/16$th inch thickness is recommended for countertops. Let the plastic laminate and the core material sit in your house (preferably in the kitchen) for at least 48 hours before beginning work on them. This acclimates the materials to the temperature and humidity in the kitchen.

Step One: Measure before Beginning. Measure the length and depth of countertop required. Most countertops are 24 to 25 inches deep, but there are exceptions, depending upon your plan. Always allow about an inch of extra material; if the counter turns a corner, allow even more extra core material and surplus laminate. When measuring and estimating materials, keep in mind that the countertop should overhang the base cabinets by an inch or so on the side edges. The overhang at the front is usually an inch but can be as much as 3 or 4 inches. Test to see whether a large overhang will interfere with the opening of drawers or doors. If interference occurs, raise the countertop on shims made of strips or blocks of wood. Be sure that the overhang in front covers the shims sufficiently to hide them from view.

If you are planning a backsplash from the same material, measure for it now. Backsplashes may be as low as 2 to 4 inches, but most people find that the neatest look and fastest cleanup comes

with backsplashes that fill the entire wall between the counter and wall-hung shelves or cabinets.

Step Two: Cutting and Joining Core and Laminate. Make sure the base cabinets are level before cutting. If not, insert wood shims to level them out, checking the results with a level.

A circular or sabre saw best cuts plywood, hardboard, or particleboard. You will probably have to join one or more pieces of your core material in order to achieve the necessary length. The floor is usually the only work space that is large enough for this. When joining two pieces, butt them together with white construction glue. Then hammer corrugated steel nails across the seams; stagger them at one- or two-inch intervals. Do this on both sides of the core material at every butt joint. Mitered corners are not recommended for turning corners.

Now working on the "wrong" or reverse side of the core, attach strips of wood 2 inches wide and ¾ inch thick to cover all the butt joints. Use construction glue; nail with coated nails. Hammer the nails in an irregular, alternating pattern along the wood strip, which is called a "batten". In the same manner, apply wood battens around the entire perimeter of the reverse side of the countertop core. To create a higher or thicker countertop, use thicker pieces of wood as battens. Generally, these battens are held even with the front and exposed edges to allow for laminating. Those along the back and ends against the walls are held back ½ inch or so to permit easier scribing of the countertop to an irregular wall surface. Even if you are not joining pieces of wood, but are using one solid piece, apply battens around the perimeter.

Clamp plastic laminate to a piece of plywood, which you can then use as a straightedge to guide your cut. The plywood will also support the laminate as you cut.

Cutting Laminate. Once the core for the top has been assembled, cut the plastic laminate. A laminate scriber, a razor blade in a holder, a fine-toothed saw, or a fine blade in a power jigsaw are recommended for cutting. To cut a straight line, scribe a line on the wrong or reverse side of the laminate with the razor or laminate scriber, and then break off the piece against a straightedge. As an alternative, you can cut the laminate from the side that will show, using a very sharp fine-toothed saw or a fine blade in a power jigsaw. First try either or both on some scrap plastic laminate to make certain that your tools are adequate and that the material will not chip.

Cut out the plastic laminate about ¼ inch larger in all dimensions than your final measurements. Lay out the pieces, which you have cut to size, over the completed core just as they will be finally assembled. With a wax pencil, mark "A", "B", "C", and so on, onto the finish sides. This allows you to put the pieces in place quickly, without puzzling as to which goes where. If there is a pattern, make sure it lines up correctly.

Edgings. If you wish to edge the top in the same laminate as the deck, it will be necessary to cut some long strips of edg-

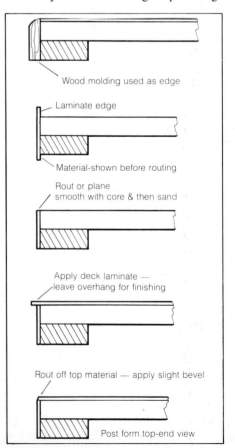

Wood molding used as edge

Laminate edge

Material-shown before routing

Rout or plane smooth with core & then sand

Apply deck laminate — leave overhang for finishing

Rout off top material — apply slight bevel

Post form top-end view

ing, again about ¼ inch larger than the size of the edge. Cutting these strips usually is done on a table saw. If you don't have one, ask your laminate supplier to precut them for you. Many outlets will do this. Edges may also be covered with metal strips designed for the purpose; these are readily available. Metal edges generally go on after the deck has been

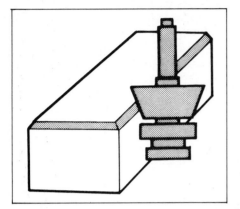

The bevel trim bit is used to finish plastic laminate edges at an angle.

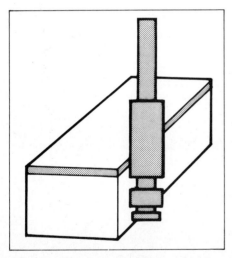

The flush trim bit cuts a perfectly vertical face on the laminate and base.

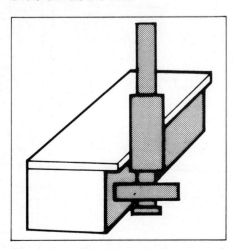

The overhang bit is used to trim base beneath laminate to leave laminate overhang.

laminated, whereas plastic laminated edging is applied before the deck is laminated. To apply the plastic edge, apply adhesive to the strips and to the countertop edge, using a narrow brush. With two hands, hold each strip by the edge and set it into place carefully. Allow a slight overhang, top and bottom. Press firmly, or use a wood block against which you can tap the edge. The edge must then be trimmed even with the deck using a router, laminate trimmer or plane. Finally, it should be sanded along the top edge to assure a good fit with the deck material. Laminate trimmers can usually be rented from a tool rental company. If you find one, be sure to first experiment using it, to get the feel of it before working on your top.

As an alternative to using plastic laminate for the edges, you can apply wood (after the deck has been laminated) to the front edge. It can be nailed and glued, stained and coated with polyurethane. This is not hard to do, and can add a very distinctive look to your countertop.

For thicker-looking counters, 1x2s may be nailed to or underneath the sanded edges. They may then be laminated as above, or the wood edge may be finished with a wood stain and coated with polyurethane.

Step Three: Attaching Laminate to Countertop Deck. Spread the adhesive onto the core surface, using a notched trowel, paint brush, or roller. Cover all surfaces. It will be least cumbersome if the core is now resting on sawhorses. Many adhesives must be spread on both the core and the back of the plastic, but the directions that come with your adhesive will make it clear whether or not this

Cut and trim plastic laminate to fit the entire counter area. Then mark each piece so you can re-assemble them quickly when you glue the laminate to the countertop.

is necessary. These adhesives bond quickly, usually on contact.

The easiest means of assuring proper alignment is to allow another ⅛ to ¼ inch all around the edges. Position as carefully as possible, but if not exactly square you can adjust the outer trim by sanding off the excess until you have the final dimensions. This will not work, however, if the laminate has any pattern.

Other techniques require some means of delaying contact until the two materials are aligned perfectly. One way to achieve this is to let the coat of adhesive dry (if using contact cement) and then to place a series of thin wood slats (strapping or lathing, for instance) on top of the core. Then position the plastic laminate very carefully over the slats. When it is exactly right and the laminate aligns with the core corner to corner, remove the slats. The easiest method is to remove one slat at a time, starting from one end. Press down each portion as you go along.

Another procedure, which sometimes is preferred, uses a paper barrier. Here are the steps involved.

(1) Brush contact cement onto the bottom of the sheet of laminate.

(2) Brush a coat of the contact cement onto the area where the laminate will be bonded.

(3) Let both surfaces dry. The required drying time will vary; you can determine if the cement is dry by placing brown wrapping paper against the dried cement. If the paper will not stick to the cemented surface when pressure is applied, then the cement has dried sufficiently.

(4) For each piece of laminate to be applied, cut 2 sheets of kraft paper, with one piece twice as long as the other. The 2 sheets, when overlapped by about one inch, should be about one inch larger in both dimensions than the surface area to be covered by that piece of laminate. Overlap the 2 sheets. The longer one will cover ⅔ of the surface; the shorter piece will cover ⅓ of the area for this piece of laminate.

(5) With the cement side down, place the laminate on the kraft paper. You can adjust as much as necessary, because the paper will prevent contact.

(6) Once you have the laminate exactly in position, have a helper firmly hold down the laminate near but not on the overlap, pressing on the longer piece of paper. By clamping down on the longer of

the two pieces of kraft paper near (but not on) the overlap, you can pull the shorter piece of kraft paper out. The area that has now bonded acts as your clamp and anchor. Carefully pull out the longer sheet of paper.

(7) Roll the top with a rubber roller, which is designed to add pressure and ensure a good bond of the laminate to the core. If you do not have a roller, a flat board, about 2 inches thick, can be used by placing it on the deck and striking it lightly as you move it around the surface. Cover the block with carpet or felt to prevent damage to the laminate.

(8) Bevel all top plastic laminate edges and corners to about 30°, using a plane or laminate trimmer. If any portion of the plastic laminate on the countertop or the vertical edges fails to adhere, use a clamp to hold it in place until it bonds.

All inside corners should be left with a slight radius. This applies to cut-outs made for sinks or burners, and also inside corners on "L" shaped tops. This helps prevent cracks due to expansion and contraction of the laminate and core.

The Sink Cut-out

If yours is a brand new sink, it probably arrived from the manufacturer with a template and instructions. If not, you can make your own template. To do so, you will need to place the countertop on top of the base cabinets. Make sure to have the assistance of a helper — or even two — when lifting the core; it can be very heavy. Position the sink upside-down on the surface of the laminated countertop, exactly where it will fit. Leave about 2 inches behind the sink. Trace the sink's outline with a wax pencil, or use some other easily erased marker. With your helper, remove the countertop back to the sawhorses. With a ruler, draw a new line ¼ inch inside the original outline. If using a sabre saw, draw the line on the wrong side of the core; plastic laminate may chip if cut from the finish side with a sabre saw. If using a keyhole saw, mark the outline of the sink on the plastic laminate side.

To help make the first cut, drill a starter (pilot) hole an inch or so inside the new outline. Some carpentry instructors advise making holes at each of the four corners of the sink outline. Beginning at the pilot hole, cut along the inner line to make the opening. Bevel and sand the edges of the opening before inserting the sink.

All openings in the countertop may be made in the same way, whether these are for butcher blocks, top burners, barbecues, marble pastry slabs, and so on. Just make sure that no opening is less than 2 inches away from any edge, front, back, or sides. All openings in countertops are cut after the plastic laminate has been applied, but before the counter has been installed. To ensure exact positioning, place the countertop in its exact and final position before placing the sink onto it in order to draw the template.

The Backsplash

Plastic laminate is mounted onto the backsplash core in exactly the same way as for the countertops. Construct the backsplash separately from the countertop core. Make it of the same materials as the core and to the measurements you prefer — it may be as low as three inches or it can reach all the way up to the wall cabinets. A backsplash may be omitted entirely when the wall behind the countertop is window glass, tile, or any other material that will not be damaged by occasional splashes of liquids. If you do not use a backsplash, apply caulking between the back edge of the counter and the wall to prevent seepage. Another technique for

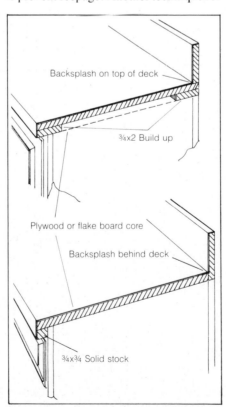

Shown are two methods for building up counter and attaching the backsplash. Backsplash may be as low as 4 inches, or up to cabinets.

a countertop without a backsplash is to finish the back edge of the top before installing it with a ready-made metal cove molding. Spread silicone sealant on the back of the molding and then install the entire counter and backsplash.

Once you have cut the backsplash core, apply plastic laminate to it before attaching it to the countertop core. In the same way that you bonded plastic laminate to the countertop, apply adhesive to the backsplash. Laminate the sides first, then the front, then the top.

With the countertop on the sawhorses, place the backsplash in its final position on the countertop. It must be held there while you work, either by your helper or a pair of C clamps. Hammer in drivescrews (also called screwnails) about eight inches apart, ½ inch from the back edge of the countertop, driving them from under the countertop. Predrill the holes before putting the backsplash in place. Seal the edge where the backsplash meets the countertop. Silicone is good for this. Seal also between the top of the backsplash and the wall; this can be done with caulking.

Post-formed Cores. If you are recovering old plastic laminate in a post-formed core, which curves up into the backsplash and curves over the front edge, you will not have a seam between the countertop and the backsplash. Instead, you will want to bend the plastic laminate to shape. Plastic laminate can be made to curve gently by placing it in hot water and then bending it to shape.

Attaching Countertop to Base

Countertops can be screwed or glued to the base cabinets. A screwed-on top is usually recommended because it can be removed with relative ease for repair or replacement. A glued top is easy to install, but it is difficult to remove, with both the top and the base cabinets usually damaged in the process.

Glue. When using glue to attach the finished countertop, apply a product such as panel adhesive to the top edges of the cabinets, both front and rear. With the assistance of your helper, lift the countertop up from the floor or sawhorses, turn it right side up, and set it into place on the base cabinets. After you have checked to see that the top's alignment is perfect, press down. Remove excess glue, if any, and allow the glue to dry before proceeding with the sink installation or any other work that might jar the top. Usually, the weight of the top is enough to hold it in place until the glue sets up. If you need some additional braces, you can improvise these by cutting lengths of 1x2 wood to wedge between the counter deck and either the ceiling or the wall cabinets. Be sure to put padding on each end of the brace to prevent damage to the top, ceiling or cabinet.

Screws. If you are screwing the top onto the base cabinets, first examine the corners of your base cabinets for triangular gusset plates or braces near the top. If there are none, holes can be drilled through the front sides of the cabinets or braces can be fabricated and glued in place. Factory-made cabinets have corner gussets that have been provided with holes at their center. These are designed to accept the screw necessary to attach the top. If there is no hole, drill one in each corner at the center of each brace.

Return the countertop to its permanent position on top of the base cabinets. Working from below, through the openings for the doors of the base cabinets, drive a screw through each of the prepared holes into the battens on the underside of the countertop. Check that the screws are long enough to go through the battens but not so long that they will come up through the countertop surface and ruin it. When your countertop is firmly in place, insert the sink into the opening that you cut earlier.

Inserting the Sink

Apply a bead of plumber's putty or caulking around the rim of the cutout. Lower the sink into the opening with the assistance of your helper. New sinks will have come from the manufacturer with directions specifying the type and number of clamps or clips, which must be spaced along the special channels that rim the underside of modern sinks. If yours is a used sink or otherwise has no instructions, slide about a dozen clips or clamps made for the purpose around the channels under the sink. Space them evenly around all four sides. In order to create a watertight seal, tighten the clamps so that the putty is compressed. Do not screw in so tightly that the sink or the countertop is distorted.

Stainless steel sinks often do not have a rim, but the procedure described above would still apply. Certain porcelain sinks are self-rimming and do not require clamps, as they are designed to overlap the counter opening. They remain in place with use of an adhesive, which comes with the sink.

CERAMIC TILE COUNTERTOPS

Ceramic tile can be laid over most of the materials usually found on a countertop, including old ceramic tile, plastic laminate and, of course, a plywood support as would be found on a new countertop installation.

The edge of the countertop may be trimmed in a number of different ways, and the first step is to decide which type of trim you will utilize. Shown are the trim pieces. There are also different methods of setting the sink in place, if the countertop has a sink. Estimate the amount of tile you will need, allowing for some waste during cutting.

We will give a basic installation for tile over a new plywood top, with the variation for installing over existing plastic laminate. Installation over existing ceramic tile is the same, once the old tile has been sanded with carborundum stone.

Step One: The Underlayment

Because ceramic tile is heavy, and kitchen countertops are exposed to moisture, you need an underlayment of either ¾ inch Exterior plywood (minimum B-D) or of backerboard. Underneath this surface, at intervals of 3 feet, add cross braces to support the top. Use 1x2s on edge or 2x4s laid flat, on inside cleats. To hold an apron or other drip edge trim, nail a 1x1 below the front edge of the counter. This will be covered with tile. Check that this edge strip does not interfere with clearances of drawers or appliances beneath.

In the installation shown here, the right side of the countertop has been cut ½ inch shorter than the base cabinet upon which it sits. The tile will follow around the cut edge of the plywood top, to give a flush finished edge so that a dishwasher can be stored in the opening next to the counter. If that small space were not left there, the tile would protrude, risking scratches to the appliance whenever it slid in or out. The other alternative, of course, is to extend the countertop over the dishwasher, after removing any existing dishwasher top. Most portables are built with this option in mind. In this latter case, the

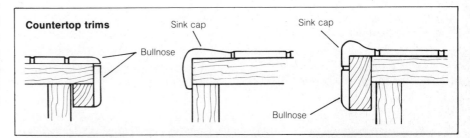

Countertop trims   Sink cap   Sink cap
Bullnose
Bullnose

This homeowner installation shows tile up to cabinets. The cost of this type of job depends upon the type amount of trim tile used; trim tile costs considerably more than field tile.

dishwasher trim tile must be adjusted to allow clearance of the dishwasher door.

Inspect the plywood surface (or any existing surface). It must be smooth, sound, and flat. No nails or other obstructions should protrude. All holes and defects must have been filled with patching material and sanded smooth.

Step Two: Dry Layout

Proper planning is probably the most important part of the tile-laying process. Careful attention to it can prevent problems later on. Rather than applying your adhesive and beginning to set the tile, first try a dry run. This will enable you to do the final setting with the least amount of cut tiles and avoid cutting tiles into very tiny pieces. As you get your trial layout, remember that you will be working from the front to the back, so that cut tiles will be at the back rather than the front of the countertop.

The starting point of your plan will depend mainly upon whether or not you are working around a sink and, if you are, where the sink is located in the counter.

Layout, Countertop Without a Sink. Measuring from end to end, find the center of the countertop. Mark this line from front to back. Then lay out the tile along the line, front edge tiles first, then the next row back, until you reach one row back from the backsplash. This last row must be cut to fit. If the tile comes with self-spacers, you need not worry about the grout line. If it does not, you will have to allow for the grout line as you go along. Grout lines usually vary from $1/16$ to $1/8$ inch, and can be adjusted to avoid tile cutting. The layout stick, or other spacer devices, can help you do this. Use a carpenter's square to ensure that the courses you are laying are perpendicular. Once you lay the tile up to the side edges you will be able to see what cutting is necessary. If any tiles at the sides must be cut to less than half their width, go back and shift the original center line so this situation can be avoided. Take your time; shift the tiles around like a crossword puzzle until you get the result you desire.

Layout, Countertop With a Sink Set Parallel to the Wall. Rather than working with the center line of the countertop, in this case you will work from the center line of the sink itself toward the sides of the countertop. Again you *dry* set the tile and work for an arrangement that will call

for the fewest cut tiles. Of course, there is no way to avoid cutting tile in order to allow for the sink opening. Use bull nose or sink rim tile around the sink opening.

Layout, Countertop with a Corner Sink. An L-shaped countertop corner sink must be handled differently than the two earlier settings. Since there is no way to avoid odd cuts of tile around the sink, the best method is to work from the sides of the countertop toward the sink opening.

Step Three: Laying Tile.

Begin placing tile on the countertop at the front edging row. If you wish, remove a few of the front row tiles from their layout positions; apply adhesive; stick them back down. This leaves the rest of your dry-laid tile in place, and prevents shifting of the tile or disruption of your layout during later adhesive application.

Setting the Tile. Apply the proper adhesive according to instructions on the can. Set the tiles using the same procedures as for setting floor tile (see Chapter 7). Again, first set the edge or trim pieces, such as sink caps. Space them properly, with spacers if they don't have spacing lugs on them. Note that the method shown utilizes a bullnose tile for the top edge, which overlaps the flat apron tile of the apron. This ensures a waterproof joint once the mortar has been packed in.

Again, when applying adhesive, do not spread out more than you can readily cover before it starts to harden. Typical adhesive for countertops is organic mastic. Although some people use epoxy, it generally requires a great deal more skill.

In most cases a cove tile will be added at the back, and the tile later will be continued up the wall to the cabinets. If a cove tile is not used, the spacing must be planned so the backsplash tile sits behind the countertop tile. This spacing must be determined during the dry layout.

Lay the field tile, following the line marked across the countertop, made by using a square. As an alternative method, position the square against the front edging tile and use it to position the first front-to-back course. Install the remainder of the field tile, until there is one row left between the cove tile or the wall, paying careful attention to spacing of the tile and ensuring that each is laid square to the next.

Keep laying your carpenter's square

across the tops of the tiles to check that they are square, with no wobbly or wiggly lines. As you set the tiles in place, use a block of wood covered with carpet or felt, and a hammer, to tap tiles firmly into the adhesive. This is done by sliding the plywood block over the surface of the tile, tapping with the hammer. Don't hammer so hard that you break the tile, or push the tiles out of alignment while sliding the block.

Cut the tile pieces that need to be cut for the last row. Use a rented tile cutter, or a glass cutter and the thin wire as mentioned earlier, and fit all cut pieces in place.

Now install the backsplash tiles on the wall. Work from the lower courses up toward the cabinets. In most instances a little adhesive is buttered on the back of the backsplash wall tiles, as well as on the wall. Then press tiles firmly in place, and twist back and forth to set them firmly. Sometimes the tiles are propped to prevent their sliding down before the adhesive sets. The continuation of the tile to the cabinets provides for continuity in design; the minimum is one course up, ending with a row of bullnose. Cut the tile to fit around outlets, light switches, window sills, using the tile-cutting pliers or other similar methods mentioned earlier.

Let the tile set for 24 hours. Then apply masking tape under the front edging to prevent the grout from running out the bottom edges of the spacers. Masking tape also should be applied over any surrounding wood surfaces, to avoid grout stains. Mix the grout and apply over the surface of the tile, using a squeegee. Clean the surface with a damp sponge to remove excess grout. Polish the tile with a soft cloth.

Install the sink, caulking well. If the sink rim is to be covered by the tile, install the sink first.

Use squeegee to apply grout to fill in joints. Application varies by type of grout.

Ceramic Tile Over Plastic Laminate

Tile can be installed over a plastic laminate counter, after removal of the backsplash and the sink. Prepare the surface by sanding with coarse sandpaper. Instructions for mosaic tile sheet installation are given here.

In order to get a good bond, roughen the surface of existing plastic laminate countertop before applying tile. Use a power sander for quickest job.

Lay out the tile sheets dry in order to determine the best layout arrangement. Use cove tile at the back corner of the countertop. After determining the best layout, draw the working lines using a carpenter's square. Once all working lines have been drawn, begin spreading the mastic, using a notched trowel.

The front edger tiles are installed first on the edge of the countertop. Install the strip of cove tile at back of countertop first and then fit the main field tile sheets between the front trim and the edge of the cove tile. Keep the sheets square, with all joints properly aligned. Fit special corner cove trim in the corner to finish it out.

Once the counter has been completed, spread newspapers over the surface and apply adhesive to the backsplash area. Use cove molding at the corners, then set the sheets in place for the deck of the counter.

Set all finish trim pieces. Lightly tap in the entire area, using the padded block of wood and hammer. Let adhesive set for 24 hours. Then apply the grout.

INSTALLING KITCHEN CABINETS

However beautifully finished or perfectly arranged, a set of cabinets is of little use if it appears to be pulling off the wall or tipping over every time you open a door or drawer.

Securing to the Wall

The strongest and most secure way to hang wall cabinets is to attach them to wall studs. If you have added a wall or done major repairs to your old walls — such as removing old plaster or wallboard and installing new — you are aware of the location of your studs. If you are removing your old cabinets and installing new ones, there is a strong chance the old cabinets were attached to studs. If not, you will have to locate them.

Finding Studs. Some wall studs are easy to find because the nails in the wallboard are easy to see. Even carefully finished wallboard walls show nail locations when a light is bounced off the surface at an angle. However, if your walls are plaster or have been painted frequently or with a texture paint, this will not usually work.

Another means of locating studs is to knock on the walls, listening for a solid rather than a hollow sound. The studs give a solid sound. Unfortunately, this method is not always reliable. If there is a baseboard around the room, you may be able to find stud locations by observing the nailing patterns of the baseboard.

When all else fails and you are still in doubt, find a place on the wall that will be covered by new cabinets or new wall paneling. Drive a 10d nail into the wall where you believe the stud is located. If the nail goes in firmly, you have struck the stud. However, if the nail goes directly through the plaster or wallboard after you have tapped it a couple of times, you have missed the stud. Pull the nail out and move it over one inch and try again. Keep trying until you hit the stud. Since studs are usually 16 inches on center (o.c.), you should have to drive no more than a dozen holes in order to locate your stud. After you have found the first stud, use a yardstick or other long measure and a level to locate your other studs. If your home is relatively new, you should find studs every 16 inches. Older homes have studs located every 24 inches. Occasionally, because of positions of doors or windows, an extra stud or double studs may

be used in the walls. This will change the locations of the wall studs after this point.

Removing Old Cabinets

This is a job which few people enjoy. It requires strength and determination more than anything else (except the right tools), which include a large wastebasket, a pry bar, a butt chisel, pipe or adjustable wrenches, hammer, screwdriver, crosscut and hack saws, and electrician's tape.

Wall Cabinets. Remove any molding around the bottom of your wall cabinets. Locate the screws or nails which hold the cabinets to the walls. If the cabinets have been attached to masonry walls or to hollow walls, you will be removing screws from either lead anchors or Mollys. Remove the doors and any movable shelves for easier handling. Brace the cabinets and have a helper steady the units as you remove the screws. If you have several cabinets which are attached, remove the screws that join them. Cabinets that are hung beneath a soffit are usually attached to the soffit studs. Be sure to remove these screws. Lift units carefully from bracing and remove.

If your cabinets have been hung with nails, you will have to use a pry bar. This is quicker but messier and will definitely require another person to help you. Brace the cabinets and remove any between-unit fasteners. Slip the pry bar behind the cabinet as far as possible and pull. You will undoubtedly damage the plaster or wallboard, but this damage will usually be hidden by the new cabinets. If these cabinets are nailed into the soffit as well as the wall, you will have to pry them free from both places. Be sure the cabinet is well braced. If it is not, it will fall suddenly as you free the last nails, or the weight of the cabinet itself may pull the unit free.

Removing a Range Hood. This step is covered in Chapter 9.

Removing Base Cabinets. This is easier than removing the wall cabinets because you do not have to worry about dropping the unit. However, base cabinets are larger and heavier than wall cabinets, so an assistant may be helpful.

First remove the countertop. If you have a laminated countertop, it will be attached to the base with screws and small brackets. Back out the screws and lift the countertop off. If your countertop is of ceramic tile, however, you will have to remove the tile from the countertop with a cold chisel and sledge hammer. This is a messy process, but it is necessary. The countertop will be very heavy and will probably crack if you attempt to remove it with the tile still attached.

Remove all molding and trim from around the base cabinets. Remove the doors, lift out any movable shelves, and detach any fasteners which join the separate cabinet units. If the cabinets are attached to the wall or floor, remove any screws or pry out any nails. Work from end cabinets toward the sink unit, removing each base cabinet as you free it. However, before you remove the base cabinets, you will have to detach the sink.

Removing the Sink Unit. This job is saved until the last moment because it involves several steps. It also requires your shutting off the water. If you do not have individual shutoff valves for the sink lines, you will probably have to cut off the water supply to the rest of the house.

After you have shut off the water to the sink, and the electrical power if you have a garbage disposer, a flash heater water tank or dishwasher, you may begin removing all the plumbing and electrical equipment. Locate the wiring for each of the electrical units attached to the sink, and disconnect. Tape any wire ends with electrician's tape. Cover all exposed wires very well. Next, disconnect the plumbing. You will have to disconnect the supply lines to the sink faucets, the dish-

washer and the flash heating unit. Use an adjustable wrench for copper tubing and appropriately sized pipe wrenches for galvanized steel. Disconnect the drain lines from the sink, the disposer and the dishwasher. Detach the disposer from the sink by removing the mounting screws and the mounting ring. Remove any other appliances. Remove the faucets from the sink.

The sink is usually held in place by a combination of mounting screws and plumber's putty. You should be able to see how the sink is installed by examining it from below after you have removed the disposer and drain pipes. If the sink is of cast iron and porcelain, you will need help to lift and carry the unit. A sink of enameled tin, stainless steel or fiberglass will be lighter, and easier to handle.

Installing Base Cabinets

Now that your kitchen is empty, you can clean up any mess, patch any damage to the walls or floor that might show after the

cabinets are in place and repair any damage to the soffit.

Next, check the corners and walls for square and plumb. Your new cabinets must hang or sit level. At a corner, snap a chalkline using a plumb bob to give a straight vertical guide line. Scribe a level horizontal base line on your wall. If your walls are out of plumb, you will not be able to butt the cabinets against a wall, and have them hang or sit level.

Positioning. Install the base cabinets first, unless there will be no backsplash. Bring the cabinets into the final position and, using Number 2 undercourse wood shingles, shim each cabinet to level. Each cabinet must be leveled until all units are at an identical height.

If there is a variation of less than ¾ inch, the cabinets may be shimmed at the base and fastened. However, if there is more than a ¾ inch variance, it is better to trim the base. To do this, scribe a level mark on the base of the cabinet(s) with a scribing tool. Cut off one half of the

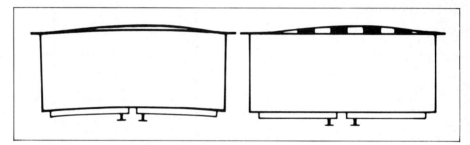

If the cabinet back is against an uneven wall, the cabinet doors may become misaligned. Shim out the back to level in order to restore doors to plumb alignment.

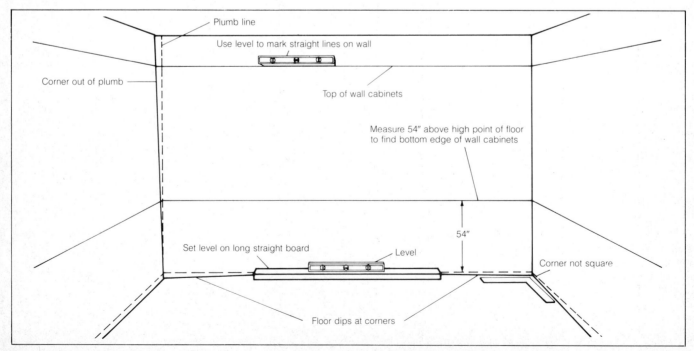

Always install cabinets so they are level. Locate plumb and square and mark your kitchen walls. Shims often will be needed to level cabinets.

thickness required for level. That is, if the cabinet is one inch off level, cut away ½ inch. The remainder of the leveling will be done with shims.

When you have determined that the cabinets are all level, scribe a line on the wall at the top edge of the units. Then pull the units away from the wall and attach a nailing strip at that location. The top of the nailer will be just below the scribed line. Put the cabinets back into position and attach to the nailer with Number 10 flathead screws. There should be a screw every 16 to 18 inches. The fronts of your base cabinets should join tightly. A filler piece may be used to hide any space between the end cabinets and the walls due to problems with plumb and level. Join the cabinets with Number 10 screws driven through the side stiles. These should be counterbored so they will not interfere with door or drawer opening.

Leveling at the Countertop. If your base cabinets are nearly level, you do not have to shim the bases. If the variation is slight, you can level at the countertop by placing small wood shims between the countertop, which is attached after the base cabinets are in position, and the cabinet edges. Attach the countertop to the base, checking level and reshimming if necessary.

The Backsplash. If you do plan a backsplash, this must be installed before the wall cabinets, or you will have too much difficulty maneuvering with your tools.

Hanging Wall Cabinets. All kitchen cabinets carry a great deal of weight. It is imperative that your hanging cabinets be secured to the studs in the wall. Mark stud positions so that you can see the marks after you have lifted the cabinets into position. Use T-braces to hold the cabinets up, and quickly drive a 10d nail through the top rail into a stud to help hold the unit in place while you check for plumb and level. Keep the T-brace in position. If the back of the cabinet is not flush with the wall, shim the cabinet back until the frame is plumb. If you do not, the cabinet doors will not hang correctly and will either stick or not close.

When you are certain that the unit is level and plumb, secure it to the studs — and to the soffit if you have one — with Number 10 screws. These screws must be long enough to bite at least one inch into the studs.

Lift the next unit into place and check that the faces meet evenly. If they do not, trim the second cabinet down to fit. Plane the edges at an angle so only the front edges meet snugly for an easier fit. Trim, shim and secure with screws. Use a filler

strip at walls to close any gaps. Secure each cabinet to the adjacent units with screws driven through side stiles.

Installing Cabinets without a Backsplash. if your base cabinets have no backsplash, you can install the hanging cabinets first. After determining plumb and level, attach nailer strips to the wall at the desired cabinet positions. Use T-braces to support the cabinets if you do not have a strong helper. Attach the cabinets with screws to the studs and through the nailers.

Soffits. If you have no soffit in your kitchen, you may create an "instant

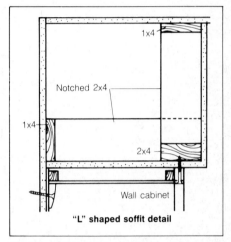

"L" shaped soffit detail

A soffit can be built using "L" or "U" shaped frames covered with wallboard.

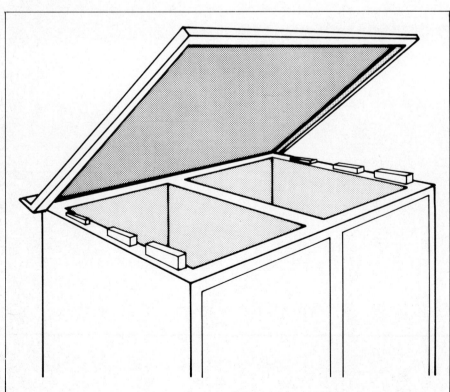

You may shim for level from underneath the cabinet countertop instead of at floor level. Place shims on the cabinet base below the countertop and secure.

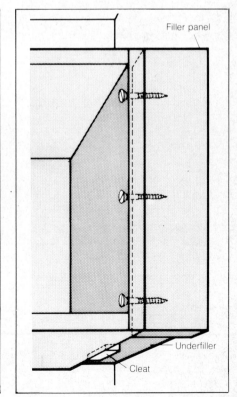

When cabinets do not meet the wall, disguise the space left open with a filler panel.

soffit" by attaching wallboard or paneling to lengths of 1x2 that have been attached to the top of your cabinets, up to the ceiling. Nail lengths of 1x2⅜ of an inch back from the front of the cabinet and in the same position on the ceiling. Nail wallboard to the 1x2, add molding at ceiling and cabinet joints. Finish as desired. Alternative — but more complicated — soffits, are shown in accompanying drawings.

INSTALLING THE SINK
Attaching Fittings
If you have not already done so, attach the faucets, spray hose, tailpiece, and drainer to the sink before inserting it into the countertop. It is easier to do now than later because you have more room in which to work. (The following instructions must be altered according to manufacturers directions if you will be installing a food waste disposer or a spray hose.)

Most faucet bodies are provided with rubber gaskets, which fit over the sink attachment stems. They make a seal which prevents water from leaking out. If the faucet for your sink did not come with rubber gaskets, use plumber's putty instead. Apply a bead around the base of the faucet openings, and then slip the stems through the holes.

Next spread a ⅛ inch bead of plumber's putty to the underside of the lip of the strainer. Set the strainer body into the opening provided for the drain. Now take the metal and rubber washers, as well as the lock nut that came with your faucet fittings, and slide them onto the bottom of the body of the strainer. With a pair of pliers, hold the strainer body to prevent it from turning while, with the other hand you straighten the lock nut. (The sink should be held upright on its side on the floor or on sawhorses during this operation. Your assistant will continue to be helpful during this portion of the job.) Now you can fit together the strainer sleeve, lock nut, and the tailpiece, after which the tailpiece should be connected to the strainer body.

Connecting the Sink to the Trap
New sinks come with full instructions for installation. Manufacturers' instructions should always be followed wherever they may differ from those given here.

Shut off the water main. Drain the cold water lines. Shut off the hot water main and then drain the hot water lines. This will prevent drips that could interfere with your work. Install shut-off valves on the water pipes entering the kitchen on the wall behind and below the sink if they are not already there (kits come with instructions).

The water pipes from the wall are horizontal (perpendicular to the wall). New water pipes can now be connected to these, running from the faucet body to the union with the shut-off valve. These pipes for hot and cold water will run parallel to the wall. Joints in pipes are sealed in different ways, depending upon the piping material used. Iron and steel pipes require pipe joint compound at the union, plus tightening. Copper pipe necessitates soldering with the proper equipment, unless flare joints or special compression fittings are used. Both compression fittings and flare joints are more expensive than soldering, but can be worthwhile when pipes need to be jointed in places that are cramped. Two types of plastic pipe used most frequently for kitchen sink installations are: CPVC (chlorinated polyvinyl chloride) and PB (polybutylene, a flexible thermoplastic). They are simple to work with and are reliable but they are not acceptable to building codes everywhere. Check as to whether your community permits their use. Joints in CPVC are

The standard kitchen sink drain fitting includes a removable basket closure.

glued together with the solvent method; PB requires a clamp technique. Instructions come with the pipe.

Attaching Waste Pipes
Attach a P-trap to the tailpiece that comes from the drain. Use an escutcheon, slip nut, and washer to make the union. After tightening and/or sealing joints, turn on the main water supply. Run the water to test the new system for leaks.

This drain combines a removable basket and a tight-sealing pop-up closure. Substitute the handle for a spray-hose unit or drill an extra hole in the sink.

RECESSED SHELVES

It is possible to find unexpected storage areas when remodeling your kitchen. A commonly overlooked area for shelf space is inside the walls. You can store a wide variety of items in the shallow space between studs; one of the best uses is storage for canned goods.

The design shown recesses a shelf unit between each of three studs, but size may vary depending upon your storage requirements. The depth of the shelf will be the same as the broad face of the stud (usually 3⅝ inches).

Constructed as shown, the space can hold fifty or more cans, depending on size. Standard soup size cans easily sit five on a shelf. Some jars and larger cans would probably fit four to a shelf. These shelves offer quick access and visual inventory of your stock of canned goods.

The height of your opening may depend upon what you plan to put beneath the shelves, but you can open the wall to the full height of the studs. Bear in mind, however, what the traffic pattern will be, especially if you plan to add doors. You do not want to place doors in such a way that anyone could be injured, or a traffic pattern disrupted, if one were left open.

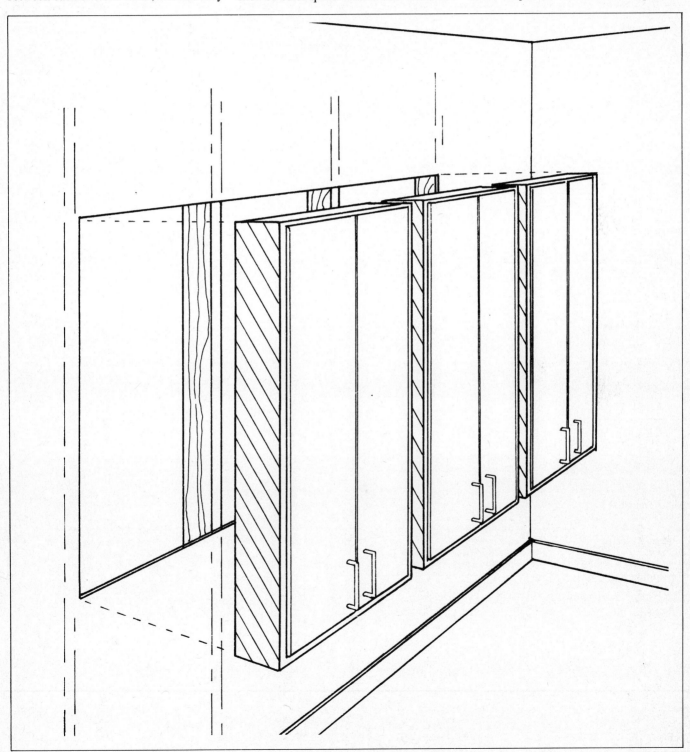

Paneling or wallboard can be applied directly to the studs to create facing. Units of plywood, lumber, or wallboard may be prebuilt and nailed in place from the inside of the box. Countersink and cover nailheads. Shelving inside can be supported with nails or cleats.

PRODUCT SOURCES

Below is a selected list of manufacturers, distributors and retail outlets of given products. Omission from this list does not indicate nonapproval, but merely the space limitations imposed on any list of this type.

ALL-IN-ONE KTCHEN
Dwyer Products Corp.
Michigan City, IN 46360
"World's Smallest Kitchen"
Douglas-Crestlyn-International, Inc.
1241 East Lake Drive
Fort Lauderdale, FL 33316

BASKETS & RACKS,
FREE STANDING
(for cabinet interiors)
Elfa Trading Co.
395 Broadway
New York, NY 10022

BINS
Mail Order Plastic, Inc.
302 Canal Street
New York, NY 10012

BRICK, FABRICATED
Z-Brick
Woodinville, WA 98072
WonderBrix
222 Wisconsin Building
Lake Forest, IL 60045

BUILDING MATERIALS,
OLD AND NEW
Robert W. Belcher
1753 Pleasant Grove Drive, N.E.
Dalton, GA 30720
Broad-Axe Beam
RD 2, Box 181E
West Brattleboro, VT 05301
Dale Carlisle
Route 123
Stoddard, NH 03464
Castle Burlingame
RD 1, Box 352
Basking Ridge, NJ 07920
Diamond K. Co., Inc.
150 Buckland Road
South Windsor, CN 06074
Guyon Industries
65 Oak Street
Lititz, PA 17543
The House Carpenters
Box 217
Shutesbury, MA 01072
Kensington Historical
PO Box 87
East Kingston, NH 03827
Period Pine, Inc.
PO Box 77052
Atlanta, GA 30309
Restorations Unlimited
24 W. Main
Elizabethville, PA 17023

BUTCHERBLOCK
H & W Products, Inc.
1200 Summer Street
Stamford, CN 06905

J & D Brauner Butcher Block
316 E. 59 St.
New York, NY 10022
298 Bowery
New York, NY 10012
455 Central Ave.
Scarsdale, NY 10583
35 Plaza
Paramus, NJ 07652
1735 North Ashland
Chicago, IL 60622
Elm Brook Plaza
Brookfield, WI 53005
Valley Wood Products
Sugarloaf, PA 18249
Workbench
470 Park Avenue South
New York, New York 10016

CABINETRY
Allmilmo
c/o Hayes-Williams, Inc.
261 Madison Avenue
New York, NY 10016
Wood-Mode Cabinets
c/o Foltz-Wessinger, Inc.
800 New Holland Avenue
Lancaster, PA 17604

CEILING FANS
Casablanca Fan Co.
182 S. Raymond
Pasadena, CA
Georgetown Fan Co.
Box 2128
Denver, CO 80201
Good Time Stove Co.
Rt. 112
P. O. Box F
Goshen, MA 01302
"Hunter Fan"
Hunter Division
Robbins and Myers, Inc.
P. O. Box 14775
Memphis, TN 38114

CEILINGS
Armstrong Cork Co.
Liberty and Charlotte
Lancaster, PA 17604

CEILINGS, SUSPENSIONS FOR
Chicago Metallic Corp.
4849 S. Austin Avenue
Chicago, Il 60638

CERAMIC TILE
American Olean
Lansdale, PA 19446
Childcrest Distributing
6045 North 55th Street
Milwaukee, WI 53218

CERAMIC TILE,
GEOMETRIC PATTERNS
Conran's
145 Huguenot Street
New Rochelle, NY 10021

CERAMIC TILE, IMPORTED
Country Floors, Inc.
300 East 61st Street
New York, NY 10012

COAL STOVE
Woodland Stoves of America
1460 W. Airline Highway
Waterloo, IA 50704

CORNICES, READY-MADE,
WITH WIRING
Lightolier, Inc.
346 Claremont Avenue
Jersey City, NJ 07305

FLOORCLOTHS
Floorcloths, Inc.
P. O. Box 812
Severna Park, MD 21146

FLOORING
Armstrong Cork Co.
Liberty and Charlotte,
Lancaster, PA 17604

FLUORESCENTS
FOR HOUSEPLANTS
Verilux, Inc.
35 Mason Street
Greenwich, CN 06830

FOLDING TABLES
"Floating Fold"
Sico, Inc.
7525 Cahill Road
Minneapolis, MN 55435
"19th Century Folding Table"
Pennsylvania Station
340 Poplar Street
Hanover, PA 17331

GLASS WINDOW SHELVES
FOR PLANTS
Buzza
P. O. Box 136 NM
Cambridge, MA 02142

HARDWARE, CABINET
Ball & Ball
463 West Lincoln Highway
Exton, PA 19341
Horton Brasses
P. O. Box 95
Nooks Hill Road
Cromwell, CN 06146

MERCURY LAMP
FOR HOUSEPLANTS
Wonderlite Division
Public Service Lamp Corp.
410 West 16th Street
New York, NY 10011

PLANT HANGERS
"Clinger Clips"
J. Franklin Styers
Route U. S. 1
Concordville, PA 19331

RANGE, RESTAURANT
Garland Commercial Industries
Freeland, PA 18224
South Bend Range Corp.
201 South Cherry Street
South Bend, IN 46627

REFRIGERATOR, PORTABLE
Williams-Sonoma
Mail Order Department
P.O. Box 3792
San Francisco, CA 94119

RUBBER SLICING BOARD
Park Rubber Co.
80 Genesee Street
Lake Zurich, IL 60047

SHELVES
Closet Maid
720 South West 17th Street
Ocala, FL 32670
"Kitchen Jeani" — powerdriven
Rich-Maid Kitchens, Inc.
Drawer B
Wernerville, PA 19565

SKYLIGHTS
Ventarama Skylight Corp.
74 Channel Drive
Port Washington, NY 11050
Velux-America Inc.
74 Cummings Park
Woburn, MA 01801

STENCIL KITS
Adele Bishop, Inc.
P.O. Box 577
Manchester, VT 05254
Craftswomen
Box 715
Doylestown, PA 18901
Pamela Friend
Hand Stencilled Interiors
590 King Street
Hanover, MA 02339
Historic Design Services
P. O. Box 857
Woodland, CA 95695
Janovic/Plaza
1292 First Avenue
New York, NY 10021
Stencil Magic
8 West 19th Street
New York, NY 10011
Stencilled Interiors
Hinman Lane
Southbury, CN 06841

TANKLESS WATER HEATER
"Instant Flow"
Chronomite Labs
21011 South Figueroa Street
Carson, CA 90745
Thorn Company
General Mail Corp.
25 Valley Drive
Greenwich, CN 06830

TRACKLIGHT
"Plugmold Track"
Wiremold Company
906 Summit Avenue
Jersey City, NJ 07307

WALLPAPERS
(with matching fabric)
Laura Ashley, Inc.
714 Madison Avenue
New York, NY 10021
Birge Wallcoverings
P. O. Box 27
Buffalo, NY 14240
Hinson and Company
General Offices
251 Park Avenue South
New York, NY 10010
Marimekko
7 West 56 Street
New York, NY 10019
Papier Peints, Inc.
979 Third Avenue
New York, NY 10022

WET BAR/ICEMAKER
Exec-Q-Bar
1241 East Lake Drive
Fort Lauderdale, FL 33316

**WINDOW GREENHOUSE,
DO-IT-YOURSELF**
Greenhouse Specialties Co.
9849 Kimker Lane
St. Louis, MO 63127

**WINDOW GREENHOUSE,
READY-MADE**
Aluminum Greenhouses, Inc.
14615 Lorain Avenue
Cleveland, OH 44111
Feather Hill Industries
Box 41
Zenda, WI 53195
Four Seasons Greenhouses
672 Sunrise Highway
West Babylon, NY 11704
General Aluminum Corp.
P.O. Box 34221
Dallas, TX 75234
Grow House Corp.
2335 Burbank Dr.
Dallas, TX 75235
Janco Greenhouses
J. A. Nearing Company
10788 Tucker Street
Beltsville, MD 20705
Lord & Burnham
Irvington, NY 10533
Peerless Products
2534 Madison Avenue
Kansas City, MO 64108
Rohm & Haas
Independence Mall
Philadelphia, PA 19106

WOOD COOK STOVE
Enheat Ltd.
100 East Main Street
Sachville, N.B.
Canada E0A 3C0
Enterprise Foundry
Sackville, N. B.
Canada E0A 3C0
**Lunenberg Foundries
& Engineering, LTD**
16 Brook Street
Lunenberg, N. S.
Canada B0J 2C0
Malleable Iron Range Co.
Beaver Dam, WI 53916
"Waterford Stove"
Capitol Export Corp.
8825 Page Blvd.
St. Louis, MO 63114

METRIC CHARTS
Lumber

Sizes: Metric cross-sections are so close to their nearest Imperial sizes, as noted below, that for most purposes they may be considered equivalents.

Lengths: Metric lengths are based on a 300mm module which is slightly shorter in length than an Imperial foot. It will therefore be important to check your requirements accurately to the nearest inch and consult the table below to find the metric length required.

Areas: The metric area is a square metre. Use the following conversion factors when converting from Imperial data: 100 sq. feet = 9.290 sq. metres.

METRIC SIZES SHOWN BESIDE NEAREST IMPERIAL EQUIVALENT

mm	Inches	mm	Inches
16 x 75	⅝ x 3	44 x 150	1¾ x 6
16 x 100	⅝ x 4	44 x 175	1¾ x 7
16 x 125	⅝ x 5	44 x 200	1¾ x 8
16 x 150	⅝ x 6	44 x 225	1¾ x 9
19 x 75	¾ x 3	44 x 250	1¾ x 10
19 x 100	¾ x 4	44 x 300	1¾ x 12
19 x 125	¾ x 5	50 x 75	2 x 3
19 x 150	¾ x 6	50 x 100	2 x 4
22 x 75	⅞ x 3	50 x 125	2 x 5
22 x 100	⅞ x 4	50 x 150	2 x 6
22 x 125	⅞ x 5	50 x 175	2 x 7
22 x 150	⅞ x 6	50 x 200	2 x 8
25 x 75	1 x 3	50 x 225	2 x 9
25 x 100	1 x 4	50 x 250	2 x 10
25 x 125	1 x 5	50 x 300	2 x 12
25 x 150	1 x 6	63 x 100	2½ x 4
25 x 175	1 x 7	63 x 125	2½ x 5
25 x 200	1 x 8	63 x 150	2½ x 6
25 x 225	1 x 9	63 x 175	2½ x 7
25 x 250	1 x 10	63 x 200	2½ x 8
25 x 300	1 x 12	63 x 225	2½ x 9
32 x 75	1¼ x 3	75 x 100	3 x 4
32 x 100	1¼ x 4	75 x 125	3 x 5
32 x 125	1¼ x 5	75 x 150	3 x 6
32 x 150	1¼ x 6	75 x 175	3 x 7
32 x 175	1¼ x 7	75 x 200	3 x 8
32 x 200	1¼ x 8	75 x 225	3 x 9
32 x 225	1¼ x 9	75 x 250	3 x 10
32 x 250	1¼ x 10	75 x 300	3 x 12
32 x 300	1¼ x 12	100 x 100	4 x 4
38 x 75	1½ x 3	100 x 150	4 x 6
38 x 100	1½ x 4	100 x 200	4 x 8
38 x 125	1½ x 5	100 x 250	4 x 10
38 x 150	1½ x 6	100 x 300	4 x 12
38 x 175	1½ x 7	150 x 150	6 x 6
38 x 200	1½ x 8	150 x 200	6 x 8
38 x 225	1½ x 9	150 x 300	6 x 12
44 x 75	1¾ x 3	200 x 200	8 x 8
44 x 100	1¾ x 4	250 x 250	10 x 10
44 x 125	1¾ x 5	300 x 300	12 x 12

METRIC LENGTHS

Lengths Metres	Equiv. Ft. & Inches
1.8m	5′ 10⅞″
2.1m	6′ 10⅝″
2.4m	7′ 10½″
2.7m	8′ 10¼″
3.0m	9′ 10⅛″
3.3m	10′ 9⅞″
3.6m	11′ 9¾″
3.9m	12′ 9½″
4.2m	13′ 9⅜″
4.5m	14′ 9⅓″
4.8m	15′ 9″
5.1m	16′ 8¾″
5.4m	17′ 8⅝″
5.7m	18′ 8⅜″
6.0m	19′ 8¼″
6.3m	20′ 8″
6.6m	21′ 7⅞″
6.9m	22′ 7⅝″
7.2m	23′ 7½″
7.5m	24′ 7¼″
7.8m	25′ 7⅛″

All the dimensions are based on 1 inch = 25 mm.

Contributors,
Picture credits

We wish to extend our thanks to the individuals, associations and manufacturers who generously provided information, photographs, line art, and project ideas for this book. Specific credit for individual photos, art and projects is given below with the names and addresses of the contributors.

Special appreciation must be given to Donald O'Connor, Director of Training, Wood-Mode Cabinets, Kreamer, Pennsylvania. Many of the design ideas in this book were originated by him and some are drawn from *Advance Design Notes*, the training manual he wrote for Wood-Mode.

Allmilmo Corporation c/o Hayes-Williams, Incorporated, 261 Madison Avenue, New York, New York 10016 cover, 12 upper left, 21 upper right, 22 left, 22 upper right, 25 upper right and right center, 26 lower right, 27 upper right, 28 upper left, 29 lower right, 30 lower, 45 right, 48 center right, 51 upper

American Olean Tile 2583 Cannon Avenue, Lansdale, Pennsylvania 19446 page 7 column 3 top, 8 lower left, 24, 31 lower left, 43 lower left, 66, 84 left, 91 line art, 92, 93, 150, 151

American Standard Box 2003, New Brunswick, New Jersey 08903 42

Armstrong Cork Co. Liberty Street, Lancaster, Pennsylvania 17604 82, 83, 90 left

Adele Bishop, Inc. Box 577, Manchester, Vermont 05254 80 center and left

Michael Bliss, landscape architect, 221 Sunset Drive, Encinitas, California 92024 62 upper right

James Brett, Architectural Photography, 1070 West Orange Grove Tucson, Arizona 85704 page 7 column one top, 9, 15 upper and left, 62 lower, 67 right, 75 lower left

Broan Manufacturing Co., Inc. 926 State Street, Hartford, Wisconsin 53207 129 left

Craig Buchanan, photographer, 490 2nd Street, San Francisco, California 94107 Foreword, page 7 column 2 top, 6, 35, 48 lower right 63 upper, 75 upper, 79 upper, 105 right

Childcrest Distributing Inc. 6045 North 55th Street, Milwaukee, Wisconsin 53218 page 7 column 1 middle, 8, 10 upper left, 11 upper, 13 center, 70 upper left

General Electric Company Appliance Park, Louisville, Kentucky 40225 46

Georgia-Pacific Corp. 900 SW 5th Street, Portland, Oregon 97204 99 upper

Alan Horowitz 2266 N. Prospect #410 Milwaukee, Wisconsin 53202 149

Herb Hughes 3033 Willow Lane, Montgomery, Alabama 36109 page 7 column 1 bottom, 17, 18 center, 19 upper right, 31 lower right, 32, 33

The Kohler Company Kohler, Wisconsin 53044 23 right center, and lower right, 155

Leviton Manufacturing Co., Inc. 59-25 Little Neck Parkway, Little Neck, New York 11352 118

William Manley, Interior Design 6062 North Port Washington Road, Milwaukee, Wisconsin 53217 page 7 column 2 middle, 57 upper

Milwaukee Electric Tool Corporation 13135 West Lisbon Road, Brookfield, Wisconsin 53005 108 left and upper center

Modern Maid East 14th Street, Chattanooga, Tennessee 37401 36 upper right, bottom center

Richard V. Nunn Media Mark Productions Falls Church Inn 6633 Arlington Blvd., Falls Church, Virginia 22045 84 center and right, 85, 86, 87 88, 89, 90 center and lower center, 91 upper right, 96, 97, 98, 102, 103, 109, 110 left, 111 left, 115 upper right, 120 right center, lower right, 122, 123, 128, 132 center, 145, 147 center

Laura Odell Kitchen Design 130 East 75th Street, New York, New York 10021 10 left, 12 left, 13 lower left, 16, 21 center right, 25 center and lower right, 26 lower left, 45 lower center

Park Rubber 80 Genessee Street, Lake Zurich, Illinois 60047 48 upper right

Tom Philbin 14 Lakeside Drive, Centerport, New York 11721 142 lower right, 146 left

Photocraft/Butler 54 E Main Street, Ramsey, New Jersey 07446 28 lower left, 37 center

Roland Scharfspitz, A.I.A. 10 Virginia Street, Tenafly, New Jersey 07670 65 upper

Season●all Industries, Inc. Indiana, Pennsylvania 15701 133

James Seeman Studios, Division of Masonite c/o Harold Imber 60 Thorn Avenue, Mount Kisco, New York 10549 81, 99 left

Cecile Shapiro RD 77, Cavendish, Vermont 05142 67 upper left

Tile Council of America/Lis King Box 503, Mahwah, New Jersey 07430 18 lower, 19 lower left, 61 upper, 71 lower left, 75 lower right, 130 right

David Ulrich & Neal DeLeo, Ulrich Inc. 100 Chestnut Street, Ridgewood, New Jersey 07450 page 7 column 3 bottom, 10 upper right, 11 left, 12 upper right, 13 lower right, 14 center left and lower right, 19 lower right, 21 lower right, 22 lower center, 29 lower left, 30 upper left, 38, 40, 41, 44, 47 lower left, 50, 52, 53, 54, 55, 56, 57 lower, 58, 59, 60, 61 center and lower, 63 lower, 64, 65 lower, 67 lower left, 68, 69, 71 right, 72 center and lower, 73, 74, 76, 77, 78, 79 lower, 80 upper, 106, 107, 111 right, 112 lower, 113, 130 left, 134, 135, 136, 138, 139, 143 left, 146 right, 148, 154

U.S. School of Professional Paperhangers 16 Chaplin, Rutland, Vermont 05701 100, 101, 110 center

James Eaton Weeks Interior Designs, Inc. 223 East Silver Spring Drive, Milwaukee, Wisconsin 53117 105, 62 upper left and center, 112 top

Wood-Mode Cabinets c/o Faltz-Wessinger, Inc., 800 New Holland Avenue, Lancaster, Pennsylvania 17604 28 center, 49

Waterford Stoves/Capitol Export Corp. 8825 Page Boulevard, St. Louis, Missouri 63114 39

Tom Yee 114 East 25th Street, New York, New York 10010 14 upper right, 47 lower right, 51 lower, 72 upper

Z-Brick Woodinville, Washington 98072 104

Passage from *From My Mother's Kitchen* by Mimi Sheraton quoted on page 35 by special permission of Harper & Row, Publishers, Inc.

Index